ENVIRONMENTAL EDUCATION IN THE 21ST CENTURY

Environmental education is a field characterised by a paradox: whilst few would doubt the urgency and importance of learning to live in sustainable ways, environmental education holds nowhere near the priority position in formal schooling around the world that this would suggest. This book seeks to unravel some of the causes and tensions involved in this situation.

The text explores the complexities of environmental education; explains what is actually happening in this field at the close of the twentieth century; and considers aspects of environmental education's priorities and potential as we enter the twenty-first. It contains a wealth of references and source material, and an outline of the core ideas of all the major global initiatives and documents that have influenced the progress of environmental education.

The reader is provided with a wide-ranging overview of thinking and writing that has been of influence, a guideline framework for planning, a summary of priorities for action, case studies of good practice, and up-to-date accounts of the 'state of the world' in environmental education in the late 1990s.

Joy A. Palmer is Reader in Education, Director of the Centre for Research on Environmental Thinking and Awareness, and Chair of the Environmental Policy Committee at the University of Durham.

ENVIRONMENTAL EDUCATION IN THE 21ST CENTURY

Theory, practice, progress and promise

Joy A. Palmer

Routledge
Taylor & Francis Group

LONDON AND NEW YORK

First published 1998
by Routledge
2 Park Square, Milton Park, Abingdon, Oxon, OX14 4RN

Simultaneously published in the USA and Canada
by Routledge
270 Madison Ave, New York NY 10016

Routledge is an imprint of the Taylor & Francis Group

Transferred to Digital Printing 2006

© 1998 Joy A. Palmer

Typeset in Garamond by Keystroke, Jacaranda Lodge, Wolverhampton

British Library Cataloguing in Publication Data
A catalogue record for this book is available from the British Library

Library of Congress Cataloging in Publication Data
Palmer, Joy A.
Environmental education in the 21st century : theory, practice,
progress and promise / Joy A. Palmer.
p.   cm.
1. Environmental education. 2. Environmental sciences—Study and
teaching. I. Title.
GE70.P33 1997
363.7'0071—dc21   97–15814
CIP

ISBN 0–415–13196–0 (hbk)
ISBN 0–415–13197–9 (pbk)

Publisher's Note
The publisher has gone to great lengths to ensure the quality of this
reprint but points out that some imperfections in the original
may be apparent

CONTENTS

CONTENTS

Part IV

Part V

Part VI

FIGURES

TABLES

PREFACE

This is not a recipe book. If readers are hoping to find here the ultimate answers and practical tips for the successful implementation of environmental education, they will be disappointed. Perhaps this is because there *are* no definitive answers and foolproof tips. Environmental education is a relatively young, dynamic and immensely complex field for study and interpretation. Indeed, it concerns itself with teaching and learning relating to complex issues that at times themselves defy human understanding. It is a field characterised by a paradox: Few would doubt the urgency and importance of learning to live in sustainable ways . . . of conserving the world's natural resources . . . and of taking care of the Earth today so that future generations may not only meet their own needs, but also enjoy life on our planet. Yet environmental education holds nowhere near the priority position in formal education programmes around the world that this scenario suggests should be the case. It seems that it constantly has to 'engage in battle' with the intricacies and demands of 'education' in general rather than be a core element of it.

This text attempts to unravel some of the causes of and tensions involved in this paradoxical situation; to explore the complexities of the subject matter of the field; to explain what is actually happening in the world of environmental education at the close of the twentieth century; and to consider aspects of the field's priorities and potential as we enter the twenty-first.

The book is divided into six parts. The first presents a concise history of the development of environmental education from an international perspective. Landmark events, conferences, publications, definitions and key concepts are introduced in the hope that readers may direct attention to critical review, interpretation, refinement, implementation and development of already established ideas, rather than to re-inventing them. This section also serves as important background information for understanding and evaluating the effectiveness of environmental education today.

Part II provides a succinct and comprehensive overview of 'the global agenda' or the subject knowledge of environmental education. Each of the major issues affecting our planet today is outlined, including 'development and environment'; and an analysis follows of key environmental problem impacts and causes, and priority solutions. This account provides a valuable introduction to the issues themselves, to their complexities, inter-relationships and inter-dependence. The part reviews key global initiatives that have led to progress in achieving sustainable development – e.g. the World Conservation Strategy, the World Commission on Environment and Development, the United Nations Conference on Environment and Development – and their priority messages for education.

In Part III, perspectives on theory and research in environmental education are introduced and discussed. Core ideas presented include differences of understanding of, and dilemmas associated with, the concepts of sustainability and sustainable development, typologies and approaches to environmentalism, the gap that exists between the rhetoric and reality of environmental education, proposed solutions to this gap, and trends in environmental education research.

This part 'bridges the gap' between theoretical and practical perspectives of the text. It provides an overview of important theoretical issues and viewpoints, and introduces the two levels at which progress may be made in terms of increasing the effectiveness of environmental education in the 'macro' level of radical rethinking and paradigm shift, and the less radical level of small-scale steps to improvement within existing frameworks and paradigms for education.

Part IV moves very much more into the realm of educational practice, and considers the current effectiveness of formal programmes of environmental education, and the various 'structural components' of it that should be considered when planning programmes. An integrated model for structuring environmental education is presented, and various case studies illuminate aspects of this model in practice.

In the fifth part, attention turns to what is actually happening in environmental education in the world today. Invited contributors, all experts in the field, present a summary of developments in their own countries, including views on progress, potential and prospects. These contributions make fascinating reading and open numerous avenues for debate on, for example, whether progress appears to be 'even' around the world, whether priorities in developing and developed countries are the same, the organisational and structural differences between countries, whether the 'rhetoric–reality gap' is a world-wide phenomenon, and so on.

Finally, in Part VI, the text returns to the core questions of how progress can be made, and how environmental education can be encouraged to maximise its potential in the twenty-first century. Steps to success are described, including taking on board concern for the content of programmes, concern for professional development and concern for those significant life experiences, formative influences and informal sources of environmental education that no formal programmes should ignore. Indeed it is concluded that only by combining formal programmes with the promotion of other significant experiences in people's lives and their informal engagement with the environment, can any real progress be made.

Whilst containing no instant recipes for success, the volume as a whole is intended to be thought-provoking and, above all, practically useful. It contains a wealth of references and source material, and an outline of the core ideas or 'essence' of all of the major global initiatives and documents that have influenced the progress of environmental education. References are also made to a wide range of papers and studies by individual authors and researchers in the field – providing the reader with a wide-ranging overview of thinking and writing that has been of influence. The usefulness of the text is also reflected in its guideline framework, or 'model' for planning (published here in its revised form for the first time), its summary of priorities for action, its wide-ranging case studies; and up-to-date accounts of the 'state of the world' in environmental education in the late 1990s.

Perhaps never before has so much material been brought together in one volume on the theme of environmental education. Inevitably, then, many aspects are given rather brief attention; but that is by design. For those wishing to pursue matters in greater depth, it may be regarded as a source book. The text as it stands aims to demonstrate how so many complex variables (background history, content, concepts, ideologies, theories, research, practical constraints, and so on) have come together to shape the field of environmental education as it exists today – and to steer it into the new century. There is ample opportunity to debate the direction in which it should be steered.

ACKNOWLEDGEMENTS

The author's international research project *Emergent Environmentalism* is referred to on various occasions in the text. This is funded primarily by the Economic and Social Research Council in the UK, with related grants from the European Commission, the British Council in Slovenia and the British Council in Greece.

Sincere thanks are due to the authors of the statements on developments in environmental education in various locations contained within Part V and of the case studies described within Parts IV and VI – their biographical details are incorporated in the text in the appropriate places; also to Ian Robottom and Paul Hart for permission to include Table 4.2; and to Susan Metcalf, Tom Taylor and other colleagues in the School of Education at the University of Durham for their meticulous work in preparing the manuscript and its figures for publication.

Finally, I am extremely grateful to David Cooper and Chris Oulton for their helpful comments on various drafts of Figures 6.1 and 6.2 and to Neil Fletcher for the design of Figure 6.3.

KEY TO ACRONYMS

CEC	Council of the European Community
CEE	Council for Environmental Education (UK)
DES	Department of Education and Science
DfEE	Department for Education and Employment
ENSI	Environment and School Initiative Project (of OECD)
FAO	(United Nations) Food and Agriculture Organisation
HMI	Her Majesty's Inspectors of Schools (in Britain)
ICCE	International Centre for Conservation Education
IEEP	International Environmental Education Programme
IUCN	International Union for the Conservation of Nature and Natural Resources (The World Conservation Union)
JEE	*Journal of Environmental Education* (USA)
NAAEE	North American Association for Environmental Education
NAEE	National Association for Environmental Education (UK)
NCC	National Curriculum Council
NFER	National Foundation for Educational Research
NGO	Non-governmental Organisation
OECD	Organisation for Economic Co-operation and Development
OFSTED	Office of Standards in Education (replaced HMI as official body for undertaking schools' inspection in Britain)
SCAA	School Curriculum and Assessment Authority
UNCED	The United Nations Conference on Environment and Development: The Earth Summit
UNEP	United Nations Environment Programme
UNESCO	United Nations Educational, Scientific and Cultural Organisation
WCED	World Commission on Environment and Development
WWF	World Wide Fund for Nature (World Wildlife Fund)

Part I

HISTORY AND DEVELOPMENT OF ENVIRONMENTAL EDUCATION

JOURNEY TO THE PRESENT DAY

Re-inventing the wheel?

Does it really matter when the two words 'environment' and 'education' were first used in conjunction with each other? Indeed, does it matter at all whether the term 'environmental education' has been in common or casual use in educational circles for one, two, three or several more decades? Surely the critical matter that should concern us as a new century unfolds is what is going on *now* to educate the world's citizens about our relationship with Planet Earth. Of course it is; yet I would argue strongly for three reasons that an overview of the history and development of the field is relevant and important in a text of this kind. Firstly, it is necessary to dispel the illusion held in the minds of some contemporary educators, that environmental education is new; a product of our growing concern for the environment, born out of recent curriculum initiatives. On the contrary, the environmental education movement around the globe has evolved over many years. Secondly, I believe that we owe it to the pioneers of the past: those with such great educational and environmental vision, whose efforts resulted in the landmark events, the conferences, publications, definitions, concepts, curricula, and case studies of good practice that are documented on the pages which follow. Thirdly, it is hoped that this book will go some way towards helping the prevention of re-inventing wheels. On my travels around the world I have many times encountered the frustration of discovering dedicated groups of people spending a great deal of valuable time devising aims, objectives and guidelines for environmental education. Worthy as the outcomes of their strenuous efforts may be, they often do little more than replicate the products of previous workshops, conferences and publications. It is my hope that by including a description and, where appropriate, the text of some of the world's landmark publications on the subject, then readers may direct their energy to refinement, criticism, implementation and development of the ideas they contain, rather than to re-invention of their core content.

3

So, where and when did it all begin? Whilst the words 'environment' and 'education' do not appear to have been used in conjunction with each other until the mid-1960s, the evolution of environmental education has incorporated the significant influence of some of the 'great' eighteenth- and nineteenth-century thinkers, writers and educators, notably Goethe, Rousseau, Humboldt, Haeckel, Froebel, Dewey and Montessori. While such influential pioneers clearly contributed to environmental thought and practice, many writers (e.g. Sterling, 1992) attribute the 'founding' of environmental education in the UK to a Scottish Professor of Botany and an originator of town and country planning – Sir Patrick Geddes (1854–1933). He is regarded by many as being the first to make that all important link between the quality of the environment and the quality of education. Geddes pioneered instructional methods which brought learners into direct contact with their environment. In 1892, he opened an Outlook Tower in Edinburgh, which can still be seen today as the original 'field' studies centre. Here, he developed the methods of 'Civic and Regional Surveying', with its innovative ideas and field survey methods.

> These approaches, and his concern for education of the whole person anticipated and set the foundation for modern environmental education. Geddes' ideas were disseminated through the Le Ploy society, to which many teachers and teacher trainers belonged in the second quarter of the century.
>
> (Sterling, 1992)

Whilst Geddes developed studies in an urban location, the nature studies movement gained momentum in its growth out of the Victorian era's preoccupation with the natural world and its life. In 1902, the School Nature Study Union was founded, and by the 1940s this area of study had broadened into rural studies, with the founding of a number of local associations of rural studies teachers. It was from this rural studies movement that the term 'environmental studies' evolved. Indeed the present day National Association for Environmental Education in the UK (NAEE as from 1970) developed from a National Rural Environmental Studies Association formed in 1960, which became the National Rural and Environmental Studies Association, and then the NAEE. By the mid-1940s, the term 'environmental studies' was well in use, largely consisting of a mixture of teaching elements of geography, history and local nature study. The term and practice of 'field studies' also increased in popularity around this time. The teaching of history, geography and biology in the field was well enhanced by the establishment of the Council for the Promotion of Field Studies in 1943 (now the Field Studies Council) and the opening of the first residential field study centre in the UK at Flatford Mill, Suffolk, in 1946. The establishment of the Nature Conservancy in 1949 was also significant for the ongoing development of environmental teaching.

The first recorded use of the term 'environmental education' in Britain may be traced to a conference held in 1965 at Keele University, Staffordshire, with

4

the purpose of investigating conservation of the countryside and its implications for education. This conference was significant for the UK in that it marked the first occasion where educationists and conservationists came together, and led to the establishment of the Council for Environmental Education (CEE), which first met in July 1968 (CEE, 1970). The CEE was founded as a focus for organisations involved or concerned with environmental education, having three broad goals:

Development: CEE aims to facilitate the development of the theory and practice of environmental education.

Promotion: CEE aims to promote the concept of environmental education and facilitate its application in all spheres of education.

Review: CEE aims to monitor the progress of environmental education and assess its effectiveness.

Whilst the first attributed use of the term 'environmental education' in the UK was at the 1965 Keele Conference, internationally it is claimed (Disinger, 1983) that it was first used in Paris, in 1948, by Thomas Pritchard at a meeting of the International Union for the Conservation of Nature and Natural Resources (IUCN); whilst Wheeler (1985) suggests that the term first appeared in the book *Communitas* by Paul and Percival Goodman, published in 1947.

Formulation of a definition

After acknowledgement of the term, organisations concerned with the development of environmental education moved towards defining its meaning and promoting its legitimacy. Key events on the development timeline, discussed below, are summarised in Figure 1.1. The IUCN was to, and indeed still does, play a critical role in this process. The IUCN, otherwise known as the World Conservation Union, was established in 1949 as a major international union of both government and non-governmental organisations (NGOs) concerned with conservation. As early as September 1965, a meeting of IUCN's Education Commission's North West Europe Committee called for 'environmental education in schools, in higher education, and in training for the land-linked professions' (Wheeler, 1985).

In 1968, the United Nations Educational, Scientific and Cultural Organisation (UNESCO) organised a Biosphere Conference in Paris, and in a later report on the event IUCN declared that 'perhaps for the first time, world awareness of environmental education was fully evidenced' (IUCN, 1971). The 1968 UNESCO Conference called for the development of curriculum materials relating to studying the environment for all levels of education, the promotion of technical training, and the stimulation of global awareness of environmental problems. It also advocated the setting up of national co-ordinating bodies for environmental education around the globe. The UK was at the forefront of

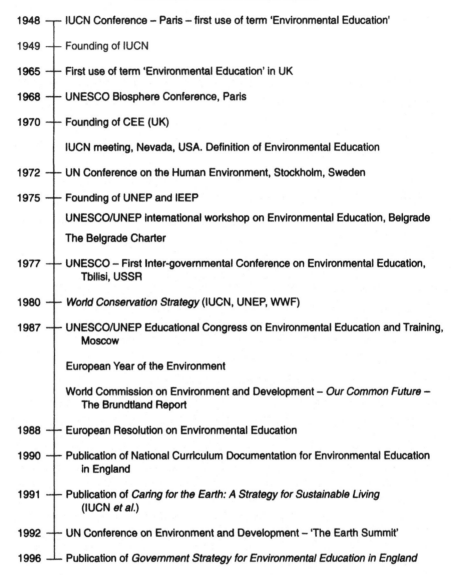

1948	IUCN Conference – Paris – first use of term 'Environmental Education'
1949	Founding of IUCN
1965	First use of term 'Environmental Education' in UK
1968	UNESCO Biosphere Conference, Paris
1970	Founding of CEE (UK)
	IUCN meeting, Nevada, USA. Definition of Environmental Education
1972	UN Conference on the Human Environment, Stockholm, Sweden
1975	Founding of UNEP and IEEP
	UNESCO/UNEP international workshop on Environmental Education, Belgrade
	The Belgrade Charter
1977	UNESCO – First Inter-governmental Conference on Environmental Education, Tbilisi, USSR
1980	*World Conservation Strategy* (IUCN, UNEP, WWF)
1987	UNESCO/UNEP Educational Congress on Environmental Education and Training, Moscow
	European Year of the Environment
	World Commission on Environment and Development – *Our Common Future* – The Brundtland Report
1988	European Resolution on Environmental Education
1990	Publication of National Curriculum Documentation for Environmental Education in England
1991	Publication of *Caring for the Earth: A Strategy for Sustainable Living* (IUCN *et al.*)
1992	UN Conference on Environment and Development – 'The Earth Summit'
1996	Publication of *Government Strategy for Environmental Education in England*

Figure 1.1 Environmental education: key events on a development timeline

this initiative with its founding of the CEE as an umbrella body to co-ordinate environmental education initiatives at all levels and in all sectors of society.

Probably the greatest landmark in the history of attempting to define the term 'environmental education' was an IUCN/UNESCO 'International Working Meeting on Environmental Education in the School Curriculum' held in 1970 at the Foresta Institute, Carson City, Nevada, USA. There an influential and what might be described as the 'classic' definition of environmental education was formulated and adopted:

> Environmental education is the process of recognising values and clarifying concepts in order to develop skills and attitudes necessary to understand and appreciate the inter-relatedness among man, his culture, and his biophysical surroundings. Environmental education also entails practice in decision-making and self-formulation of a code of behaviour about issues concerning environmental quality.

(IUCN, 1970)

IUCN continued to promote this definition and its meaning around the world. A series of conferences and workshops on environmental education was set up, including meetings in the UK, India, The Netherlands, Canada, Kenya and Argentina. The IUCN 'Nevada' definition was adopted by the National Association for Environmental Education in Britain. In that same year (1970) an Environmental Education Act passed in the USA gave a welcome stimulus to the promotion of environmental awareness there.

Milestones of the 1970s – Stockholm, Belgrade and Tbilisi

The support of key international institutions continued to raise the profile of environmental education during the 1970s, leading to a great deal of common understanding of the aims, objectives and approaches to the subject. Principle 19 of the United Nations Conference on the Human Environment held in Stockholm, Sweden, in 1972 declared that:

> education in environmental matters for the younger generation as well as adults . . . giving due consideration for the underprivileged is essential.

A key recommendation of this first world meeting on the state of the environment endorsed the need for environmental education, thus greatly enhancing its international status and perceived importance. This Stockholm Conference reflected the rapidly growing global interest in and concern for the environment of the 1970s. It led to the establishment in 1975 of the United Nations Environment Programme (UNEP), which together with UNESCO founded the UNESCO/UNEP International Environmental Education Programme in 1975.

The IEEP was launched at an International Workshop on Environmental Education held in Belgrade by UNESCO/UNEP. IEEP produced the first inter-governmental statement on environmental education. It listed the aims, objectives, key concepts and guiding principles of it in a document prepared at the meeting known as 'The Belgrade Charter – A Global Framework for Environmental Education'. The brief but comprehensive set of objectives for environmental education prepared at Belgrade are summarised as follows:

1 To foster clear awareness of and concern about economic, social, political, and ecological inter-dependence in urban and rural areas;

2 To provide every person with opportunities to acquire the knowledge, values, attitudes, commitment and skills needed to protect and improve the environment;

3 To create new patterns of behaviour of individuals, groups and society as a whole towards the environment.

(UNESCO, 1975)

A key feature of the Belgrade event is that whilst it was attended by education-ists, it was planned to hold a follow-up conference with the crucial involvement of politicians. Thus it was hoped that recommendations would be:

translated into policy at national levels in those countries where environ-mental education is not yet integrated into development strategies.

(Tolba, 1977)

Belgrade also saw the launch of *Connect*, the UNESCO/UNEP international periodical on environmental education.

The plan to involve government representatives in environmental education policy and debate came to fruition at a milestone event held in Tbilisi, Georgia, USSR in October 1977. This was the UNESCO First Inter-governmental Conference on Environmental Education, attended by official government delegations of 66 UNESCO member states together with representatives of numerous NGOs. The Conference prepared recommendations for the wider application of environmental education in formal and non-formal education. Its Final Report contains a Declaration – largely based on the principles outlined at the Belgrade Conference. This established a framework for an international consensus which without doubt has been the seminal influence on the devel-opment of environmental education policies around the globe. Indeed, the Tbilisi event and the subsequent publications based on it continue to provide the blueprint for the development of environmental education in many countries of the world today.

Such is the historic significance of the Tbilisi Conference that there follows an extract from the Introduction to the Papers prepared as part of the UK delegation's contribution to the event. Following this extract is a set of state-ments based on the Conference's Recommendation 2, which may be regarded as guiding principles of environmental education, and the 'Three Goals' of environmental education as agreed at Tbilisi.

Environmental education in the UK: extract from Introduction to Papers prepared as part of the UK delegation's contribution to the UNESCO inter-governmental conference, Tbilisi, 1977

While a science-based and inter-disciplinary approach to environmental education is the first consideration of many, there are also important initiatives from the side of the humanities and from the full spectrum of individual subjects. A report of the Council for Environmental Education sums up the situation like this: 'As an educational approach it (environmental education) can permeate a range of disciplines, both traditional and new, as well as form the mainspring of many integrated courses. With its methodology firmly inter-related it can impart the balanced understanding of, and active concern for, the whole environment which alone can enable man to plan and realise a world fit to live in.' Environmental education is regarded as the embodiment of a philosophy which should be pervasive, rather than a 'subject' which might be separately identified.

An important review was provided by the report *Environmental Education* published by the Scottish Education Department in 1974. Some of its recommendations, quoted here in adapted form, are:

1a Both formal and informal education should use the local and distant environments to provide knowledge, training in appropriate skills, and first hand experience;

b pupils and young people should be introduced to environmental concepts and values, given practice in decision-making and afforded opportunities for personal involvement;

c pupils and young people should be trained to assess critically the many views being expressed today on current environmental issues;

2a environmental education should permeate the whole curriculum both inside and outside the school;

b every school should have adequate arrangements for planning and implementing a programme of environmental education;

c to make environmental education a separate subject is neither desirable nor possible;

d the programme of environmental education begun in primary school and pursued into secondary school should continue into informal education and later life; and

e efforts should be made to co-ordinate the total programme of environmental education.

Examination of the processes which take place in the practice of formal environmental education in the UK reveals a complexity of teaching strategies falling into three overlapping categories. These are:

1 The use of the environment as a medium for education. The environment is used as a source of stimulation for realistic activities in language, mathematics, science, art and the humanities and with the development of skills and abilities as an important purpose. This is known as 'environmental studies'.

9

2 The use of the environment as a subject for investigation. Here the educational objectives are essentially cognitive, and may be achieved through science, geography, history and other subjects; or through a specifically 'non-fragmented' approach such as is analytically treated in *Environmental Education – A Statement of Aims*, published in 1976 by the National Association for Environmental Education. This document identifies operational objectives under chosen headings as a guide to syllabus construction.

3 The conservation and improvement of the environment as a goal of education. This is concerned above all with values and attitudes. The Scottish Report referred to concludes: 'The ultimate aims of environmental education are the creation of responsible attitudes and the development of an environmental ethic.' This echoes, *How Do You Want To Live?*, published in 1972 by the Department of the Environment. 'It is essential to realise', it is stated, 'that the world of the human habitat is not just a world of objects; it is a world of values. The moral purpose of environmental education is to enable the citizen to understand these values, to criticise them and where necessary to change them.'

It is only within the last ten years that the term 'environmental education' has come into general use. It would be surprising if so youthful a movement were not characterised by uncertainties and diversions; but a significant re-orientation of educational objectives does seem to be taking place. The fact that such a variety of approaches exists is a reflection of the opportunities there are for innovation, and the number of viewpoints seeking expression. There is a need to devise more intellectually satisfying syllabus structures, and research and evaluation will be needed if future work is to be directed to best effect. But the developments recorded here reflect not only the recent wave of enthusiasm and concern but also aspects of the UK experience which go back many years, and it is hoped that on both counts they will be of interest to others.

Tbilisi recommendations

The following set of statements is based upon the Tbilisi Report Recommendation 2 (1978):

Environmental Education:

- is a life-long process;
- is inter-disciplinary and holistic in nature and application;
- is an approach to education as a whole, rather than a subject;
- concerns the inter-relationship and interconnectedness between human and natural systems;

- views the environment in its entirety including social, political, economic, technological, moral, aesthetic and spiritual aspects;
- recognises that energy and material resources both present and limit possibilities;
- encourages participation in the learning experience;
- emphasises active responsibility;
- uses a broad range of teaching and learning techniques, with stress on practical activities and first hand experience;
- is concerned with local to global dimensions, and past/present/future dimensions;
- should be enhanced and supported by the organisation and structure of the learning situation and institution as a whole;
- encourages the development of sensitivity, awareness, understanding, critical thinking and problem-solving skills;
- encourages the clarification of values and the development of values sensitive to the environment;
- is concerned with building an environmental ethic.

These goals and principles were carried forward into and underpin the content of preliminary papers and final documentation for environmental education in the National Curriculum for schools in England, as described later in this text.

The Tbilisi goals of environmental education

The final report of the Tbilisi Conference set out three 'goals of environmental education', clearly reflecting those identified at Belgrade. They are:

(i) To foster clear awareness of, and concern about, economic, social, political and ecological inter-dependence in urban and rural areas.

(ii) To provide every person with opportunities to acquire the know-ledge, values, attitudes, commitment and skills needed to protect and improve the environment.

(iii) To create new patterns of behaviour of individuals, groups, and society as a whole, towards the environment.

(UNESCO, 1977)

The decade leading up to Tbilisi was certainly a remarkable one. In 1967 the term 'environmental education' had just been introduced into the UK. By 1977 an inter-governmental conference was calling for 'new patterns of behaviour of individuals, groups and society as a whole towards the environment'. Such far-reaching thinking and speed of its development no doubt led Wheeler (1985) to remark:

11

perhaps there is no other example in the history of world education when a term expressing a complex of ideas disseminated as rapidly as environmental education from country to country.

(reported in Sterling, 1992)

Key publications in Britain during the 1970s included the Schools' Council *Project Environment* (1974) which defined the components of environmental education as education 'in', 'about' and 'for' the environment; the National Association for Environmental Education's original *Statement of Aims*, quoted below; an HMI Report *Environmental Education* published in Scotland in 1974, and the HMI document 'Environmental Education' in *Curriculum 11–16, Supplementary Working Papers* published in London in 1979.

Statement of Aims of the National Association for Environmental Education (UK) 1976 (revised 1982, 1992)

This statement sets out learning targets or performance objectives for all school age groups. For example:-

Objectives in Environmental Education for Primary and Middle Schools (5–12)

AREA AND LOCATION

Experiences basic orientation within the local and national environments. Perceives the Earth as the home of man but shrinking in terms of time, distance and limits of resources. Observes how man uses and influences the environment. Learns the use to be made of local and world maps.

ATMOSPHERE AND COSMOS

Can describe and measure simple climatic factors in the local environment and appreciates their significance for food production. Recognises the role of the atmosphere in the life of the plants and animals. Can identify the major climatic and vegetative patterns of the world.

LANDFORMS, SOILS AND MINERALS

Knows that soil is dynamic: (a) it forms, (b) it contains living things and supports plant growth, (c) it erodes or becomes less fertile. Can identify different soil types, sees the interaction between soil and living things. Understands that mineral resources are limited. Can point out on a map the general arrangement of landforms in Britain and the World.

PLANTS AND ANIMALS

Knows from first hand experience various kinds of plants and animals in their own environment. Recognises inter-dependence among soil,

12

atmosphere, plants (producers), animals and man (consumers). Knows what is meant by the food chain. Is aware of some endangered species and measures for their conservation, particularly food species important to man.

WATER

Knows the necessity of water for life and its importance as a natural resource. Knows the water cycle. Is aware of water pollution.

PEOPLE

Recognises the varieties and similarities among people. Knows how people live in and use different environments. Knows of rural depopulation as a world-wide phenomenon. Is aware of population growth and its relation to the quality of life.

SOCIAL ORGANISATION

Learns individual and group responsibility concerning environment. Uses environmental experience to gain self-discipline. Recognises agencies working on environmental problems and recognises international co-operation as a means of solving world environmental problems.

ECONOMICS

Relates food, clothing and shelter needs to available resources in various societies. Recognises the organisation of resources into farming, forestry, fishing, mining, manufacturing, servicing, transportation and communication.

AESTHETICS, ETHICS, LITERACY, NUMERACY

Uses environmental experience to acquire basic skills. Builds a basic vocabulary of environmental terms. Uses the visual arts and music to describe and interpret various environments. Develops an appreciation of art and design factors in the built environment.

BUILT ENVIRONMENT

Recognises different buildings and functional areas in the locality (residential, shopping, work places, leisure provision). Knows the main local services (police, fire brigade, hospital).

ENERGY

Recognises manifestations of energy in various forms, and the control of energy by man. Knows that energy arrives from the sun. Knows the origin of fossil fuels.

(NAEE, 1976)

A similar range of objectives is provided for the secondary level of schooling, also objectives to be attained by the individual at the appropriate level and in varying degrees throughout formal education, e.g.

PLANTS AND ANIMALS

Acts so as to create and preserve conditions under which ecologically balanced ecosystems can evolve in his local environment.

(NAEE, 1976)

The document also provides a more general statement of aims for each level of schooling (pre-primary, primary, middle, secondary, sixth form, tertiary), e.g.

PRIMARY 5–10

At the primary stage environmental education is seen as involving pupils in personal experience of the environment by direct exploration with all their senses, using the school and its immediate surroundings and going further afield when necessary. Such environments will involve both the living environment in small nature reserves, school gardens or in the countryside and the built environment in streetwork. At this stage emphasis should be placed on the development and deepening of concepts. Teachers are expected to use these experiences to develop language in all its aspects, numeracy, scientific methods of enquiry, aesthetic appreciation and creative expression as well as to encourage the development of value judgements and an environmental ethic. Children at this stage should be introduced to the statutory and accepted codes of environmental behaviour.

It is not suggested that a specific subject should be established for this area of study in primary schools but that environmental education should involve the children's total learning. It is felt that it is important to keep in mind during this period of education the sequential development of concepts whereby understanding is built on previous experiences, and stress the need to build up basic vocabularies and skills which will be needed in studies leading to an appreciation of variations and the ecological significance of phenomena in the environment.

(NAEE, 1976)

The *Statement of Aims* was a strategically critical document. Not only did it achieve a move towards the all important task of practical interpretation of the theoretical principles of environmental education set out in earlier documents; it also had a very direct influence upon the production of guidelines for

14

environmental education produced within certain counties or Local Education Authorities of the country (e.g. Birmingham, Hertfordshire). Furthermore, and perhaps surprisingly, the document had little competition – it stood as the definitive national guide to the interpretation of environmental education in England and Wales until the emergence of the National Curriculum for Schools well over a decade later.

Consolidation in the 1980s

In 1980 the *World Conservation Strategy* was launched; the next major international initiative, by IUCN, UNEP and (then) World Wildlife Fund (WWF). This key document stressed the importance of resource conservation through 'sustainable development', and the idea that conservation and development are mutually inter-dependent. The *World Conservation Strategy* included a chapter on environmental education, containing the message:

> Ultimately, the behaviour of entire societies towards the biosphere must be transformed if the achievement of conservation objectives is to be assured . . . the long term task of environmental education [is] to foster or reinforce attitudes and behaviour, compatible with a new ethic.
>
> (IUCN, 1980)

From the mid-1980s onwards, work at the international level continued on preparing supplements to the *World Conservation Strategy*, dealing with environmental education and ethics and culture, among other matters.

1987 was another critical year on the international scene, marking the tenth anniversary of the first Tbilisi Conference with the holding of a 'Tbilisi Plus Ten' Conference, jointly organised by UNESCO and UNEP, and held in Moscow. A number of major themes emerged from the deliberations of this event, including the vital importance of environmental education as summed up in the opening address:

> In the long run, nothing significant will happen to reduce local and international threats to the environment unless widespread public awareness is aroused concerning the essential links between environmental quality and the continued satisfaction of human needs. Human action depends upon motivation, which depends upon widespread understanding. This is why we feel it is so important that everyone becomes environmentally conscious through proper environmental education.
>
> (UNESCO, 1987)

Thus in 1987 the principles of environmental education laid down in Tbilisi a decade earlier were endorsed.

Also in that year, the essence of the *World Conservation Strategy* was substantially reinforced and expanded by the publication of *Our Common Future* (WCED, 1987) otherwise known as the *Brundtland Report*, the outcome of the

15

deliberations of the World Commission on Environment and Development. This report presented a major statement on a 'global agenda' to reconcile environment with development, thus reinforcing and extending the core message of the *World Conservation Strategy*. Further references to the Report of WCED will be found in Part II of this text. Education was seen as a focal point in its agenda:

> The changes in human attitude that we call for depend on a vast campaign of education, debate and public participation.
>
> (WCED, 1987)

Whilst 1987 was another milestone year, 1987/88 marked the European Year of the Environment within the European Community, and in May 1988 a resolution was passed within the European Community when the Council of Ministers agreed on 'the need to take concrete steps for the promotion of environmental education so that this can be intensified in a comprehensive way throughout the community'. The adopted resolution concluded that 'environmental education should be an integral and essential part of every European citizen's upbringing'. It had the following objective and guiding principles:

> The objective of environmental education is to increase the public awareness of the problem in this field, as well as possible solutions, and to lay the foundations for a fully informed and active participation of the individual in the protection of the environment and the prudent and rational use of natural resources. For the achievement of the objectives environmental education should take into account particularly the following guiding principles:
> – the environment is a common heritage of mankind,
> – the common duty of maintaining, protecting and improving the quality of the environment, as a contribution to the protection of human health and the safeguarding of the ecological balance,
> – the need for a prudent and rational utilisation of natural resources,
> – the way in which each individual can, by his own behaviour, particularly as a consumer, contribute to the protection of the environment.
>
> (*Journal of the European Communities*, 6/7/88)

It was resolved that Member States would make every effort to implement certain measures, including:

> The promotion of environmental education in all sectors of education ... giving consideration to the basic aims of environmental education when drawing up curricula ... taking appropriate measures to develop teachers' knowledge of environmental matters in the context of their initial and in-service training. ...

It is very likely that the European Resolution of 1988 played a critical role in the adoption of environmental education as a cross-curricular theme of the National Curriculum of the 1990s in England.

The groundwork for the new National Curriculum was set out in the publication of *The National Curriculum 5–16: A Consultation Document* by the Department of Education and Science in 1987. A campaign by the CEE, NAEE and other interested parties set out to ensure that environmental education was properly represented in the National Curriculum debate of the turn of the decade.

In September 1988, the then Prime Minister Mrs Margaret Thatcher made a speech on the environment to the Royal Society. Overnight, the environment and its related issues were high on the political agenda. This, together with other notable events, including the resolution of the Council of Ministers of the European Community (CEC) in May 1988 requiring each Member State to:

> promote the introduction of environment education in all sectors of education, including vocational training and adult education
>
> (CEC, 1988)

led to the publication in England and Wales of the HMI document *Environmental Education from 5 to 16* (1989) and the movement towards the 'official status' of Environmental Education in the National Curriculum for Schools.

Rio and beyond: The 1990s

Debate arising from *Our Common Future*, report of the WCED (WCED, 1987), led to the second, and very much larger, conference of the United Nations, two decades after Stockholm. This was the United Nations Conference on Environment and Development – The Earth Summit – staged in Rio de Janeiro, Brazil, 3–14 June 1992. It was attended by some 120 heads of state and government, together with delegates from over 170 countries. Parallel to the governmental Summit was the Global Forum, involving representatives from several hundred special interest groups and NGOs in a series of presentations, displays, seminars and workshops on a wide range of environmental issues and topics. Several important documents were signed at the Summit, representing the beginning of a long process of interpreting, responding to and implementing recommendations and agreements designed to change the future of planet Earth. The centrepiece of the Rio agreements is *Agenda 21*, a major action programme setting out what nations should do to achieve sustainable development in the twenty-first century. The 40 chapters of *Agenda 21* cover topics ranging from poverty, toxic waste and desertification to youth, education and free trade. Its content is described in greater detail in the following part of this text. There are implications for environmental education throughout this document, but of particular significance are Chapters 25, on Children and Youth in Sustainable Development, and Chapter 36, on Promoting Education, Public Awareness and Training. A second crucial document produced and signed at the Summit is the *Rio Declaration*, this being a statement of 27 principles for sustainability which provide the basis for the programmes of international

17

co-operation in *Agenda 21* (see also Part II). In other words, *The Rio Declaration* sets out a blueprint for a sustainable future, whilst *Agenda 21* provides a guiding programme for its interpretation. The UNCED also agreed: *The Climatic Change Convention*, the first international treaty to acknowledge the threat of global warming; *The Biodiversity Convention*, the first treaty to deal with ownership of genetic resources (signed by 153 governments excluding the USA) and *Forest Principles*, a non-legally binding text on principles for sustainable forest management. One of the key outcomes of the Conference for educators is the recommendation that environment and development education should be incorporated as an essential part of learning, within both formal and non-formal education sectors:

> A proposal is made that:
> Governments should strive to update or prepare strategies aimed at integrating environment and development as a cross-cutting issue into education at all levels within the next three years.
>
> (Agenda 21, Chapter 36, UNCED, 1992)

The turn of the decade saw positive plans for the inclusion of environmental education as an officially recognised cross-curricular theme of the National Curriculum for Schools in England. It was one of the original five themes to be documented, alongside health education, education for citizenship, careers education and guidance, and economic and industrial understanding. Themes were to be regarded not as an appendage to be 'tacked on' to the Curriculum's core and foundation subjects, but as a central element of the curriculum as a whole, having progression and continuity like all other subject areas. By definition, they are cross-curricular, and thus can feature in or arise out of a number of other areas of the curriculum. The themes share the ability to promote thinking and discussion on questions of values and belief; they add to knowledge and understanding; and they rely on practical, experiential learning and decision-making.

The working group convened by the National Curriculum Council (NCC) to examine the theme of environmental education and to prepare official documentation relating to it believed strongly that it should be an entitlement for every school-aged pupil. Hence, in 1989 the group drew up a statement of proposed Entitlement of pupils in environmental education. This formed part of a collection of key papers (unpublished) that were circulated widely for consultation and response. It suggests that a pupil's learning should be founded on knowledge, understanding and skills. A summary follows:

By the age of 16 all pupils should have had educational experiences, which range from local to global in scale, and which enable them to:

1 Understand the natural processes that take place in the environment, including the ecological principles and relationships that exist.
2 Understand that human lives and livelihoods are totally dependent on the processes, relationships and resources that exist in the environment.

3 Be aware of the impact of human activities on the environment, including planning and design, to understand the process by which communities organise themselves, initiate and cope with change; to appreciate that these are affected by personal, economic, technological, social, aesthetic, political, ethical and spiritual considerations.

4 Be competent in a range of skills which help them to appreciate and enjoy, communicate ideas and participate in the decision-making processes that shape the environment.

5 View, evaluate, interpret and experience their surroundings critically so that a balanced appreciation can be reached.

6 Have insights into a range of environments and cultures, both past and present, to include an understanding of the ways in which different cultural groups perceive and interact with their environment.

7 Understand the conflicts that may arise over environmental issues, particularly in relation to the use of resources, and to consider alternative ways to resolve such conflicts.

8 Be aware of the inter-dependence of communities and nations and some of the environmental consequences and opportunities of those relationships.

9 Be aware that the current state of the environment has resulted from past decisions and actions and that the future of the environment depends on contemporary actions and decisions to which they make a contribution.

10 Identify their own level of commitment towards the care of the environment.

Underpinning this Entitlement is a clear emphasis on values and attitudes. Indeed a critical component of cross-curricular issues in general is their ability to promote discussion or questions of values, belief and personal decision-making as a response to interaction with the environment.

Learning

Further to the above statement of Entitlement, a broad outline structure for every child's learning in environmental education was articulated (unpublished NCC Task Group papers, 1989). This is based on two broad dimensions which relate to other subject areas of the curriculum. Each of these areas is further divided into three sub-sections as follows:

1 Knowledge and Understanding

(a) Knowledge about the environment at a variety of levels, ranging from local to global.

(b) Knowledge and understanding of environmental issues at a variety of levels, ranging from local to global; to include understanding of different influences, both natural and human, on the issues.

(c) Knowledge of alternative attitudes and approaches to environmental issues and the value systems underlying such attitudes and approaches.

2 Skills

(a) Finding out about the environment, either directly through the environment or by using secondary courses.

(b) Communicating:

    (i)   Knowledge about the environment.

    (ii) Both the pupil's own and alternative attitudes to environmental issues, to include justification for the attitudes or approaches advanced.

(c) Participation:

    (i)   As part of group decision-making.

    (ii) As part of making a personal response.

The three-fold aims of this Entitlement, as built into the final National Curriculum documentation, are:

- To provide opportunities to acquire the knowledge, values, attitudes, commitment and skills needed to protect and improve the environment.
- To encourage pupils to examine and interpret the environment from a variety of perspectives – physical, geographical, biological, sociological, economic, political, technological, historical, aesthetic, ethical and spiritual.
- To arouse pupils' awareness and curiosity about the environment and encourage active participation in resolving environmental problems.

In so doing environmental education promotes the long-term aims of improving management of the environment and promoting satisfactory solutions to environmental issues.

The official documentation for the cross-curricular theme of environmental education, *Curriculum Guidance* (NCC, 1990), sets out objectives for it that reflect the three dimensions of learning, namely, knowledge, skills and attitudes. The content of this is elaborated upon in Part IV of this text.

A little further north, 1993 marked the date of publication of a keynote and influential publication *Learning for Life* in Scotland (Working Group on Environmental Education, 1993). This was prepared by a working group set up by the Secretary of State for Scotland in 1990. The official response from the Secretary of State to *Learning for Life* came in June 1995, entitled: *A Scottish Strategy for Environmental Education* (Scottish Office, 1995). A new Education for Sustainable Development group was set up by the Government to assist its implementation.

Another notable step forward in the UK was the publication in 1993 of the Toyne Report – *Environmental Responsibility: An Agenda for Further and Higher*

Education (Committee on Environmental Education in Further and Higher Education, 1993). This recommended that every further and higher education institution should adopt and publicise:

1 a comprehensive environmental policy statement;
2 a policy and strategy for the development of environmental education; and
3 action plans for their implementation.

At last, environmental education above school level was seriously on the agenda. Then, in 1996, the UK Government's strategy for environmental education in England was published: *Taking Environmental Education into the 21st Century*. This strategy provides a general framework which encompasses the National Curriculum, the 16–19 sector, further and higher education, training and informal education. The strategy's objective is

> to instill in people of all ages, through formal and informal education, and training, the concepts of sustainable development and responsible global citizenship; and to develop, renew and reinforce their capacity to address environment and development issues through their lives, both at home and at work.
>
> (DfEE, 1996)

On the international scene, probably the most significant publication of the early 1990s is *Caring for the Earth: A Strategy for Sustainable Living* (IUCN, UNEP, WWF, 1991). This was welcomed as a new and thoroughly revised version of the *World Conservation Strategy*. It set out to endorse the key message of the strategy, namely that the conservation of nature and natural resources and human development need not necessarily be in opposition to each other, forever irreconcilable. Rather, the protection and rational use of natural resources is essential for the welfare of present and future human generations, and for the future of the whole planet. The notion of sustainable development, well and truly on the environmental agenda by the 1990s, permeates the text. *Caring for the Earth* is organised into three parts. The first begins by setting out nine principles that point the way to sustainable living; it then identifies actions that can help translate principles into reality. The second part focuses on the main components of the biosphere and organised human activity within them, together with a series of priorities for action. The final part sets out guidelines that aim to help people and organisations adopt and develop the *Caring for the Earth* strategy in their own circumstances. *Caring for the Earth* provided a timely contribution to international debate about environmental education, with its focus on translating ideas and principles of sustainable living into practical actions that may influence governments and individuals alike. Further reference to this publication will be found in Part II of this book.

A stream with many tributaries

No overview of the history and development of environmental education would be complete without reference to many other 'educations' and fields of study that have, in some way, contributed to or conflicted with its evolution. Regrettably, present space dictates that it can only be a brief reference, and so trends are presented in diagrammatic form. I choose the terms 'contribute' and 'conflict' carefully. For example, in terms of contribution, there can be little doubt that environmental education evolved out of, and was significantly influenced by, the rural studies movement. Members of the National Rural Studies Association in the UK formed the core element of the newly named NAEE. Similarly, outdoor education, global education and humane education have clearly influenced (and been informed by) developments in environmental education. Such 'educations' have a great deal in common. Their aims, objectives and content merge and overlap to a considerable degree. If environmental education is my metaphorical stream, then the likes of nature studies, rural studies, fieldwork, urban studies, streetwork, and a host of 'adjectival' educations: outdoor, adventure, earth, humane, heritage, peace, development, global and futures among them, have fed as welcome tributaries into the steady and increasing flow of influence.

By 'conflict' perhaps I really mean fragmentation. Yes indeed, these numerous 'educations' have commonly identifiable attributes, goals and content. If the last four decades could be relived, maybe it would make a great deal of sense for various of them to unite and go forward into the twenty-first century as one influential movement which strives to promote sustainability and quality of life for all on our planet.

Figure 1.2 summarises in a far from precise fashion some key trends in environmental education over the past four decades; whilst Figure 1.3 (p. 27) provides an equally rough 'map' of environmental and related educations, together with some explanatory notes for those wishing to pursue studies of these.

In conclusion to this section, I add, by way of postscript, that the title of this text incorporates the words 'environmental education': no doubt many readers will regret that the phrase 'education for sustainability' does not appear on the cover instead. The reason for the choice is simple. The book is about what the majority of education and policy makers around the globe recognise as environmental education – an element of education relating to the environment that has evolved throughout four decades, which has gained significantly in global impact, and which thus deserves recognition with familiar terminology. As discussed on later pages of the text, perhaps the twenty-first century will herald a revised language of the relationship between people and the environment, and hence a new terminology for teaching and learning about it.

1960s **Nature study**
       Learning about plants and animals, and the physical systems that
       support them

       Fieldwork
       Led by 'experts' with a particular academic focus – biology,
       geography, etc.

1970s **Outdoor/Adventure education**
       Increasing use of the natural environment for first-hand experiences

       Field studies centres
       Growth of field and environmental/outdoor education centres –
       centres for developing awareness through practical activity and
       investigation

       Conservation education
       Teaching about conservation issues

       Urban studies
       Study of the built environment, streetwork

1980s **Global education**
       A wider vision of environmental issues

       Development education
       Environmental education has a political dimension

       Values education
       The clarifying of values through personal experience

       Action research
       Community problem-solving. Pupil-led problem-solving, involving
       fieldwork

1990s **Empowerment**
       Communication, capacity-building, problem-solving and action, aimed
       at the resolution of socio-environmental problems

       Education for a sustainable future
       Participatory action. Relevant approaches to changing behaviours
       and resolving ecological problems

2000s **Community of partners?**
       Pupils, students, teachers, NGOs, politicians – working together to
       identify and resolve socio-ecological problems?

Figure 1.2 Key trends in environmental education

REVIEW AND PROSPECTS

So far, this part has presented an overview of facts, with little in the way of critique. So, to what extent *has* the development of environmental education over the past half century been successful? That is really intended to be a rhetorical question: readers are invited to judge the evidence themselves; to stand aside, and evaluate the real impact and progress of the major national and international initiatives described throughout this book. Some evidence and views are presented below in order to help a judgement to be made; yet maybe the most appropriate time to consider the question is after perusing the content of Part V... or indeed, at the end of the volume... the choice is yours. Meanwhile, I offer some comments on the developmental timeline and events in the UK, so far presented, which at face value read as an extremely positive catalogue of events, as indeed they should. A review of the past four decades shows an ongoing sequence of major international meetings, initiatives and publications, each in the series building upon those that have gone before. The speed of development of thinking and documentation relating to environmental education in the 1970s and 1980s was quite remarkable – once again, attention is drawn to the comment by Wheeler (1985) reported on p. 12, who cites environmental education as being perhaps unique in the history of world education in terms of its speed of progress as a term. In my opinion the late 1980s and 1990s saw no reduction in that speed. Yet what exactly do we mean by dissemination of the term? The last few decades have without doubt seen a great proliferation of documentation pertaining to teaching and learning about the environment. We have access to definitions, aims, guidelines and ideas for interpretation, at national and international levels; we have, equally without doubt, international acknowledgement at all levels (including by many governments) of the importance of environmental education and the entitlement of all to receive it. We have witnessed a substantial refinement of the language used to talk about environmental education, and of appropriate modes of delivery. But what is the effect of all this upon everyday practice?

Let us take some sobering figures from the UK, where there is a lot of evidence (see below) that environmental education is still not being planned or taught in a coherent and comprehensive way in schools. In the mid-1990s, this fact prompted the CEE to prepare a document, *Develop an Environmental Policy: A Call to Action for Schools* (CEE, 1995), and a follow-up practitioners' guide providing advice, guidance, and case studies of good practice. At the launch of the 'Call to Action', the HMI with national responsibility for environmental education reported that, based on official government (OFSTED) inspections of schools, in his own survey carried out in autumn 1994 of 682 primary and secondary schools:

- only 17% referred to environmental education
- only 2% of schools had any policy for environmental education
- 1% had undertaken an audit

- 10 schools had a co-ordinator in post
- where there is a policy there is not necessarily a management plan to achieve it

(CEE, 1996)

It should be noted that over 4,000 schools had responded to the Call to Action by late 1995.

Also in the 1990s, the National Foundation for Educational Research (NFER) undertook a number of specific research projects in environmental education whose results included the following:

- The majority of school managers saw environmental education as either a 'quite' or 'very' important part of the school curriculum. A small minority saw it as essential.

- Only 7% of schools had produced a specific environmental education policy. Forty-two per cent had no environmental education of any sort.

- Less than 25% of schools had a co-ordinated, cross-curricular approach across many subjects. Geography and science curricula were used as the main vehicles for environmental education. Seventy-five per cent of schools also used their personal and social education curriculum.

- The main constraints were identified as: lack of timetable time (because of the need to meet the statutory requirements); lack of resources; lack of staff expertise; lack of staff motivation. Other needs identified were teacher training and increased resources to deliver environmental education.

(Tomlins and Froud, 1994)

These conclusions are sobering, yet are well substantiated by my own experiences as teacher educator and educational researcher. The numbers of teachers attending in-service education courses on environmental education at my own institution fell sharply with the advent of the original National Curriculum documentation and local financial management of schools. The reasons are straightforward: acute lack of time and resources to devote to anything but the curriculum's core subject areas. Almost overnight, before copies of *Curriculum Guidance 7* (NCC, 1990) had had time to gather dust on the shelves, cross-curricular themes were marginalised to the point (in many though thankfully not all institutions) of being relegated to semi-permanent residence on the 'back burner'. With equal speed, it was realised that the National Curriculum and its related assessment arrangements in general were far too burdensome. A new 'slimmed down' set of documents for the core and foundation subjects was rapidly produced, with no mention or reinforcement of the five cross-curricular themes. Whilst the useful content of *Curriculum Guidance 7* continues to form the basis for interpretation of environmental education in England (see also Part IV), the document itself was perceived as being redundant by many schools.

In some senses, the slimming down and reorganisation of the National Curriculum may be regarded as a gloomy chapter in the history book of environmental education: no longer was it a recognised 'theme' or element of the curriculum in its own right. On the other hand, the curriculum revisions placed a great deal of what had traditionally been regarded as the content of environmental education at the heart of two of the statutory subjects – geography and science. In theory then, all pupils following the National Curriculum for schools should receive teaching in environmental education through their programmes of study in geography and science, and as a result of whatever initiatives are taken by individual schools and teachers to pursue this content in cross-curricular ways. This position is reinforced in the School Curriculum and Assessment Authority document *Teaching Environmental Matters Through the National Curriculum* (SCAA, 1996), published with the aim of supporting schools in planning and teaching environmental matters through National Curriculum subjects and religious education for pupils aged 5–16.

- The National Curriculum subject Orders require teaching about environmental matters. The original subject Orders were complemented by the National Curriculum Council's curriculum guidance on environmental education (NCC, 1990, p. 3).

- It is for schools to decide how to teach environmental matters through the National Curriculum and how far to go beyond statutory obligations (p. 4).

- In some National Curriculum subjects, notably geography and science, the programmes of study ensure that environmental matters are taught. ... Environmental matters may also feature in other National Curriculum subjects, not because they are required, but because schools choose to take up opportunities to include an environmental dimension (p. 4).
(SCAA, 1996)

To an extent, then, environmental education is on the statutory agenda; how far it is actually pursued in practice remains, as it always has done in Britain, with the enthusiasm and motivation of individuals. Sterling (1992), when commenting on the NAEE's 1976 publication *Statement of Aims*, points out that

strangely this document stood alone for many years and other key issues relating to the development and implementation of environmental education were not to be addressed by any substantive study. In many respects, the health of environmental education was entirely in the hands of enthusiastic individuals in voluntary organisations, some colleges of education, LEAs and schools.
(Sterling, 1992)

Another (at this stage) rhetorical question: is the situation any different today?

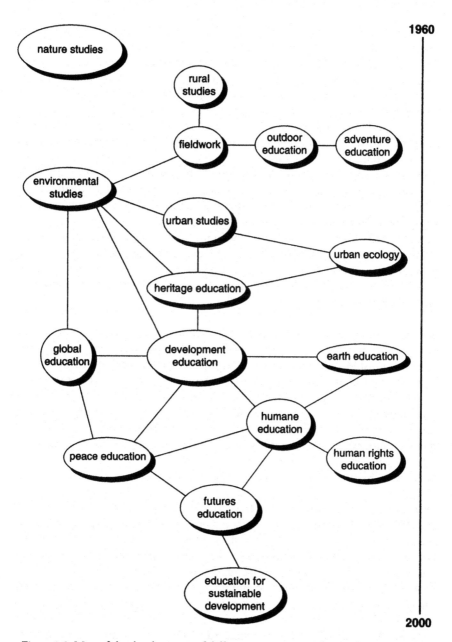

Figure 1.3 Map of the development of different aspects or emphases of environmental education

Figure 1.3 Notes of Explanation (suggested further reading is indicated at the end of the section)

Nature studies, rural studies, fieldwork, environmental studies, outdoor education and adventure education seem almost self-explanatory, being a group of approaches to education that share a focus on 'in' the environment experiences. In the early days of 'nature' and 'rural' studies, emphasis was very much on teacher-directed 'show and tell' techniques. In more recent years, fieldwork and environmental studies have encompassed more of what might be described as participatory, problem-solving techniques, but with a strong emphasis on scientific approaches involving detailed observations, measurements, and the gaining of empirically derived knowledge. 'Outdoor' and 'adventure' education are broader in scope and encompass outdoor activities in which students engage with the environment, such as canoeing, mountain-walking and climbing. They aim to provide opportunities that encourage enjoyment, appreciation and awareness of the environment. Those working in the outdoor and adventure education fields strive to help change attitudes by exposing young people to new and relevant experiences which will lead to a better understanding of themselves as well as their environment. Such activities often operate from centres or specialist bases, rather than schools.

Urban studies promote and advance the study and understanding of the social, physical and natural characteristics of the urban environment and their inter-relationships. Aims include fostering concern about the built environment, improving understanding of the conservation of nature in urban areas, developing wasteland as an education resource and providing city children with experiences of the 'natural' world. Closely linked to urban studies is *heritage education*, which focuses particular concern on the educational use of historic buildings and estates, and the study of our historic heritage. Both of these movements involve close links between educators and other professionals – architects, planners and other local government professionals.

Development education grew out of the increasing concern in the 1960s and 1970s of the United Nations, the churches and charitable organisations about 'Third World' poverty. Originally, development education focused on the plight of certain developing countries. In more recent years it has concerned itself with understanding the level of development in a particular country, necessitating a study of global economic and political systems; understanding development processes within and between all countries, rich and poor; showing that what is appropriate development in one context is not necessarily appropriate in another; showing that the 'West' has much to learn from non-Western perspectives on development; and showing that the 'Third World' is not just a term to describe economically poor nations, but also encompasses areas and groups that have been marginalised by the workings of economic and political systems (e.g. women, the aged, the homeless, the unemployed, ethnic minorities, indigenous peoples, and poor, remote or uninfluential parts of wealthy countries).

Peace education originated in the post-Second World War era. It aimed to help students create more positive attitudes to the people of other nations and so foster international understanding. In more recent years its focus has broadened to include not only 'negative peace' (i.e. absence of war) but also 'positive peace' (i.e. ways of creating more just structures in and between societies). It concerns itself with questions of violence/non-violence, poverty/economic welfare and injustice/justice. It also embraces the study of conflict, conflict avoidance and resolution between individuals, groups and nations, and explores the question of humanity's relationship with the environment.

Human or **human rights education** also had a fairly limited original focus – on civil and political rights (e.g. freedom of speech, freedom of movement of individuals). More recent approaches have broadened to include social and economic rights (e.g. those that ensure material and bodily well-being such as the right to food and shelter) and non-Western concepts of rights and 'new rights' issues such as racism, sexism, the right to development and the rights implications of environmental abuse.

Global education developed out of the proliferation of 'educations' (i.e. development education, environmental education, human rights education, peace education) in an attempt to cluster them all under a more inclusive title. It was recognised that while these separate educations had their own distinctive features and starting points, their concerns are actually complementary and inter-dependent.

Earth education is an approach to environmental education that has been developed by the Institute for Earth Education. The overall goal is 'the process of helping people of all ages live more harmoniously and joyously with the natural world'. A range of structured programmes aims to 'break down barriers in the natural world, encourage an understanding of how ecosystems work, and develop positive caring attitudes to the Earth'.

Humane education is a broad field, ranging from the humane treatment of animals to world peace. It aims to 'provide the basis for responsible planetary citizenship' and to 'achieve compassionate change which challenges the selfish and anthropocentric attitudes that have encouraged exploitation of each other, animals and the world to the point where we are now threatening our very survival on this planet'. Core concepts and attitudes addressed include a reverence for life, respect for animals as living creatures, and an understanding of and concern for keeping the environment safe and natural for all life.

Futures education aims to provide a more 'future-orientated' approach to the curriculum, and bridges the gap between environmental education and 'future studies'. Two inter-linked questions relevant to this field are 'what sort of images do people hold of a *probable* future?' and 'what are people's ideas of *preferable* futures?' In other words, it is concerned with individuals' ideas about the future, how their ideas influence the way they act in the present, and how their present actions influence the future.

Education for sustainable development or sustainability aims to help people understand the inter-dependence of life on Earth, the effects of actions and decision relating to resource use, and factors which foster or impede sustainable development. It is concerned with developing people's awareness, values and attitudes, thus enabling them to be involved effectively in sustainable development.

Suggested Further Reading on related 'Educations' (see Figure 1.3)

Greig, S., Pike, G. and Selby, D. (1987) *Earthrights. Education as if the Planet Really Mattered*, London: WWF, Kogan Page.

Hicks, D. (1996) 'Envisioning the Future: The Challenge for Environmental Educators', *Environmental Education Research*, 2 (1) 101–108.

Pike, G. and Selby, D. (1988) *Global Teacher, Global Learner*, London: Hodder & Stoughton.

Selby, D. (1995) *Earthkind: A Teacher's Handbook on Humane Education*, Stoke on Trent: Trentham Books.

Sterling, S. and EDET Group (1992) *Good Earth-Keeping. Education, Training and Awareness for a Sustainable Future*, London: UNEP-UK.

Van Matre, S. (1979) *Sunship Earth: An Acclimatisation Programme for Outdoor Learning*, Martinsville, Ind.: American Camping Association.

REFERENCES

CEC (1988) Resolution of the Council of Ministers of Education Meeting within the Council, *Environmental Education* (88/C177/03) EC 24 May 1988, Brussels.

CEE (1970) *Environmental Education*, Report of the Council for Environmental Education, No. 9, presented to the Standing Committee of 'The Countryside in 1970', London.

CEE (1995) *Develop an Environmental Policy: A Call to Action for Schools*, Reading: CEE.

CEE (1996) *Annual Review of Environmental Education 1995*, Reading: CEE.

Committee on Environmental Education in Further and Higher Education (Chairman, Peter Toyne) (1993) *Environmental Responsibility: An Agenda for Further and Higher Education*, London: HMSO.

DES (1987) *The National Curriculum 5–16: A Consultation Document*, London: HMSO.

DfEE (1996) *Taking Environmental Education into the 21st Century*, London: HMSO.

Disinger, J. (1983) 'Environmental Education's Definitional Problem', *ERIC Information Bulletin No. 2*, Ohio: ERIC.

HMI (1974) *Environmental Education*, Scottish Education Department, London: HMSO.

HMI (1979) 'Environmental Education' in *Curriculum 11–16*, Supplementary Working Papers, London: DES.

HMI (1989) *Environmental Education from 5 to 16*, London: HMSO.

IUCN (1970) *International Working Meeting on Environmental Education in the School Curriculum*, Final Report, September 1970, Gland, Switzerland: IUCN.

IUCN (1971) *Commission on Education: Report on Objectives, Actions, Organisations and Structures Working Programme*, Gland, Switzerland: IUCN.

IUCN (1980) *World Conservation Strategy*, Gland, Switzerland: IUCN, WWF, UNEP.

IUCN, UNEP, WWF (1991) *Caring for the Earth: A Strategy for Sustainable Living*, Gland, Switzerland: IUCN.

NAEE (1976) *A Statement of Aims*, Walsall, Staffordshire: National Association for Environmental Education.

NCC (1990) *Curriculum Guidance 7 – Environmental Education*, York: NCC.

SCAA (1996) *Teaching Environmental Matters Through the National Curriculum*, London: SCAA.

Schools Council (1974) *Project Environment – Ethics and the Environment*, Harlow: Longman.

Scottish Office (1995) *A Scottish Strategy for Environmental Education: The Statement of Intent by the Secretary of State for Scotland*, Edinburgh: Scottish Office.

Sterling, S. (1992) *Coming of Age – A Short History of Environmental Education*, Walsall: NAEE.

Tolba, M. (1977) 'Opening Statement', *The International Workshop on Environmental Education*, Final Report, Belgrade, Yugoslavia, October 1974, Paris: UNESCO/UNEP.

Tomlins, B. and Froud, K. (1994) *Environmental Education: Teaching Approaches and Students' Attitudes: A Briefing Paper*, Slough: NFER.

UNCED (1992) *Agenda 21, The United Nations Programme of Action from Rio*, New York: UN.

UNESCO (1975) *The International Workshop on Environmental Education Final Report*, Belgrade, Yugoslavia. Paris: UNESCO/UNEP.

UNESCO (1977) *First Intergovernmental Conference on Environmental Education Final Report*, Tbilisi, USSR. Paris: UNESCO.

UNESCO (1987) *International Congress on Environmental Education and Training*, UNESCO/UNEP, Moscow. Paris: UNESCO.

WCED (1987) *Our Common Future*, Oxford: Oxford University Press.

Wheeler, K. (1985) 'Environmental Education: An Historical Perspective', *Environmental Education and Information*, 4 (2), The Environmental Institute, University of Salford.

Working Group on Environmental Education (1993) *Learning for Life: A Report of the Working Group on Environmental Education to the Secretary of State for Scotland*, Edinburgh: Scottish Office.

Part II

THE GLOBAL AGENDA

THE ISSUES

So what *is* the case for the promotion and development of environmental education on a major global scale? In a nutshell, the ever-increasing threats to the resources of the Earth and to the health and stability of its societies justify an urgent need for an informed global citizenship. The pace of change has been very rapid. Our planet is around 4.5 billion years old, and life on Earth has existed for more than 3.5 billion years. Human life has inhabited the planet for some 2 to 3 million years, and for almost all of that time, existed in harmony or sustainable equilibrium with other forms of life. It is only within the last two centuries that human activity has had what might be described as a significant impact upon the environment and its resources; and perhaps only in the last half century has it been evident that this impact is extremely serious. As the impacts of human activities and influences have escalated, so too have the risks and threats associated with those impacts. As the significance of the threats to the Earth's resources, natural systems and populace has become apparent, so too has the need for widescale education relating to our responsibilities towards the environment. Public concern about the state of the Earth and our relationship with it has increased at a pace over the past two decades. There is a high demand for information of the 'what can we do?' variety from the public at large, and also from many industries and businesses in the so-called developed world. In its publication *State of the World 1989*, the Worldwatch Institute (Brown *et al.*, 1989) predicted that historians may look back on the 1980s as a turning point for public concern about the environment.

Presumably, if one is to design and implement educational programmes aimed at producing an informed population of citizens who care about the future of the planet and engage in appropriate pro-environmental behaviours, then some *subject* knowledge of the issues concerned is essential. So we now turn to an overview of the problems and their impacts that threaten the resources and stability of our planet. Of course the overview is extremely brief, and it is certainly not comprehensive; this is not a textbook on environmental issues. The purposes of including this 'taster' of the issues involved is to provide a framework for discussion and further research; to provide indicative content for teacher education courses on the subject knowledge background to environmental education; and to emphasise the complex inter-relationships that exist among issues affecting the global environment. An overview of some of the major points to be considered will be given for each topic, followed by some key remarks made about the topic in *Agenda 21*. The overview focuses on the key issue in each case, and some of its problem or negative impacts. There are of course many examples and case studies of successful remedies and good practice relevant to each topic, which readers will wish to pursue and debate.

Population growth, poverty and inequality

Key issue: global population explosion

- The world's population, currently 5.5 billion, has grown from around 2 billion in 1920 and 3 billion in 1960. At the present time, it increases by some 90 million each year, and is expected to exceed 8 billion by the year 2020 unless the use of birth control methods increases dramatically.

- Over 90 per cent of the projected increase in global population between now and the year 2020 will occur in developing nations in Asia, Latin America and Africa. It is likely that these countries will double their present population in the next 30 years.

- The population increase together with the world's unsustainable consumption pattern is putting ever-increasing stress on the land, water, air, energy and other essential resources of the planet. Rapid population growth is usually accompanied by serious environmental degradation, including soil erosion, desertification and deforestation. It can put a region well beyond its economic and natural resource limits or 'carrying capacity' – threatening its long-term ability to support life.

- Countries with rapid population growth tend to rate very highly on measures of human suffering and very poorly on measures of the physical quality of life. The Population Crisis Committee (Camp and Speidel, 1987) compiled an index of human suffering for each of 130 countries based on 10 measures of human welfare. A high correlation is found between level of suffering and rate of population increase. For example, 30 countries falling in the 'extreme' suffering range are all in Africa and Asia, and have an annual population increase of nearly 3 per cent.

- Rapid population growth can put great stress on political institutions and stability, particularly in regions where there are established ethnic differences. Also there are many links between population growth and social conflict. Declining health and living standards lead to unrest and civil war.

- There are enormous differences in rates of population growth, wealth, education, employment opportunities, health and sanitation, and general standards of living between the so-called 'developed' and less-developed nations of the world. Thus there are serious differences in levels of environmental stress and degradation. Such differences can be addressed only by extensive international co-operation and defrayment of the 'Third World Debt'.

Comments from Agenda 21

- Population concerns should be part of national sustainable development strategies, and countries should establish population goals and programmes. Countries need to assess how the age structure of their populations will create future demands for resources.

- Countries need to know their national population-carrying capacity. Special attention should be given to critical resources, such as water and land, and environmental factors, such as ecosystem health and biodiversity.

- The world needs to do a better job of forecasting the possible outcomes of current human activities, including population trends, per capita resource use and wealth distribution.

- Sustainable development will require reproductive health programmes to reduce maternal and infant mortality, and provide men and women with the information and means to plan family size.

- Population programmes need to be part of broader policies that also deal with such factors as ecosystem health, technology and human settlements, and with socio-economic structures and access to resources.

- Population programmes will require the support of political, indigenous, religious and traditional authorities, the private sector and the scientific community. The programmes will also need adequate funding, including support to developing countries.

- Every country needs a health action plan that includes a national public health system. All countries should have programmes to identify environmental health hazards and reduce the risks. They need to make environment and health safeguards part of national development programmes, and train people to deal with environmental health hazards.

- Every nation needs its own programme to eradicate such root causes of poverty as hunger, illiteracy, inadequate medical and childcare, lack of employment and population pressures. The actions of individual governments must receive support, including financial assistance, because the struggle against poverty is the shared responsibility of all countries.

(Keating, 1993, pp. 8–9)

Food and agriculture

Key issue: growing demand for food; limits to increasing supply

- Each year, some 60–70 million people die from hunger and hunger-related diseases. Around a fifth of the world's population do not consume sufficient calories for a 'normal' active working life.

- Grain production per person is declining at a serious rate in Latin America, Africa and India (26 per cent decline in India since 1983, 24 per cent in Africa since 1974, 12 per cent in Latin America since 1980). Land degradation is a serious cause of this. Soil erosion is seriously degrading croplands in many of the world's most important agricultural regions, and so grain acreage is diminishing.

- Other negative environmental impacts are leading to serious decline in productivity of food-producing areas. In addition to soil erosion, salination, waterlogging and loss of soil fertility are increasing throughout the world. Inefficient or inappropriate crop irrigation is depleting underground water supplies and damaging soils in a number of places. Increased ultraviolet radiation resulting from thinning of the stratospheric ozone layer may also reduce food production.

- The amount of food lost to pests has been estimated at 25 per cent of world harvests. Chemical control of food pests has been widely used but is a very costly method and is harmful. Agricultural chemicals (fertilisers, pesticides, herbicides) are polluting groundwater and surface waters and harming both people and wildlife in many locations. Each year, hundreds of thousands of accidental pesticide poisonings are reported world-wide, including some 45,000 in the USA alone.

- As the availability of fertile cropland declines under pressure from increasing populations, nations depend more and more on genetic manipulations of plants and animals to provide enough food. The genetic base needed to improve crops and livestock is found in the natural and bred genetic diversity of local and wild species or varieties. These crucial genetic resources are rapidly disappearing as a result of habitat destruction, plus reliance on a few highly inbred livestock and crops.

- Social and economic factors have major impacts on the world's food production and distribution systems. In many locations, pressures from increasing populations have already diminished the land's carrying capacity.

Comments from Agenda 21

- Sustainable agriculture and rural development will require major adjustments in agricultural, environmental and economic policies in all countries, and at the international level. This requires co-operation involving rural people, national governments, the private sector and the international community.

- Techniques for increasing production, reducing food spoilage and loss to pests and for conserving soil and water resources are already available but are not widely or systematically applied.

- By the turn of the century, governments should have sound food policies, based on an awareness of the environmental costs and benefits of various policy choices.

- More energy will have to be used to increase food production. This should involve a cost-effective mix of fossil and renewable energy resources, including fuels from wood and plants.

- Better use of the world's great variety of plant and animal genetic resources is essential to diversify and increase food production and improve the quality of draught animals. There is a steady loss of invaluable plant and animal species, and efforts to promote genetic diversity are underfunded and understaffed.

- The best option (for agricultural pest control) is integrated pest management, which combines biological controls, host-plant resistance and appropriate farming practices, to minimise pesticide use. This technique guarantees food production, reduces costs and is environmentally less harmful.

- The world's long-term ability to meet the growing demand for food and other agricultural products is uncertain.

(Keating, 1993, pp. 24–25)

Tropical forests

Key issue: tropical deforestation

- The Earth's tropical rainforests cover around 7 per cent of its land surface, yet contain over two-thirds of all plant and animal species. They are a tremendously rich and essential source of food plus the raw materials upon which agriculture and medicines depend. They also yield a variety of products that have commercial or industrial value.

- A good half of the world's original area of tropical forest land has now gone, and each year some further 11 million hectares are destroyed. Tropical forests are removed for the creation of farm land, for logging, cattle-ranching, and large-scale development projects. Pressures on many forests are increasing rather than decreasing.

39

- Deforestation causes the near or complete extinction of numerous plant and animal species, plus the loss of many valuable forest products, including fuelwood, timber and other products available for human development.

- Deforestation affects the lives of hundreds of millions of people. It causes soil erosion, increased flooding and silting of waterways; shortages of timber and fuelwood; drought; and the displacement of whole societies and cultures.

- Deforestation may alter both regional and global climate. It reduces the number of trees that can retain carbon dioxide, a greenhouse gas.

- There are a number of ways of slowing down or halting the practice and consequences of deforestation, including establishing forest reserves, preventing unsustainable development projects, improving the management of vulnerable forests for sustainable use, reducing pressures for deforestation by making appropriate social and economic changes, and increasing rates of reforestation.

Comments from Agenda 21

- Forests are renewable, and when managed in a way that is compatible with environmental conservation, can produce goods and services to assist in development.

- The survival of forests depends on our recognising and protecting their ecological, climate-control, social and economic values. These benefits should be included in the national economic accounting systems used to weigh development options.

- There is an urgent need to conserve and plant forests in developed and developing countries to maintain or restore the ecological balance, and to provide for human needs.

- National governments need to work with business, non-governmental organisations, scientists, technologists, local community groups, indigenous people, local governments and the public to create long-term forest conservation and management policies for every forest region and watershed.

- Governments should create national action programmes for sustainable forestry development.

- In order to get more value from their forests, some countries will need international co-operation in the form of advice on modern technologies, and the use of fair terms of trade, without unilateral restrictions and bans on forest products.

- In addition to encouraging sustainable use of forests, countries need to create or expand protected area systems to preserve some forests. Such forests are needed to preserve ecological systems, biological diversity, landscapes and wildlife habitat.

- Forests also need to be preserved for their social and spiritual values, including that of traditional habitats of indigenous people, forest dwellers and local communities.

(Keating, 1993, pp. 19–20)

Biological diversity

Key issue: extinction of biological resources (genes, species, populations and ecosystems)

- The normal rates of extinction of many of the world's biological resources have accelerated, and still are rapidly accelerating – as a result of the ongoing destruction of tropical forests and other biologically rich habitats; plus over-harvesting, pollution, and inappropriate introduction of foreign plants and animals.

- It is estimated that by the year 2020, a million or more species of plants, animals and other micro-organisms will have been lost to the planet.

- Biodiversity is essential for human survival. Biological resources provide food, medicines, clothing, housing and a wide range of raw materials. They are important for the future improvement of livestock and crops, and for the development of new medicines and products. Plants and animals are also essential in the maintenance of soil productivity, the degradation of waste, and in pest and flood control.

- Around 1.4 million living species have been identified and named. Some 750,000 are insects, 41,000 are vertebrates (mammals, birds, amphibians, reptiles, fish) and 265,000 are plants. The remainder includes other invertebrates, algae, fungi and micro-organisms. Estimates of the true number of species on the planet range from 5 to over 30 million. It is estimated that the world may be losing biodiversity at the rate of one species per day.

- Habitat loss by human activities, notably destruction of tropical forests, is the major cause of species extinction and planetary loss of biodiversity.

Comments from Agenda 21

- Urgent and decisive action is needed to conserve and maintain genes, species and ecosystems.

A number of recommendations are made for governments, with the co-operation of the United Nations, non-governmental organisations, the private sector and financial institutions. These include:

- The conduct of national assessments on the state of biodiversity.

- The development of national strategies to conserve and sustainably use biological diversity and make these part of overall national development strategies.

- The encouragement of traditional methods of agriculture, agroforestry, forestry, range and wildlife management which use, maintain or increase biodiversity. The involvement of communities, including women, in conserving and managing ecosystems.

- The development of sustainable uses of biotechnology, and ways of safely and equitably transferring it, particularly to developing countries.

- Governments, business and development agencies need to learn more about how to evaluate the impact of development projects on biological diversity, and how to calculate the costs of losing this diversity.

(Keating, 1993, pp. 26–27)

Desertification and drought

Key issue: human impact on the land is causing serious degradation, and increasing poverty and starvation

- Land degradation in the forms of soil erosion, desertification, and loss of soil fertility is having a most serious impact on food production, and on world levels of poverty and starvation.

- Desertification is the process of land degradation caused by human impacts, notably the use of unsustainable agricultural methods (see below), and variations in climate. Drylands of the world that are already ecologically fragile are particularly vulnerable.

- The key short-term impacts of desertification and drought are degradation of grazing lands and decline in food production.

- Seventy per cent of all the world's drylands, which amount to some 3.6 billion hectares or a quarter of the world's land, are already affected by degradation.

- From time to time, notably when rains fail for several consecutive years, the problem becomes extremely serious. Drought conditions along with land degradation contributed to severe famine in sub-Saharan Africa in 1975. An estimated 3 million people died in the same region in the 1980s because of drought.

- Much of the land at high risk of desertification is in Africa and Asia, but substantial at-risk areas are in the south-west of the USA, northern Mexico, Australia and South America.

- Desertification is caused almost entirely by human misuse and overuse of land. Major causes are overgrazing by livestock and deforestation for fuelwood. Other important factors include overcultivation of marginal lands and salinisation from poorly managed irrigation. Even in areas of moderate rainfall, overgrazing and the production of livestock feed can lead to serious losses of topsoil from water erosion.

Comments from Agenda 21

- To stop desertification from spreading, land use, including farming and grazing, must be made environmentally sound, socially acceptable, fair and economically feasible.

- In areas prone to desertification and drought, traditional farmland and grazing styles are often inadequate and unsustainable, particularly in the face of increasing populations. Rural dwellers should be trained in soil and water conservation, water harvesting, agroforestry and small-scale irrigation.

- Poverty is a major factor in accelerating the rate of degradation and desertification. To reduce pressure on the fragile lands, it is necessary to rehabilitate degraded lands, and provide alternative livelihoods for people.

- It is necessary to establish an international drought emergency-response system equipped with food, healthcare, shelter, transport and finances.

(Keating, 1993, pp. 21–22)

Fresh water

Key issue: growing water demand, declining water quality

- Fresh water is essential for the maintenance of life on Earth. It is vital for drinking, sanitation, industry, food production, urban developments, power generation, transportation, inland fisheries and recreation. Adequate supplies of fresh water are available to satisfy projected world-wide demands into the twenty-first century if the resource is used efficiently. However, in many parts of the world there are widespread shortages of water, coupled with gradual destruction and increased pollution of supplies.

- The main causes of current and projected lack of availability of adequate amounts of fresh water include poor management, linked to lack of adequate conservation, inadequately treated sewage and industrial waste, loss of natural water catchment areas, deforestation, dams, river diversions and irrigation schemes; pollution, linked to poor agricultural practices which release pesticides and other harmful chemicals into groundwater; and rapid local increases in demand in some areas.

- In developing nations, less than half of the population has access to safe drinking water and sanitation. Over 10 million deaths occur each year in the world as a result of water-borne intestinal diseases. It is estimated that 80 per cent of all diseases and one-third of deaths in the developing world are caused by drinking contaminated water.

- In industrial nations, surface and underground water supplies are being polluted by industrial and municipal wastes as well as by surface run-off of toxins from agricultural and urban activities.

Comments from Agenda 21

- Many of the problems are the result of a development model that is environmentally destructive, and a lack of public awareness and education about the need and the ways to protect water resources. There is widespread failure to understand the linkages between various forms of development and their impact on water resources.

- Ways must be found of supplying everyone on the planet with an adequate supply of good quality water. To do this, human activities must be adapted to fit within the limits of nature, so that the healthy functioning of ecosystems can be preserved.

- The way to provide all people with basic water and sanitation is to adopt the approach 'some for all, rather than more for some'. A realistic strategy to meet present and future water needs is to develop low-cost but adequate services that can be installed and maintained at the community level.

- Better water management will require innovative technologies, including the improvement of indigenous technologies, to make full use of limited water resources and to safeguard the water from pollution.

- A realistic target date for universal water supplies is 2025.

It is suggested that various approaches are needed to provide adequate water supplies and sanitation, for example:

- There should be mandatory assessment of the environmental impact of all major water-resource development projects that have the potential to impair water quality and aquatic ecosystems.

- Alternative sources of fresh water must be developed. These include de-salting sea water, catching rain water – particularly on small islands – reusing waste water and recycling water.

- In developing and using water resources, priority has to be given to satisfying basic human needs and to safeguarding ecosystems. Beyond these requirements, water users should be charged appropriately.

(Keating, 1993, pp. 32–34)

Oceans and coasts

Key issue: degradation of marine resources

- Oceans cover more than two-thirds of the Earth's surface and, like tropical forests, are vital for the maintenance of biodiversity. Areas such as coral reefs, mangroves and estuaries are among the most highly diverse and productive of the planet's ecosystems.

- Marine fisheries yield some 80 to 90 million tons of fish and shellfish each year. Fishing has increased greatly over the past few decades. There have been significant increases world wide in overfishing, unauthorised fishing, ecosystem degradation and in the use of inappropriate equipment that catches too many fish. Furthermore, there has been too little co-operation among nations to prevent overfishing and related problems.

- Oceans and coastal zones are delicately balanced ecosystems. As well as overharvesting, they are threatened by construction and development; and by pollution from oil, municipal and industrial wastes, and other land- and sea-based sources.

- Oceans influence climate, weather and the state of the atmosphere. They provide not only food, but many other resources for the world's population.

- Some 70 per cent of marine pollution comes from sources on land, including towns, cities, industry, agriculture, forestry, construction activities and tourism.

- The main pollutants include sewage, chemicals, sediments, plastics, metals, oil and radioactive wastes. Many of these substances are toxic; they may be very slow to break down in the water environment, and may accumulate in living creatures, thus entering food chains.

- Many pollutants are deliberately dumped at sea, including radioactive materials. Some 600,000 tons of oil enter the oceans each year as a result of regular shipping, accidents, and illegal discharges.

- There is currently no global scheme to address marine pollution from land-based sources.

Comments from Agenda 21

- The Law of the Sea provides an international basis for the protection and sustainable use of the seas. However, oceans are under increasing environmental stress from pollution, overfishing and degradation of coastlines and coral reefs. It is necessary to:

- Anticipate and prevent further degradation of the marine environment and reduce the risk of long-term or irreversible effects on the oceans.

- Ensure prior assessment of activities that may have significant adverse impact on the seas.

- Make marine environmental protection part of general environmental, social and economic development policies.

- Apply the 'polluter pays' principle, and use economic incentives to reduce pollution of the seas.

- Improve the living standards of coast-dwellers, particularly in developing countries, so people can help to protect the coastal and marine environment.

Other recommendations include:

- Nations need to build and maintain sewage-treatment systems, and avoid discharging sewage near shell fisheries, water intakes and bathing areas. Industrial discharges also need to be controlled and properly treated.

- Countries should change sewage- and waste-management, agricultural practices, mining, construction and transportation to control the run-off of pollutants from diffuse sources.

- Nations should commit themselves to the conservation and sustainable use of marine life, including fish and marine mammals, which include whales, dolphins, porpoises and seals.

- Global warming caused by climate change is likely to cause sea levels to rise, and even a small increase could cause significant damage to small islands and low-lying coasts. Precautionary measures should be undertaken to diminish the risks and effects, particularly on small islands and low-lying coastal areas.

(Keating, 1993, pp. 29–31)

Energy

Key issue: growing energy demand, unsustainable use, pollution of the environment

- Energy stands as one of the most essential of all the Earth's resources. Human life would not exist without the heat, light and food that depend on it. The world's consumption of energy has quadrupled in the past five decades. There has been a very great increase in the use of non-renewable energy sources, notably fossil fuels, yet most energy is used inefficiently.

46

- Air pollution from the increased use of fossil fuels is harming human health, causing acid rain, which in turn damages whole ecosystems, and increases the build-up of atmospheric carbon dioxide and the likelihood of global warming and climate instability.

- Accessing and developing adequate and affordable energy supplies in the long term presents serious economic and environmental problems for both developed and developing nations. Patterns in world energy use are character-ised by sharp contrasts and inequalities.

- Oil accounts for 44 per cent of the world's commercial energy production, coal and other solid fuels 30 per cent, natural gas 21 per cent, and electricity from nuclear and hydropower 5 per cent. Over 2 billion people in developing countries rely on diminishing fuelwood supplies for energy.

- Until recently, the traditional and simplistic approach to energy supply and consumption policies in most nations of the world was to meet increasing demands by expanding supply. Various factors have combined to change this approach, notably the vulnerability of the world economy to oil supply disruptions, fluctuating oil prices, anti-nuclear arguments (see below), greatly increasing environmental damage caused by fossil fuel use, and realisation that many resources being used are non-renewable. As a result of these various factors, policies are gradually shifting towards consideration of sustainable energy production, at the lowest cost, and with the least environmental damage.

- The increase of nuclear power as an energy source has highlighted its potential for nuclear accidents, its high costs, technical and waste disposal problems. This trend has also expanded the world's stock of nuclear weapons and poten-tial for nuclear terrorism.

- It is apparent that because of the complex costs and risks associated with energy obtained from traditional sources such as oil, gas, coal and nuclear materials, it is essential that all nations strive to increase energy use efficiency and conservation, and develop a variety of renewable energy sources.

Comments from Agenda 21

- Much of the world's energy is produced and consumed in ways that cannot be sustained if overall quantities increase substantially.

- Controlling emissions will depend on greater efficiency in energy pro-duction, transmission, distribution and consumption, and on creating environmentally sound energy systems.

Various recommendations are made on what governments need to do, including:

- Modernise existing power systems to gain energy efficiency, and develop new and renewable energy sources, such as solar, wind, hydro, biomass, geothermal, ocean, animal and human power.

- Help people learn how to develop and use more efficient and less polluting forms of energy.

- Co-ordinate regional energy plans so that environmentally sound forms of energy can be produced and distributed efficiently.

- Promote environmental assessment and other ways of making decisions that integrate energy, environment and economic policies in a sustainable manner.

- Promote national energy efficiency and emission standards, and increase public awareness of environmentally sound energy systems.

(Keating, 1993, pp. 15–16)

Atmosphere and climate

Key issue: air pollution, acid deposition, ozone layer depletion and climatic change

- The Earth's atmosphere is under increasing pressure from pollutants. These include the so-called 'greenhouse gases' that may change the climate of the planet, and also from chemicals that reduce the ozone layer (see below).

- Chlorofluorocarbons and other pollutants entering the atmosphere are depleting the Earth's protective ozone layer. In some locations, this depletion is causing an increase in the amount of harmful ultraviolet radiation that reaches the Earth's surface. Depletion of the ozone layer can reduce agricultural crop yields; damage human health by suppressing the immune system, causing skin cancer and cataracts; disrupt ocean food chains; and cause significant changes to the Earth's climate.

- The continuing increased combustion of fossil fuels leads to a related increase in the amount of carbon dioxide in the atmosphere. This trend, together with ever-increasing concentrations of other heat-absorbing gases in the atmosphere, is leading to a gradual but steady increase in global temperatures. The planet is likely to suffer serious alterations in weather patterns, increased storms, the destruction of natural systems, and consequent disruption of agriculture. Many scientists predict that, ultimately, global warming will lead to a melting of polar ice caps, subsequent rises in sea levels, and flooding of low-lying coastal environments.

- Other air pollutants cause 'acid rain'. Nitrogen and sulphur oxides and other pollutants from burning fossil fuels are inflicting serious environmental damage, including acidification of streams, lakes and soils; damage to buildings

48

and materials. Together with ozone these pollutants are also implicated in the death of trees. Such pollution is airborne and may travel long distances through the atmosphere, causing far-reaching damage to both terrestrial and water environments.

- Numerous toxic gases and other pollutants entering the air have been shown to cause serious damage to human health. For example, sulphur and nitrogen oxides damage lungs and cause respiratory diseases; carbon monoxide from motor vehicles can impair the ability of blood to carry oxygen, and affects cardiovascular, nervous and pulmonary systems; ozone, from atmospheric reactions between nitrogen oxides and organic compounds, can cause eye irritation, asthma, possible damage to lung tissue and reduced resistance to infection.

Comments from Agenda 21

- Governments need to develop more precise ways of predicting levels of atmospheric pollutants and greenhouse gas concentrations that would cause dangerous interference with the climate system and the environment as a whole.

- Governments should develop efficient, cost-effective, less polluting and safer rural and urban mass transport, along with environmentally sound road networks.

- Governments should encourage forms of transportation that minimise emissions and harmful effects on the environment.

- Certain uses of the land and seas can decrease the amount of plant material available to take carbon dioxide, a greenhouse gas, out of the air. Governments should promote the sustainable management and conservation of natural greenhouse gas sinks and reservoirs, including forests and salt-water ecosystems.

- Governments should create or strengthen regional agreements, such as the 1979 Convention on Long-range Transboundary Air Pollution, in order to reduce flows of pollutants that harm human health and forests and acidify lakes and rivers.

- Countries should have early-warning systems and responses for air pollution coming from industrial accidents, natural disasters, or the destruction of natural resources.

(Keating, 1993, pp. 15–16)

Managing solid wastes and sewage

Key issue: solid waste volume is exceeding disposal capacity

- The Earth has an ever-growing volume of sewage and solid waste to dispose of. Quantities could increase four to fivefold by the year 2025.

- Solid waste includes garbage, refuse and sludge as well as solids and liquids from industrial, commercial, mining, agricultural and community activities, but excludes solid or dissolved material in domestic sewage.

- This rapidly expanding quantity of waste (solid and sewage), particularly from cities, poses serious threats to human health and the environment. Each year, some 5.2 million people, including 4 million children, die from diseases caused by the improper disposal of sewage and solid waste. Solid waste disposal is also causing serious pollution of groundwater, surface water and the air in many locations.

- In developing countries, less than 10 per cent of urban wastes are treated, and only a small proportion of that treatment meets acceptable standards. At the start of the twenty-first century, around half of the urban population in developing countries will not have adequate waste disposal facilities.

- To manage this growing volume of solid waste, it will be necessary to rely on a combination of approaches to dealing with it, viz: waste reduction, recycling, composting, use of landfills, and incineration. One method alone will be insufficient. Municipal solid waste and sewage volume is exceeding disposal capacity.

Comments from Agenda 21

- The best way to cope with waste problems is through a waste-prevention approach, focused on changes in lifestyles and in production and consumption patterns.

- National plans are needed to minimise the creation of waste, and to ensure that wastes are reused, recycled and safely collected and treated. Waste-control programmes should be developed in co-operation with local governments, businesses, non-governmental organisations and consumer groups.

- Waste-management charges should ensure that those who generate wastes pay the full cost of environmentally safe disposal. This will make waste-recycling and resource-recovery more cost-effective.

- Governments need to provide incentives to recycling, and to fund pilot programmes, such as small-scale and cottage-based recycling industries, compost production, irrigation using treated waste water and recovery of energy from wastes.

(Keating, 1993, pp. 39–40)

Hazardous substances (including nuclear waste)

Key issue: management of unprecedented amounts of hazardous material, including radioactive wastes

- Hazardous substances – including toxic waste, industrial chemicals, pesticides and other toxic agricultural substances, and nuclear waste – are entering the environment in unprecedented quantities.

- Hazardous substances are affecting both human health and the environment. When they are released into the environment as waste, they may contaminate the air, soil, surface water or groundwater, and may harm people and eco-systems. They pose both short- and long-term threats to health and the biosphere in general.

- The term 'hazardous substances' includes any substance that poses a threat to human health or the environment, and encompasses a broader range of materials than those that have toxic qualities. Hazardous substances include materials that are flammable, explosive, corrosive and/or toxic.

- There are no reliable estimates of how much hazardous waste is produced in the world. Some scientists put the figure at 375 million metric tons, others at 500 million, but all agree that the quantity is constantly increasing.

- The chief producers of hazardous wastes (other than nuclear) are the chemical and petrochemical industries, which contribute some 70 per cent of such wastes in industrialised nations.

- The majority of hazardous wastes in industrialised nations are disposed of on land – into landfills, injection wells, or surface impoundments such as pits and ponds. Such disposal sites are subject to leaks that can contaminate both soil and groundwater. Other wastes are discharged into sewers or directly into streams and rivers. A minority of the waste is recycled or processed to reduce its toxicity before final disposal.

- Human exposures to pesticides and similar toxic chemicals are commonplace – through direct contact on farms or industrial sites, or through contaminated food and drinking water. Serious health threats result, including increased likelihood of developing cancer, gastrointestinal or neurological diseases. Some 2 million pesticide poisonings occur in the world each year, the majority being among farmers in developing countries.

- Nuclear waste presents the most significant challenge of all. The substances involved are extremely dangerous, many of them have no known technological

51

detoxifiers, and they will remain life-threatening for thousands of years. As yet, no completely satisfactory programme for safe, long-term nuclear waste disposal has been devised and implemented.

- The radiological and safety risk from radioactive wastes varies from very low for short-lived, 'low level' wastes, to very high for 'high level' wastes. At present, each year the nuclear power industry creates about 200,000 cubic metres of low level and intermediate level waste and 10,000 cubic metres of high level waste and used nuclear fuel. The amount of such waste is increasing, and as some nuclear power plants shut down, more start up.

- The cost to a country of managing and disposing of radioactive waste is very high, though variable according to the technology used.

Comments from Agenda 21

- All national environmental protection plans should include targets for hazardous waste reduction. Programmes are needed to identify wastes and their potential effects, and to minimise them and treat them safely. They should be based on the 'polluter pays' principle.

- Governments should immediately identify contaminated waste disposal sites and populations at high risk, and take the necessary remedial measures, including cleaning up the sites.

- Governments should build treatment centres for hazardous wastes, either at national or regional level. Industry should treat, recycle, reuse and dispose of wastes at or close to the site where they are created.

- Developed countries should promote the transfer of environmentally sound technologies and know-how on clean technologies and low waste production methods to developing countries.

- Governments should ban the export of hazardous wastes to countries that are not equipped to deal with those wastes in an environmentally sound way. Countries should create an alert system to detect illegal traffic in hazardous wastes.

- Countries should promote ways of minimising and limiting the creation of radioactive wastes ... promote the proper planning of safe and environmentally sound ways of managing radioactive wastes, including assessment of environmental impact ... provide for safe storage, processing, conditioning, transportation and disposal of such wastes ... not promote or allow storage or disposal of radioactive wastes near seacoasts or open seas unless it is clear that this does not create an unacceptable risk to people and the marine environment.

(Keating, 1993, pp. 37–38 and p. 41)

Global security

Key issue: warfare is destructive of sustainable development; excessive military spending diverts resources from other security priorities

- The world spends a vast amount of money on military activities – well over $950 billion a year. This is greater than the total income of the least wealthy half of the world population.

- Military spending absorbs a disproportionate share of critical resources and technical skills in most nations. This preoccupation with military matters has led to the neglect of urgent social, economic and environmental problems. Low-income countries spend more on military establishments than on health and education together.

- The 'arms race' is likely to gain a momentum and life of its own, even though it may be an outward entity distracting the world from underlying tensions and conflict.

- Military solutions to non-military problems are inappropriate and ineffective – human tensions and conflict are often related to such matters as environmental degradation, population pressures, lack of basic human needs, and economic decline.

- The term 'global security' should be broadened to include far more than military and economic aspects of national security. True security, including security at both national and personal levels, relates to environmental, demographic and natural resource issues.

- A preoccupation with military factors distracts attention from the underlying causes of insecurity and conflict.

Comments from Agenda 21 (from the Rio Principles)

- Warfare is inherently destructive of sustainable development, and nations shall respect international laws protecting the environment in times of armed conflict, and shall co-operate in their further establishment.

- Peace, development and environmental protection are inter-dependent and indivisible.

(Keating, 1993, p. x)

DEVELOPMENT AND THE ENVIRONMENT

Perhaps this issue should be incorporated into the above list or perhaps it should have come first – certainly the problem of 'development and the environment' is integral to and is a common link between all of the environmental issues so far described. In various and complex ways, as the above snapshot view of issues indicates, development in both 'rich' and 'poor', developed and developing, nations is seriously degrading the Earth's land, air and water resources. During the past half century, very great effort and massive amounts of cash have been devoted to so-called economic development around the world. Yet only a decade ago, developing countries, with 77 per cent of the world's population, had an average income per person of $670 per year, less than 6 per cent of the average income of $12,070 in industrial nations. The gap between the 'rich' and the 'poor' is ever widening, and the impact of development on the environment is ever increasing.

Key issue: unsustainable development

- The gap between Third World 'poor' and Western, industrialised 'rich' nations is large and widening. During the past decade, many developing countries paid out more in debt repayments to developed nations than the total amount they received from exports and development assistance. These developing nations had to reduce imports, investment and consumption, and they were less able to fight poverty at home. In some cases, the financial drain resulted in cuts in health care, education and environmental protection. Thus there is a net flow of money from developing to industrialised countries.

- Industrialised countries have unsustainable patterns of consumption and production. Such excessive demands and unsustainable lifestyles among the wealthy sectors of humanity contribute significantly to environmental degradation (see below). These patterns actually worsen poverty and degradation in the Third World, where basic human needs often remain unmet.

- The particular problems of developing countries may be summarised as: foreign debt; the need to export in order to acquire foreign currency; over-population; unmet basic human needs; poverty; inadequate or misconceived government policies; overuse or misuse of natural resources; and environmental degradation.

- Industrialised nations are also in a continual state of development. Problems associated with this ongoing process include serious environmental damage resulting from use of energy, resources and the generation and disposal of wastes; depletion of finite resources and unmet basic human needs of significant elements of the population.

Comments from Agenda 21

- Developing countries critically need investments to stimulate economic growth and meet the basic needs of their people in a sustainable manner. They should diversify exports and co-operate more among themselves in economic development plans.

- The world needs to offer assistance to developing nations in managing and diversifying their economies, and in managing natural resources for sustainability. Market forces such as interest and foreign exchange rates need to be stable. The prices of commodities in all nations need to reflect the environmental and social costs of their production.

- To be sustainable over the long term, development plans must deal with the conservation and protection of resources. A development policy that focuses mainly on increasing the production of goods without ensuring the sustainability of the resources on which production is based will sooner or later run into declining productivity.

- We must consider the need for new concepts of wealth and prosperity, which allow higher standards of living through changed lifestyles and are less dependent on the Earth's finite resources and more in harmony with the Earth's carrying capacity.

- Some economists are questioning traditional concepts of economic growth. They underline the importance of pursuing economic objectives that take account of the full value of natural resource capital.

- Achieving sustainable development will require efficiency in production and changes in consumption patterns. In many instances, this will require reorientation of existing production and consumption patterns which have developed in industrial societies and are, in turn, emulated in much of the world.

- Development strategies will have to deal with the combination of population growth, health of the ecosystem, technology and access to resources. The primary goals of development include poverty alleviation, secure livelihoods, good health and quality of life, including an improvement in the status of women.

(Keating, 1993, pp. 2–5)

As a response to ever-increasing concern about environment and development issues and the increasingly obvious detrimental impacts of human activity on the Earth and its resources, a number of major global initiatives were established. These are outlined and discussed on pp. 60–77 below, where the definition of the core concept of sustainable development will be returned to.

PROBLEM IMPACTS AND CAUSES: INTER-DEPENDENCE AND PRIORITY SOLUTIONS

What will be very apparent to the reader of the above glimpse into the array of problems and issues affecting the planet is their obvious complexity, their inter-relationships and inter-dependence. Take some examples from the above overview: rapid population growth is usually accompanied by serious environmental degradation, including soil erosion, desertification and deforestation; deforestation causes soil erosion, increased flooding, drought and the displacement of whole societies and cultures; the main causes of current and projected lack of availability of adequate amounts of fresh water include poor management, linked to lack of adequate conservation, inadequately treated sewage and industrial waste, loss of natural water catchment areas, deforestation, etc., and pollution, linked to poor agricultural practices which release pesticides and other harmful chemicals into groundwater; air pollution from the increased use of fossil fuels is harming human health, causing acid rain, which in turn damages whole ecosystems and increases the build-up of atmospheric carbon dioxide and the likelihood of global warming and climate instability. . . . The so-called environmental crisis is an incredibly complicated web or network of inter-related causes and problem impacts.

Furthermore, there are not just local and immediate links among the Earth's key natural systems of land, air and water. International or global links may be immediately apparent, or unexpected and distant in terms of both space and time. For example, the accident at Chernobyl nuclear power station in the Ukraine, USSR, which occurred in April 1986, started a great fire and released radioactive debris into the air. Uncontrollable clouds dispersed lethal deposits over the land of some 20 countries, up to 2,000 km from the reactor site. It is impossible to provide an accurate estimate of the impact of the disaster in terms of casualties. It has been estimated that 24,000 citizens of the then USSR will die from Chernobyl-caused cancer-related deaths; that during the next 50 years there will be up to 60,000 Chernobyl-caused deaths around the world, 1,000 birth defects and 5,000 cases of radioactive-related genetic abnormality. Researchers predicted that the Chernobyl disaster would cause 450–500 cancer deaths in the UK over a 40-year period, as well as thousands of non-fatal cancers (Elsworth, 1990). Whilst Chernobyl may be regarded as a tragic and extreme example – an 'accident' – the principles of its impact apply across the whole spectrum of global environmental issues. Environmental degradation, modification of ecosystems and their adverse impacts upon life-forms and societies apply to all nations. Yet the 'costs' are not equally shared among them. The polluter, the exploiter, the degrader does not necessarily pay the cost of damage or bear the responsibility of solutions. Wealthy countries do not necessarily acknowledge or bear the consequences of their actions; often it is economically developing countries that have no choice but to do so.

A fundamental question in the minds of readers will no doubt be: 'So where do we begin to break through this complex network of inter-related issues; where do the solutions begin?'

Various interesting and important attempts have been made to illustrate some of the relationships between major impacts and important causes of global problems, and to indicate the relative importance of these underlying causes. One such attempt has been made by the Global Tomorrow Coalition in the USA (Corson, 1990). This study, drawing on analysis of research on a range of global problems, assumes that two inter-related kinds of problems can be distinguished:

'Problem impacts' or visible effects that appear to be caused by or result from other factors (e.g. deforestation):
- Unmet basic human needs for safe water, food, shelter, health care, education, employment, etc.
- Species depletion (extinction of plants and animals), habitat degradation
- Land degradation: soil erosion, desertification, loss of soil fertility
- Depletion of non-renewable energy and minerals
- Depletion of fresh water (groundwater and surface water)
- Water pollution: chemical and bacterial contamination of groundwater and surface water
- Air pollution: urban air pollution, acid deposition, ozone layer depletion, greenhouse gas build-up
- Conflict and war: domestic and international

Underlying 'problem causes' that may be less visible, but seem to play a role in creating or causing the more visible impacts (e.g. population growth):
- Unsustainable population growth
- Poverty and inequality
- Unsustainable food production
- Unsustainable energy use
- Unsustainable industrial production

Analysis of relevant research relating to each of these impacts and causes (Corson, 1990) has informed tentative estimates of the relative importance of the underlying causes. These estimates are described on a four-fold linear scale, i.e. very important cause, moderately important cause, less important but significant cause, unimportant or insignificant cause. The following conclusions are drawn:

- *Unsustainable population growth* (that is, growth of human population that diminishes the Earth's long-term capacity to support life) is an important underlying cause of all eight problem impacts.
- *Poverty and inequalities* (that is, inequitable access to factors such as land, food, shelter, health care, education, employment and political power) are important causes of unmet basic human needs, depletion of plant and animal species, land degradation, and conflict and war. They are less important but significant causes of water and air pollution.
- *Unsustainable agriculture* (that is, reliance on methods of food production that emphasise maximum short-term yields while causing environmental damage and long-term loss of natural productivity) is an important or significant cause of all problem impacts.
- *Unsustainable energy use* (use that is inefficient, wastes non-renewable energy sources, releases harmful effluents, or causes deforestation or other

environmental damage) is an important cause of air pollution, depletion of non-renewable energy sources, and land degradation. It is a less important but significant cause of habitat degradation, water pollution, and conflict.

- *Unsustainable industrial production* (production that is inefficient, wastes primary resources, produces harmful effluents, or causes other environmental damage) is an important cause of energy, mineral and water depletion, and air and water pollution. It is a less important but significant cause of habitat degradation and conflict.

Based on these estimates, unsustainable population growth is clearly the single most important causal factor across the entire range of problem impacts listed. Unsustainable food production is the next most important cause across all impacts, followed by unsustainable industrial production, poverty and inequality, and unsustainable energy use.

> For each problem impact, the estimates suggest which of the five problem causes are most important. For example, for both unmet needs and species depletion, population growth and poverty are estimated to be very important causes. For land degradation, population growth and food production are very important. For water depletion, food production is a very important cause; and for water pollution, industrial production is very important. For air pollution, both energy use and industrial production are judged to be very important causal factors.
>
> (Corson, 1990)

This study then goes on to translate the five causal factors into seven priority solutions for the remedy of global environmental issues. These are:

- Slowing population growth
- Reducing poverty and inequalities
- Making agriculture sustainable
- Protecting forests and other habitats
- Making energy use sustainable
- Making water use sustainable
- Reducing waste generation

As before, for each problem impact a four-fold scale is used to suggest the likely importance or effectiveness of the seven priority solutions, i.e. very important solution, moderately important solution, less important but significant solution and unimportant or insignificant solution. Based on estimates that draw upon a wide range of sources and are detailed in the study, the following conclusions are drawn:

- *Slowing population growth* is important for alleviating all eight problem impacts.
- *Reducing poverty and inequalities* – which includes such factors as improving health, longevity, and literacy; increasing employment and political participa-

tion; and broadening opportunities for women and minorities – is important for meeting basic human needs, slowing species depletion, curbing land degradation, and reducing conflict and war. It is less important but significant for curbing water pollution.

- *Making agriculture sustainable*, which includes reducing soil erosion and decreasing the use of harmful chemicals and farming practices, is important for curbing land degradation, water pollution, and depletion of water, energy, and plant and animal species. It is less important but significant for meeting basic human needs and for reducing air pollution and conflict.

- *Protecting forests and other habitats*, which includes reforestation and protection of other living resources, is important for slowing species depletion, curbing land degradation, and reducing air pollution and fresh water depletion. It is less important but significant for slowing depletion of non-renewable energy and for meeting basic needs.

- *Making energy use sustainable*, which includes improving energy efficiency, conserving energy through means such as economic incentives, and developing renewable energy sources, is important for reducing air pollution, land degradation, depletion of energy and minerals, and conflict. It is less important but significant for reducing species depletion and meeting basic needs.

- *Making water use sustainable*, which includes improving the efficiency of water use and protecting water quality, is important for curbing water depletion and pollution. It is less important but significant for reducing energy depletion, land degradation, and conflict, and for meeting basic needs.

- *Reducing waste generation*, which includes improving production processes and recycling liquid and solid wastes, is important for reducing air and water pollution and energy and mineral depletion. It is less important but significant for meeting basic needs.

Based on these estimates, it can be concluded that slowing population growth is the most effective single measure for alleviating the range of global problem impacts. Making agriculture sustainable is the next most effective measure across the entire range of problems. Protecting forests and using energy sustainably rank next in effectiveness, followed by reducing poverty, using water sustainably, and reducing waste generation.

(Corson, 1990)

This analysis could well appear to be highly subjective and oversimplistic. The authors acknowledge that the estimates of relative importance throughout are very tentative subjective appraisals. Nevertheless, the estimates are based on a wide range of relevant supporting material, including data obtained from studies of national research councils in various locations, the United Nations, the OECD, the Worldwatch Institute and the report of the WCED. If any serious attempt is to be made to remedy the entire range of global problem impacts, and eliminate their causes, then a knowledge of priority solutions and the

59

general extent of their likely impact on the whole range of issues is surely essential. Furthermore, such knowledge can well inform decision-making in situations where limited resources are available for tackling environmental problem impacts and deploying solutions, and hard decisions have to be made about prioritisation.

What is clear is that the range, intensity and complexity of global environmental problems impacting upon the Earth continues to present an acute challenge to governments, NGOs, existing institutions and individuals alike. Key questions include: What are the most appropriate strategies for achieving sustainable development both within specific problem areas and across the whole spectrum of issues? Are our existing organisations, structures, policies and practices adequate to cope with the challenges the world faces? Various major international initiatives have addressed, either directly or indirectly, these and related questions. So we now turn to an overview of some of the most significant events or documents that have impacted upon the world in the relatively recent past. For each initiative, its main goals and outputs will be described, and, where appropriate, attention will be drawn to commonalities, limitations and evidence of progression in thinking or action within or among the initiatives.

PROGRESS TOWARDS SUSTAINABLE DEVELOPMENT

The *World Conservation Strategy*

The idea of sustainable development was first used in an international forum in the *World Conservation Strategy* (IUCN, 1980). The Strategy, published in March 1980, was a document only 70 pages long, representing the work of some 700 scientists and specialist advisers, and 450 government agencies and conservation organisations. It was the result of more than two years of intensive preparation by IUCN with the financial backing and support of the WWF, UNEP, UNESCO and the United Nations Food and Agriculture Organisation (FAO).

The concept of sustainable development as used within the Strategy may be interpreted as present development of available resources without compromising the ability of future generations to meet their needs. The Strategy argues for three priorities to be incorporated into all development programmes, namely, the maintenance of essential ecological processes, the sustainable use of natural resources, and the preservation of genetic diversity and the conservation of wild species.

> The World Conservation Strategy has been described as 'an arrow aimed at a paradox' and the paradox is this – as we increase our demands on the Earth to support us we are reducing its capacity to do so. Forests are being felled and wetlands drained. We are using up the world's irreplaceable stocks of minerals and fossil fuels at an ever-increasing rate. We dump our wastes in the oceans, rivers and atmosphere . . . and build roads and

houses on good agricultural land. We exploit wild animals and plants to the point of economic, if not total extinction. We take for today and think little of tomorrow. The World Conservation Strategy is a global remedy for this dangerous situation . . . an instruction manual for keeping the Earth alive.

(ICCE, UNEP, IUCN, 1984)

The Strategy argues that effective conservation is not merely desirable, but essential, if long-term economic growth is to be achieved. The 'essence' of the message of the Strategy is that conservation and development need each other. A key aspect of its recommendations is the integration of conservation principles and objectives with social and economic development. Governments and development agencies must be made more aware that conservation is not just another word for 'nature study' and should not be dismissed as being of little political or economic relevance (ICCE, UNEP, IUCN, 1984).

Despite that message, the main criticism made of the Strategy when launched was that it was anti-development – largely because of its emphasis on conserving the physical environment in its current state. It stressed sustainability in ecological terms, and was concerned to a far lesser extent with economic development. The Strategy tended to view economy–environment relationships rather simply, in terms of negative human impact on the environment. Hence it was seen to focus too much on the impacts or symptoms of environmental degradation, rather than the causes. For example, it suggested that clearance of tropical forest areas should be ceased – without consideration of the fact that in some instances such clearance is defensible and desirable, e.g. for essential agriculture. Further criticism of the document focused on its 'anti-poor' bias. The actions of poor nations and poverty itself were seen as underpinning some of the prime causes of unsustainable development, whilst analysis actually suggests that poverty and degradation of the environment are consequences of dominant patterns of development.

The launch of the *World Conservation Strategy* and the debate it generated represented a most important stage in the understanding and analysis of environmental issues. For the first time, the term 'sustainable development' was used in a key international forum; and with hindsight, the criticisms levelled at the document led to important developments in the world's understanding of sustainability. A reformulation of the concept incorporated a wider vision of the relationships that exist among the economy, development and the environment, and led to the creation of a World Commission on Environment and Development to examine further the issues involved.

The World Commission on Environment and Development

The WCED, chaired by the then Prime Minister of Norway, Gro Harlem Brundtland, was established in 1983. As an independent Commission of the United Nations, the WCED, or Brundtland Commission as it became known,

61

included individuals from 22 nations. Membership included 6 Commissioners from Europe (with 3 from Eastern Europe), 5 from Africa, 5 from Asia (including one from the Middle East), 3 from North America and 3 from South America. Its huge task was to investigate the state of the world, to suggest ways into the twenty-first century that would allow the planet's rapidly growing population to meet its basic needs, and to come up with a 'global agenda for change'. The Commission engaged in a great deal of research and debate. The group, composed of ministers, scientists, diplomats and law makers, studied, debated and held public hearings on five continents over almost three years. The outcome of its endeavours was a report almost 400 pages long, published in April 1987, entitled *Our Common Future* (WCED, 1987). The Commission's Chair wrote in the Report's foreword:

> Our message is directed towards people, whose well-being is the ultimate goal of all environment and development policies. Unless we are able to translate our words into a language that can reach the minds and hearts of people young and old, we shall not be able to undertake the extensive social changes needed to correct the course of development.
>
> (WCED, 1987)

Our Common Future, otherwise known as the Brundtland Report, defines sustainable development as: 'Development that meets the needs of the present without compromising the ability of future generations to meet their needs.'

> Humanity has the ability to make development sustainable – to ensure that it meets the needs of the present without compromising the ability of future generations to meet their own needs. The concept of sustainable development does imply limits – not absolute limits but limitations imposed by the present state of technology and social organisation on environmental resources and by the ability of the biosphere to absorb the effects of human activities. But technology and social organisation can be both managed and improved to make way for a new era of economic growth. The Commission believes that widespread poverty is no longer inevitable. . . . A world in which poverty is endemic will always be prone to ecological and other catastrophes. . . . Sustainable development is not a fixed state of harmony, but rather a process of change. . . . We do not pretend that the process is easy or straightforward. Painful choices have to be made. Thus, in the final analysis, sustainable development must rest on political will.
>
> (WCED, 1987)

Thus the Report identifies two key concepts that are tied to the process of sustainable management of the Earth's resources:

1 The basic needs of humanity – for food, clothing, shelter, and jobs – must be met. This involves, first of all, paying attention to the largely

unmet needs of the world's poor, which should be given over-riding priority.

2 The limits to development are not absolute but are imposed by present states of technology and social organisation and by the impacts upon environmental resources and upon the biosphere's ability to absorb the effect of human activities. But technology and social organisation can be both managed and improved to make way for a new era of economic growth.

(IIED/Earthscan, 1989)

It advanced the following list of critical objectives for sustainable development policies:

- Reviving economic growth
- Changing the quality of growth
- Meeting essential needs for jobs, food, energy, water, sanitation
- Ensuring a sustainable level of population
- Conserving and enhancing the resources base
- Reorienting technology and managing risk
- Merging environment and economics in decision-making processes

Our Common Future is sub-divided into three main sections:

Common Concerns:	A Threatened Future
	Towards Sustainable Development
	The Role of the International Economy
Common Challenges:	Population and Human Resources
	Food Security: Sustaining the Potential
	Species and Ecosystems: Resources for Development
	Energy: Choices for Environment and Development
	Industry: Producing More With Less
	The Urban Challenge
Common Endeavours:	Managing the Commons
	Peace, Security, Development and the Environment
	Towards Common Action: Proposals for Institutional and Legal Change

The Report contains many specific recommendations for institutional and legal change, which cannot adequately be described here. By way of summary, the Commission's main proposals fall within six priority areas:

- Getting at the Sources – International and regional organisations and national governments must start making bodies directly accountable for the environmental effect of their actions.
- Dealing with the Effects – Agencies formed to protect and restore the

environment should be reinforced, especially the United Nations Environment Programme.

- Assessing Global Risks – The capacity to identify, assess and report on risks to the environment must be improved. This should not only be the responsibility of individual governments; a new independent co-ordinating body should be set up.
- Making Informed Choices – The public, NGOs, scientists and industry should all have the opportunity to participate in decision-making.
- Providing the Legal Means – National and international law is being outpaced by events. Governments must fill the major gaps.
- Investing in our Future – The overall cost effectiveness in halting pollution has been shown over the last decade. But a commitment to sustainable development has large financial implications, and a new priority and focus must be taken up by financial institutions, aid agencies and governments. Developing countries need a strong infusion of financial support from international sources for environmental restoration, protection and improvement. Major lending agencies like the World Bank, the International Monetary Fund, and the regional development banks should upgrade their environmental programmes.

Our Common Future concludes with a 'Call for Action' which asks the UN General Assembly to 'transform this report into a UN Programme of Action on Sustainable Development'. Sustainable development is seen not as a fixed state, but rather as a process of change in which each nation achieves its potential for development, whilst also improving the quality of the environmental resources upon which the development is based. Throughout, the Report argues that sustainable development at a global level can be achieved only through major changes in the ways in which our planet is managed. Suggested changes include those in political systems, which allow effective citizen participation in decision-making processes; in economic systems, which lead to the ability to generate surpluses and technical knowledge on a self-reliant and sustained basis; in social systems, which provide solutions to tensions arising from our present form of development; in production systems, which respect the obligation to preserve the ecological base for development; in technological systems, which can search continuously for new solutions; in international systems, which foster sustainable patterns of trade and finance; and in administrative systems, which promote flexibility and have the capacity for self-correction.

The Report of the WCED was ambitious, and based on a vast array of accumulated evidence and wisdom. One criticism made of it is that it set a very broad and complex agenda for change in the direction of achieving sustainable development, without identifying the many and specific barriers that exist to achieving the intended goals. Mechanisms for achieving the end results appear as rather vague statements lacking in precision or guidelines for translating them into specific actions.

More fundamental criticism attacks the Report's definition of development, and this is clearly important criticism since the Commission's analysis is based on a certain conception of development, and thus of economic growth. Anupam Mishra, an Indian environmentalist, says:

> We should not assume that we can look for solutions to our problems within the framework of the current development pattern. It would be folly to think the Brundtland Commission can find solutions within the 'counter-productive framework' of governments, the United Nations, the World Bank, and so on. Because the present structures have given us the disease, is it then logical that they should also provide the cure? This seems to be the limitation of this Commission, because it itself stemmed from the current framework.
>
> (Court, 1990)

By 'the current framework' is meant that dominant pattern of development today, based on Western culture. This has created a universal order: universal values, universal economics, universal science. Critics of this culture, including Shiva and Bandyopadhyay, emphasise its emphasis on private endeavour, interests and profits and indeed its non-sustainability:

> The ideology of the dominant pattern of development derives its driving force from a linear theory of progress, from a vision of historical evolution created in eighteenth and nineteenth century Western Europe and universalised throughout the world, especially in the post-war development decades. The linearity of history pre-supposed in this theory of progress, created an ideology of development that equated development with economic growth, economic growth with expansion of the market economy, modernity with consumerism, and non-market economics with backwardness. The diverse traditions of the world, with their distinctive technological, ecological, economic, political and cultural structures, were driven by this new ideology to converge into a homogeneous monolithic order modelled on the particular evolution of the west.
>
> (Court, 1990)

According to this viewpoint, the dominant development paradigm disregards the true complexity and inter-relationships of all processes on Earth, a complexity encompassed in the Gaia Hypothesis, an alternative paradigm articulated and developed by James Lovelock (1979). For Lovelock, the

> entire range of living matter on Earth . . . could be regarded as a single living entity, capable of manipulating the Earth's atmosphere to suit its overall needs. This organism, of which human society is a part, but only one part, regulates her activities in a very complex and subtle way.
>
> (Lovelock, 1979)

This is a radically different view from that embodied in the 'dominant development paradigm', which sees the Earth and its resources merely as a place with raw materials to be used by its inhabitants. Proponents of the Gaia theory accept a concept of development that is based on restoring internal control, creating stability and peaceful co-operation.

> Such a concept doesn't allow strong external influences. It will maximise 'stocks' (physical, intellectual, ecological) and will minimise the movement and export of things (in the form of goods, natural resources, capital and so on). Essentially, it runs contrary to the open market system. Sustainable development in this sense will demand solving the problem of domination in society élites. . . . It is in this sense also a critique and action against the dominant paradigm of development. Sustainable development therefore means solving a conflict which is rooted deep in our images of the world and the organisation of our society.
> The Report of the World Commission on Environment and Development does not contain any of this critique. . . .
>
> (Court, 1990)

Such criticisms fuelled important and far-reaching dialogue. Whatever views may be held on these fundamental issues, the fact remains that the Brundtland Commission successfully steered the world's thinking and debate on the formulation and reorientation of policies relating to environment and development. Consideration of the environmental consequences of any action had been placed firmly on the agenda of governments, NGOs and international agencies alike.

By late 1989 the Report had been published in 17 languages and had generated many other publications that provided commentaries on or developed aspects of its policy recommendations. A Centre for our Common Future was established in Geneva as a focal point for the environmental activities of governments, multilateral institutions, scientific bodies, industry and NGOs.

Within the United Nations systems, the Brundtland Report inspired the planning of a major global Conference on Environment and Development to take place in 1992, marking the twentieth anniversary of the UN Conference on the Human Environment that had been held in Stockholm.

Caring for the Earth

In 1991, the IUCN together with UNEP and WWF published a completely revised and updated version of the *World Conservation Strategy* entitled *Caring for the Earth: A Strategy for Sustainable Living* (IUCN/UNEP/WWF, 1991). The foreword to this *WCS* successor indicates that it is founded on the conviction that people can alter their behaviour when they see that it will make things better, and can work together when they need to. It is aimed at change because values, economies and societies different from most that prevail today are needed if we are to care for the Earth and build a better quality of life for all.

66

The aim of *Caring for the Earth* is to help improve the condition of the world's people, by defining two requirements. One is to secure a widespread and deeply-held commitment to a new ethic, the ethic for sustainable living, and to translate its principles into practice. The other is to integrate conservation and development: conservation to keep our actions within the Earth's capacity, and development to enable people everywhere to enjoy long, healthy and fulfilling lives. It extends and emphasises the message of the World Conservation Strategy.

(IUCN/UNEP/WWF, 1991)

The text of *Caring for the Earth* is divided into three main sections. Part I, 'The Principles for Sustainable Living', begins with a chapter that defines nine principles to guide the way towards sustainable societies. These principles are:

- respect and care for the community of life
- improve the quality of human life
- conserve the Earth's vitality and diversity
- minimise the depletion of non-renewable resources
- keep within the Earth's carrying capacity
- change personal attitudes and practices
- enable communities to care for their own environments
- provide a national framework for integrating development and conservation
- forge a global alliance

Chapters that follow recommend activities that illustrate and give substance to the more abstract principles. For example, within the chapter 'Keeping Within the Earth's Carrying Capacity':

Action 5.1 Increase awareness about the need to stabilise resource consumption and population

Governments, educational bodies and non-governmental groups in all countries should support and undertake formal and informal education to make people aware that:

- the carrying capacity of the Earth is not unlimited;
- excessive and wasteful use of resources, particularly in upper-income countries, is a major threat to the Earth's carrying capacity;
- people in high-consumption countries can eliminate wasteful consumption without reducing the quality of life, and often with financial savings (for example, through energy conservation);
- consumption patterns, family health and size, and social welfare are closely inter-related;
- population stabilisation is essential, and men and women must accept their shared responsibility for achieving it;
- enhanced, but sustainable, production of agricultural and other renewable resources is essential to meet the inevitable rise in human needs.

The campaigns and programmes will be more effective if guided by the ethic for living sustainably and by the results of research on cultural attitudes to these issues.

(IUCN/UNEP/WWF, 1991)

Part II of *Caring for the Earth*, 'Additional Actions for Sustainable Living', describes actions that are required in relation to the main areas of human activity and some of the major components of the biosphere. The subjects of these chapters are energy; business, industry and commerce; human settlements; farm and range lands; forest lands; fresh waters; and oceans and coastal areas. For each topic, a brief survey of the relevant issues is provided, followed by a series of recommended priority actions.

In the single chapter that comprises Part III of the text, guidelines are proposed to help users adapt the strategy to their own needs and capabilities and implement it. For example:

Action 17.8 Building up the Global Alliance

The global alliance . . . is crucial to the human future. Few, if any, nations have the resources and skills to achieve sustainability on their own – and those tempted to try could do so only by retreating into isolation. . . . Following the UN Conference on Environment and Development governments should:

- strengthen and streamline the United Nations machinery to ensure a co-ordinated approach to environmental issues, based on an agenda whose priorities are determined by the widest practicable process of dialogue;
- build new machinery to ensure that dialogue at the national and inter-national levels reflects the knowledge, skills and concerns of all sectors of society, including NGOs, business, commerce, industry, indigenous peoples, and religious groups;
- establish new international financial mechanisms that will support technical co-operation and promote the transfer and application of the best available technology in all parts of the world, and so create the best possible conditions for sustainable resource use and protection of the global environment;
- review and adapt the world's trading system so that markets are more open to the produce of lower-income countries, and so that, taken in conjunction with the elimination of rescheduling of debt and the increase in development assistance, net resource flows are reversed and run from the higher-income to the lower-income countries;
- strengthen the global machinery for monitoring and research, so that the policies of nations are increasingly based on a common body of reliable knowledge.

(IUCN/UNEP/WWF, 1991)

Part III also sets out a series of targets of achievable, concrete steps that could be taken by specified dates. For example:

Changing Personal Attitudes and Practices

By 1995 Clearinghouse for information on environmental education established.
By 2000 National plans to promote sustainable living adopted in at least 50 countries.
Support for environmental education and training doubled (from 1990) by development assistance agencies.
By 2005 Incorporation of environmental education in school curricula in all countries.
By 2010 Support for environmental education and training quadrupled (from 1990) by development assistance agencies.
National plans to promote sustainable living adopted in all countries.

(IUCN/UNEP/WWF, 1991)

Caring for the Earth was prepared through a wider process of consultation than was possible when the *World Conservation Strategy* was written. Its strength is its accessibility: it is a document intended to restate current thinking about conservation and development in a way that will persuade people at all levels – governments, NGOs, individuals and so on – that something can be done towards the achievement of sustainability.

The United Nations Conference on Environment and Development (UNCED)

In June 1992 the United Nations convened its Conference on Environment and Development in Rio de Janeiro, Brazil, the so-called 'Earth Summit' – by far the largest event of its kind ever held. Close to 10,000 delegates from 150 or more countries met in association with the official gathering of 116 national political leaders, whilst around 15,000 individual citizens, representatives of NGOs and activists participated in a parallel Global Forum. The event offered a unique opportunity to establish a global base for the major shift required to put the planet on the path towards a more secure and sustainable future. In the words of Maurice Strong, Secretary-General to UNCED:

At the core of this shift there is a need for fundamental change. Change to our economic life, a more careful and more caring use of the Earth's resources and greater co-operation and equity in sharing the benefits as well as the risks of our technological civilisation. Of particular importance is the need to integrate the ecological dimension into education and culture as well as in economics.

(Quarrie, 1992)

UNCED produced five major documents. These included two international agreements, two statements of principles and a major action agenda on world-wide sustainable development. These five documents are:

- *The Rio Declaration of Environment and Development.* Its 27 principles (detailed below) define the rights and responsibilities of nations as they pursue human development and well-being.
- *Agenda 21*, a comprehensive blueprint or agenda for global actions to affect the transition to sustainable development.
- *A Statement of Principles* to guide the management, conservation and sustainable development of all types of forests, which are essential to economic development and the maintenance of all forms of life.
- *The United Nations Framework Convention on Climate Change*, aiming to stabilise greenhouse gases in the atmosphere at all levels that will not dangerously upset the global climate system. This will require a reduction in our emissions of such gases as carbon dioxide, a by-product of the use of burning fuels for energy.
- *The Convention on Biological Diversity*, which requires that countries adopt ways and means to conserve the variety of living species, and ensure that the benefits from using biological diversity are equitably shared. Representatives from over 150 countries signed this and the Convention on Climate Change, both legally binding documents.

The Rio Declaration

The United Nations Conference on Environment and Development, *having met* at Rio de Janeiro from 3–14 June 1992, *reaffirming* the Declaration of the United Nations Conference on the Human Environment, adopted in Stockholm on 16 June 1972, and seeking to build upon it, *with the goal* of establishing a new and equitable global partnership through the creation of new levels of co-operation among States, key sectors of societies and people, *working towards* international agreements which respect the interests of all and protect the integrity of the global environmental and developmental system, *recognising* the integral and inter-dependent nature of the Earth, our home, proclaims that:

Principle 1
Human beings are at the centre of concerns for sustainable development. They are entitled to a healthy and productive life in harmony with nature.

Principle 2
States have, in accordance with the Charter of the United Nations and the principles of international law, the sovereign right to exploit their own resources pursuant to their own environmental and developmental policies, and the responsibility to ensure that activities within their jurisdiction or

70

control do not cause damage to the environment of other States or of areas beyond the limits of national jurisdiction.

Principle 3
The right to development must be fulfilled so as to equitably meet developmental and environmental needs of present and future generations.

Principle 4
In order to achieve sustainable development, environmental protection shall constitute an integral part of the development process and cannot be considered in isolation from it.

Principle 5
All States and all people shall co-operate in the essential task of eradicating poverty as an indispensable requirement for sustainable development, in order to decrease the disparities in standards of living and better meet the needs of the majority of the people of the world.

Principle 6
The special situation and needs of developing countries, particularly the least developed and those most environmentally vulnerable, shall be given special priority. International actions in the field of environment and development should also address the interests and needs of all countries.

Principle 7
States shall co-operate in a spirit of global partnership to conserve, protect and restore the health and integrity of the Earth's ecosystem. In view of the different contributions to global environmental degradation, States have common but differentiated responsibilities. The developed countries acknowledge the responsibility that they bear in the international pursuit of sustainable development in view of the pressures their societies place on the global environment and of the technologies and financial resources they command.

Principle 8
To achieve sustainable development and a higher quality of life for all people, States should reduce and eliminate unsustainable patterns of production and consumption and promote appropriate demographic policies.

Principle 9
States should co-operate to strengthen endogenous capacity-building for sustainable development by improving scientific understanding through exchanges of scientific and technological knowledge, and by enhancing the development, adaptation, diffusion and transfer of technologies, including new and innovative technologies.

Principle 10
Environmental issues are best handled with the participation of all

concerned citizens, at the relevant level. At the national level, each individual shall have appropriate access to information concerning the environment that is held by public authorities, including information on hazardous materials and activities in their communities, and the opportunity to participate in decision-making processes. States shall facilitate and encourage public awareness and participation by making information widely available. Effective access to judicial and administrative proceedings, including redress and remedy, shall be provided.

Principle 11
States shall enact effective environmental legislation. Environmental standards, management objectives and priorities should reflect the environmental and developmental context to which they apply. Standards applied by some countries may be inappropriate and of unwarranted economic and social cost to other countries, in particular developing countries.

Principle 12
States should co-operate to promote a supportive and open international economic system that would lead to economic growth and sustainable development in all countries, to better address the problems of environmental degradation. Trade policy measures for environmental purposes should not constitute a means of arbitrary or unjustifiable discrimination or a disguised restriction on international trade. Unilateral actions to deal with environmental challenges outside the jurisdiction of the importing country should be avoided. Environmental measures addressing transboundary or global environmental problems should, as far as possible, be based on an international consensus.

Principle 13
States shall develop national law regarding liability and compensation for the victims of pollution and other environmental damage. States shall also co-operate in an expeditious and more determined manner to develop further international law regarding liability and compensation for adverse effects of environmental damage caused by activities within their jurisdiction or control to areas beyond their jurisdiction.

Principle 14
States should effectively co-operate to discourage or prevent the relocation and transfer to other States of any activities and substances that cause severe environmental degradation or are found to be harmful to human health.

Principle 15
In order to protect the environment, the precautionary approach shall be widely applied by States according to their capabilities. Where there are threats of serious or irreversible damage, lack of full scientific certainty

shall not be used as a reason for postponing cost-effective measures to prevent environmental degradation.

Principle 16

National authorities should endeavour to promote the internalization of environmental costs and the use of economic instruments, taking into account the approach that the polluter should, in principle, bear the cost of pollution, with due regard to the public interest and without distorting international trade and investment.

Principle 17

Environmental impact assessment, as a national instrument, shall be undertaken for proposed activities that are likely to have a significant adverse impact on the environment and are subject to a decision of a competent national authority.

Principle 18

States shall immediately notify other States of any natural disasters or other emergencies that are likely to produce sudden harmful effects on the environment of those States. Every effort shall be made by the international community to help States so afflicted.

Principle 19

States shall provide prior and timely notification and relevant information to potentially affected States on activities that may have a significant adverse transboundary environmental effect and shall consult with those states at an early stage and in good faith.

Principle 20

Women have a vital role in environmental management and development. Their full participation is therefore essential to achieve sustainable development.

Principle 21

The creativity, ideas and courage of the youth of the world should be mobilized to forge a global partnership in order to achieve sustainable development and ensure a better future for all.

Principle 22

Indigenous people and their communities and other local communities have a vital role in environmental management and development because of their knowledge and traditional practices. States should recognize and duly support their identity, culture and interests and enable their effective participation in the achievement of sustainable development.

Principle 23

The environment and natural resources of people under oppression, domination and occupation shall be protected.

73

Principle 24
Warfare is inherently destructive of sustainable development. States shall therefore respect international law providing protection for the environment in times of armed conflict and co-operate in its further development, as necessary.

Principle 25
Peace, development and environmental protection are inter-dependent and indivisible.

Principle 26
States shall resolve all their environmental disputes peacefully and by appropriate means in accordance with the Charter of the United Nations.

Principle 27
States and people shall co-operate in good faith and in a spirit of partnership in the fulfilment of the principles embodied in this declaration and in the further development of international law in the field of sustainable development.

(United Nations, 1993)

Agenda 21

Agenda 21 is a complex document, reflecting a global consensus and political commitment at the highest level on development and environment co-operation. The Agenda deals both with the urgent problems the planet is facing today, and the need to prepare for the challenges of the twenty-first century. It recognises that sustainable development is primarily the responsibility of governments, and that this will require national strategies, plans and policies.

In total, *Agenda 21* has 40 chapters, divided, after a preamble, into four sections: Social and Economic Dimensions, Conservation and Management of Resources for Development, Strengthening the Role of Major Groups, and Means of Implementation. Its full text is available from United Nations Publications (United Nations, 1993) and abridged versions are available (e.g. Quarrie, 1992). Readers of this text will already be familiar with the 'flavour' and some of the detailed content of the document through the various quotations cited above, which are taken from the 'plain language version' of the Agenda (Keating, 1993).

Did Rio matter?

There are probably as many answers to this question as there were delegates at the event. First and foremost, UNCED was an undoubted success in so far as for the first time in history it brought together representatives from over 150 nations and many thousands of interested individuals under one umbrella event to share common interests and concerns about environment and development

74

issues. The 7,000 journalists accredited to the conference were almost certainly the largest gathering of representatives of the global communications media ever assembled. Rio mattered because it did a great deal towards raising public awareness of the need to take action. It mattered because its documents built upon and extended the excellent foundation work achieved by the *World Conservation Strategy* and *Our Common Future*, and because two key outcomes were legally binding Conventions signed by a majority of nations.

Overall, it is probably fair to describe the Earth Summit as a qualified success. Individuals and national delegations went to it with very different agendas, perceptions and goals. No doubt the rich nations of the North were looking for a blueprint for sustainable development that did not involve sacrifice, whilst the poorer states of the South had hoped for considerable financial commitments from the developed North. In reality, the Rio event ended with very little international agreement, except at the most general level of principles. It seemed to raise more questions than were answered, for example:

- What *is* a just level of aid to developing countries?
- What sacrifices can and should be made by the 'rich' in order to assist development elsewhere?
- Where should compensation come from for those persuaded not to over-exploit natural resources?
- What and how should 'the polluter pay'?
- How can the world's resources best be rationalised?
- How can individuals and societies be persuaded to move from an anthropocentric, 'human-centred' view of the planet towards a more 'life-centred', holistic view?

and perhaps the most complex questions of all:

- What *is* sustainable development?
- Is sustainable economic growth actually feasible, or even desirable?

Maurice Strong himself, reflecting after the event, admitted in an interview that 'there is no denying that the underlying conditions that have produced the civilisational crisis that the Earth Summit was designed to address did not change during the meeting in Rio . . . ' (Strong, 1993).

Inevitably, the event gave rise to fierce criticism from some sources:

Ecocentrics derided the whole approach of Agenda 21. *The Ecologist* magazine said that for grass-roots groups around the world the question was not *how* the environment should be managed – they have the experience of the past as their guide – but *who* will manage it and in *whose* interest? They reject UNCED's rhetoric of a world where all humanity is united by a common interest in survival, and in which conflicts of race, class, gender and culture are characterised as of secondary importance to humanity's supposedly common goal (Goldsmith *et al.*, 1992).

(Pepper, 1996, p. 103)

The Ecologist repudiates Rio's six mainstream responses to the environmental crisis:

> First, it is not poverty defined as absence of the American way of life which is the root cause of environmental degradation, it is American-style 'wealth'. Second, 'overpopulation' is *caused*, not cured, by modernisation, destroying the traditional balance between people and the environment. Third, the 'open international economic system' of the Declaration will extinguish cultural and ecological diversity. Fourth, the problem of externalisation of pollution, etc., is not solvable by pricing the environment, but by reversing enclosure of the commons, so there is nowhere to 'externalise' to. Fifth, Rio's calls for more 'global management' effectively constitute Western cultural imperialism. This approach would anyway be ineffective because of the impossibility of verifying and enforcing global agreements (Greene, 1993). Sixth, the attitude that transfers of Western technology to the Third World are the most urgent need smacks of traditional Western scientific imperialist arrogance – effectively presuming that ignorance and laziness characterise Third World people.
>
> (Pepper, 1996, p. 105)

And from Greenpeace activist, Curtis, the harsh words:

> The Conference was a failure of historic proportions. While there were minor successes, these were microscopic by comparison to the failure of governments to address satisfactorily the kinds of basic reforms and other actions required.
>
> (McCoy and McCully, 1993, p. 79)

From other sources, more positive assessments emerged. McCoy and McCully (1993) provide a balanced and worthwhile overview and debate on NGO involvement in environment and development and on the successes and failures of Rio from the NGO point of view.

> Most environmental activists left Rio with a strong sense that the Summit had failed. Yet they also took away a few straws of comfort. First they had fought and won the right to participate in the conference and its follow-up meetings and institutions; and they had learned a lot, made new contacts and set up or strengthened networks for international campaigning on various issues. The fact that they were granted the right to participate in official global environmentalism was hailed by many as the NGO's greatest Summit achievement.
>
> ... Many groups are now consolidating the power that the Earth Summit gave them and working hand in glove with their new government and business partners.
>
> (McCoy and McCully, 1993, pp. 95–96)

Roddick and Dodds (1993) comment favourably that *Agenda 21* encourages localism by calling for consultation, negotiation and participation among 'stakeholders' – including women, youth, indigenous people, local authorities, workers and farmers – together with world democratisation.

No doubt debate will continue for a long time over just how successful UNCED actually was, and other authors pursue this question in far greater depth than is possible here (e.g. Chatterjee and Finger, 1994). If nothing else, the Earth Summit provided a crucial forum for the opening of debate between developed and developing countries. Whilst it may well be many years before its true historic significance can be more accurately evaluated, environmentalists will continue to reflect on the key issue highlighted by Chatterjee and Finger (1994), namely that

> The major lesson to be drawn from the entire ten-year process leading up to UNCED is, in our view, that the global approach is at best a useful tool for awareness raising. But is it not at this global level that the environment and development crisis will be dealt with. . . .
>
> . . . we have no choice but to focus on the local, its people, and its communities . . . and collectively unlearn the development paradigm of which modern society is both the product and the victim.
>
> (Chatterjee and Finger, 1994, p. 172)

EDUCATION: A PRIORITY SOLUTION

All of the initiatives described above emphasised the urgent need for world-wide environmental education, and its fundamental role in the transition towards sustainability. Indeed, messages relating to education have become more power-ful and elaborate as thinking about environment and development issues has progressed.

The *World Conservation Strategy* links education to attitudes and behaviour:

> Environmental education has the task of transforming the attitudes and behaviour of entire societies if a new conservation ethic embracing plants and animals as well as people is to become a reality.
>
> (ICCE, 1984, para 67)

The Report of the World Commission on Environment and Development contains many direct and indirect references to education.

> Human resource development demands knowledge and skills to help people improve their economic performance. Sustainable development requires changes in values and attitudes towards environment and devel-opment – indeed, towards society and work at home, on farms and in factories. . . . Education should also be geared towards making people more capable of dealing with problems of overcrowding and excessive population densities, and better able to improve what could be called 'social carrying capacities'.

Most people base their understandings of environmental processes and development on traditional beliefs or on information provided by a conventional education. Many thus remain ignorant about ways in which they could improve traditional production practices and better protect the natural resource base. Education should therefore provide comprehensive knowledge, encompassing and cutting across the social and natural sciences and the humanities, thus providing insights on the interaction between natural and human resources, between development and environment.

Environmental education should be included in and should run throughout the other disciplines of the formal education curriculum at all levels – to foster a sense of responsibility for the state of the environment and to teach students how to monitor, protect and improve it.

(WCED, 1987, p. 111 and p. 113)

The sixth chapter of *Caring for the Earth*, which focuses on 'changing personal attitudes and practices', emphasises not only the need for more widespread education, but also the necessity to change its content.

Children and adults should be schooled in the knowledge and values that will allow them to live sustainably. This requires environmental education, linked to social education. The former helps people to understand the natural world, and to live in harmony with it. The latter imparts an understanding of human behaviour and an appreciation of cultural diversity. To date, this blend of environmental and social education has not been widely applied. It needs to be – at all levels.

(IUCN/UNEP/WWF, 1991, p. 53)

This chapter goes on to provide recommendations and suggested actions, and emphasises the importance of values in education.

Environmental education deals with values. Many school systems regard this as dangerous ground, and many teachers (particularly in the natural sciences) are not trained to teach values. The 'whole school' approach, in which the school tries to behave consistently with what is taught, may also be dauntingly novel. Yet no lifestyle or educational system is value-free. It is vital that schools teach the right skills for sustainable living. It is equally important that what the school does reinforces what it teaches. . . .

Development assistance agencies need to give more support to environmental education. It is the key to sustainability.

(IUCN/UNEP/WWF, 1991, p. 55)

Finally, the Earth Summit's *Agenda 21* incorporates a full chapter (Chapter 36) on 'Education, Training and Public Awareness'. This carries forward the message of the Brundtland Commission that education can give people the environmental and ethical awareness, values and attitudes, skills and behaviour needed for sustainable development. It also reinforces the notion that education needs to explain not only the physical and biological environment, but also the socio-economic environment and human development. National responsibilities are spelled out:

To improve sustainable development education, nations should seek to:

- Make environment and development education available to people of all ages.

- Work environment and development concepts, including those of population, into all educational programmes, with analyses of the causes of the major issues. There should be a special emphasis on training decision makers.

- Involve school children in local and regional studies on environmental health, including safe drinking water, sanitation, food, and the environmental and economic impacts of resource use.

(Keating, 1993, p. 57)

So far this text has provided an overview of international developments in the history, definition and promotion of environmental education over the past half century, and of the key environmental problem impacts and causes that have led to the growth of global awareness of and concern for issues affecting the planet. Major global initiatives on the theme of environment and development have been reviewed, and their call for universal environmental education highlighted.

Whilst there can be little doubt about the urgent need for promoting change in attitudes and behaviour, for encouraging people to appreciate and enjoy the world around them, and for equipping the decision makers of both present and future to adopt environmentally responsible approaches, it would seem that some fundamental questions remain unanswered. In particular, debate continues around the world on how best to achieve these goals and on what are the most successful ways of approaching environmental education in practice.

So attention now turns to these matters. The remaining parts of the text will review ongoing developments in thinking, research and theoretical perspectives in the field, and fundamental issues relating to teaching and learning in it. Insights into what is happening on the global scene in environmental education will give some indication of the extent to which *Agenda 21*'s call for environment and development education for all is being realised.

REFERENCES

Brown, L.R. *et al.* (1989) *State of the World 1989. Worldwatch Institute Report on Progress Toward a Sustainable Society*, New York: W.W. Norton & Co.
Camp, S.L. and Speidel, J.J. (1987) *The International Human Suffering Index*, Washington, DC: Population Crisis Committee 1987.
Chatterjee, P. and Finger, M. (1994) *The Earth Brokers*, London: Routledge.

Corson, W.H. (ed.) (1990) *The Global Ecology Handbook*, The Global Tomorrow Coalition, Boston: Beacon Press.

Court, T. de la (ed.) (1990) *Beyond Brundtland*, Zed Books Ltd, New York: New Horizon Press.

Elsworth, S. (1990) *A Dictionary of the Environment*, London: Paladin, Grafton Books.

Goldsmith, E., Hildyard, N., Bunyard, P. and McCully, P. (eds) (1992) 'Whose Common Future?', *The Ecologist*, 22 (4) July–August.

Greene, O. (1993) 'International Environmental Regimes: Verification and Implementation Review', *Environmental Politics*, 2 (4) 156–173.

ICCE, UNEP, IUCN (1984) *Planning for Survival*, Cheltenham, UK.

IIED/Earthscan (1989) *Our Common Future. A Reader's Guide*, London: Earthscan Publications.

IUCN (1980) *World Conservation Strategy*, Gland, Switzerland: IUCN.

IUCN/UNEP/WWF (1991) *Caring for the Earth: A Strategy for Sustainable Living*, Gland, Switzerland: IUCN.

Keating, M. (1993) *The Earth Summit's Agenda for Change – A Plain Language Version of Agenda 21 and the Other Rio Agreements*, Geneva: Centre for Our Common Future.

Lovelock, J.E. (1979) *Gaia. A New Look at Life on Earth*, Oxford: Oxford University Press.

McCoy, M. and McCully, P. (1993) *The Road from Rio*, Utrecht: International Books, World Information Service on Energy.

Pepper, D. (1996) *Modern Environmentalism*, London: Routledge.

Quarrie, J. (ed.) (1992) *Earth Summit 1992*, London: The Regency Press.

Roddick, J. and Dodds, F. (1993) 'Agenda 21's Political Strategy', *Environmental Politics*, 2 (4) 242–248.

Strong, M. (1993) Interviewed in *Earth Island Journal*, Winter 1993, p. 18.

United Nations (1993) *Agenda 21: The United Nations Programme of Action from Rio*, New York: United Nations Publications.

WCED (1987) *Our Common Future*, Oxford: Oxford University Press.

Part III

PERSPECTIVES ON THEORY AND RESEARCH IN ENVIRONMENTAL EDUCATION

SUSTAINABLE DEVELOPMENT: A POLITICAL MINEFIELD

Central dilemmas

As the previous part of this text made apparent, the concept of sustainable development or indeed of sustainability is far from straightforward. There are numerous definitions associated with the term 'sustainable development'. Pearce *et al.* (1989) document over 60 definitions, and other writers, e.g. Moffat (1992), regard this as a low estimate. Some claim (Moffat, 1996) that the forerunner to the establishment of the concept of sustainable development was the earlier idea of eco-development (Riddell, 1981). Two or three decades down its evolutionary path, there is still no agreed definition of the term, despite its widespread acceptance, and the recognition of its significance by governments, NGOs, business and academics alike. Some commentators (see below) have viewed it as a narrow economic concept; others have tried to keep it broad, as an attempt to integrate economic, social and ecological development (Barbier, 1989).

For those wishing to pursue this complex field in greater detail, Moffat (1996) provides a useful overview of the evolution of the sustainable development debate, its definitions and principles, together with a discussion of aspects of an analysis of the concept and policy implications.

Yet some further discussion of the differences of understanding and dilemmas associated with the concepts of sustainable development and sustainability is an essential prerequisite for a review of definitions and progress in environmental education.

The need for development is obvious; we live in a world where a minority of the world's population lives with practices of unsustainable, wasteful consumerism, whilst the majority of citizens of the planet live in circumstances that do not provide for basic human needs. Numerous writers (e.g. Wallace, 1990) blame the current ecological crisis on the workings of the capitalist world economy. This links the world's peoples, nation states and environments in a single process of combined and uneven development which ensures that an ever-increasing number of people use natural resources in ways that are not sustainable in the long term (O'Connor, 1989).

For many, the concept of sustainable development is inextricably interwoven with environmental economics. An influential study in the UK, *Blueprint for a Green Economy* (Pearce *et al.*, 1989), advances three themes that characterise sustainable development. The first is the need to value the environment properly. This includes valuing the natural, built and cultural aspects of the environment as well as the quality of life. Clearly this poses great problems – how does one value such things, and assess the value of degradation of resources? It is argued that, in the past, the environment has been poorly used and degraded because its true value has not been defined and understood. We cannot manage resources in a sustainable way until their 'true' price has been recognised and paid by those benefiting from them. Clearly this approach may be regarded as being extremely problematic, as it depends upon valuations of numerous 'unmeasurables' that may well be informed by assumptions, unreliable data and prejudices.

The second theme advanced by Pearce *et al.* is the need to set realistic short-, medium- and long-term timescales or frameworks for implementing desired changes. Long-term policies should consider the eventual impact of present-day decisions that include inter-generational effects of the way resources are used and managed. Again serious problems have been associated with this idea: Is it possible to predict future needs accurately, as resource values inevitably change through time? How do we know what developments in technology will occur and alter predictions? How can we predict long term change in the value of aesthetic resources? What if, in the long-term, some people gain and others lose from this policy? How does one persuade people of today to make sacrifices in their consumerist lifestyle for the benefit of future generations?

The third theme of *Blueprint for a Green Economy* concerns intra-generational equity – the need to provide for the present-day needs of society's least advantaged people, in order to reduce the chasm between the world's 'rich' and 'poor'. This requires policies involving sacrifice of economic growth and implementation of the theme at all levels – within communities, and at national and global levels. Yet whilst the world might be united on the desirability of intra-generational equity, there remain substantial differences of opinion on both the causes of and solutions to the 'rich–poor' divide.

Environmental economics play a key role in the sustainability debate, and ideas and dilemmas in the field are discussed in numerous sources (e.g. Pearce *et al.*, 1989; Barde and Pearce, 1991; Redclift, 1987; Adams, 1990; Sarre, 1991; Moffat, 1996). The problems raised are in part *technical*, and in part *ideological*. A central issue is the debate on the role of market mechanisms versus state regulations and enforced standards as mechanisms for environmental policies. Related to this is the tendency for a separation of production and distribution activities, with a welfare orientated pattern of solutions where the needs of the poor are provided for through charitable distributions from the rich. Worthy as such an approach may be, particularly in the short term, surely a truly sustainable form of development will need to be rather different. Rather than simply providing for the needs of the poor, it will give the poor the capacity to provide for their own needs in a secure and dignified manner (Mannion and Bowlby, 1992). Such an interpretation raises fundamental questions about the control of resources used in the development process and who has power over the decisions on which forms of development should take place.

> This is essentially about giving people greater control in their own lives, and as such is about a form of development which creates democracy alongside growth and equity. This means democracy in its widest sense; not just voting to elect governments, but a process whereby people can have a say in the decisions which shape their destinies.
>
> . . . This is a political minefield . . . it raises the whole question of which forms of political organisation and economic ownership will best give people real control over their own lives. . . . This is the central dilemma of sustainable development: what is the best way to confront and overcome the massively powerful vested interests that would feel threatened by structural changes to the status quo? As is true for other approaches to development, sustainable development is about power relationships, and the fine intentions of the approach will come to nothing until this central dilemma is recognised.
>
> (Mannion and Bowlby, 1992)

Environmentalism: typologies and approaches

The concept of ecological sustainability and the notion of sustainable development are by now well subsumed within the dialectic that defines and characterises modern environmentalism. Inevitably, as suggested above, they take on different meanings and are subject to very different interpretations for people of differing viewpoints or ideas. Once again, present space allows for only a brief glimpse into the complexity of leading ideas in environmentalism, which are so relevant for pursuing an understanding of the development of thinking and practice in environmental education.

For those wishing to pursue reading on key environmentalist ideas, influences and movements, Pepper (1996) presents a comprehensive introduction to this field of Western attitudes towards nature and the environment, the origins of its main beliefs and ideas, and how these relate to modern environmental ideologies.

Deep and shallow ecology

Arne Naess (1973) first made a distinction between 'deep' and 'shallow' ecology. Deep ecology fundamentally rejects the dualistic view of humans and nature as separate and different. It holds that humans are intimately a part of the natural environment – and are *one* with nature. Shallow ecology, on the other hand, considers that humans and nature are separate and that humans can dominate the world around them. Deep ecologists try to live with nature's ways and rhythms, rather than opposing them. They oppose anthropocentrism, defined firstly as seeing human values as the source of all value and secondly as wanting to manipulate, exploit and destroy nature to satisfy human material desires.

Deep ecology combines its concerns for nature with a desire to transform society (Naess, 1988). But it shuns social change by confrontation, where one side of an argument considers the other 'wrong'. There is value in all viewpoints, and consensus is possible when all sides shift their positions a little. Hence a plurality of the world is tolerated. There are no right or wrong religions – rather there are some basic principles that all religions share. These include the most important principles of deep ecology. They argue, among other points, that the richness of life on the planet is the greatest when the diversity of life forms is greatest (Pepper, 1996).

Deep ecologists focus on the transformation at the level of individual consciousness as far as social change is concerned. The prime need is for each individual to change attitudes, values and lifestyles to emphasise respect for, and peaceful co-operation with, nature. They do not rely totally on ecological science for their conclusions; they also value emotional and intuitive knowledge. They say that we can never know enough for certain, but intuition should tell us that we should not do anything that might do long-term environmental damage (Pepper, 1996).

Summarised below are the eight basic principles of deep ecology, taken from Devall and Sessions (1985), who have promoted deep ecology as the philosophical basis of 'green' practices and sustainable lifestyles. They claim that 'deep ecology begins with the unity rather than the dualism which has been the dominant theme of western philosophy'.

The eight basic principles of deep ecology

1 The well-being and flourishing of human and non-human life on Earth have value in themselves (synonyms: intrinsic value, inherent value). These values are independent of the usefulness of the non-human world for human purposes.

2 Richness and diversity of life forms contribute to the realisation of these values and are also values in themselves.

3 Humans have no right to reduce this richness and diversity except to satisfy *vital* needs.

4 The flourishing of human life and cultures is compatible with a substantial decrease of the human population. The flourishing of non-human life requires such a decrease.

5 Present human interference with the non-human world is excessive and the situation is rapidly worsening.

6 Policies must therefore be changed. These policies affect basic economic, technological, and ideological structures. The resulting state of affairs will be deeply different from the present.

7 The ideological change is mainly that of appreciating life *quality* (dwelling in situations of inherent value) rather than adhering to an increasingly higher standard of living. There will be a profound awareness of the difference between big and great.

8 Those who subscribe to the foregoing points have an obligation directly or indirectly to try to implement the necessary changes.

(Devall and Sessions, 1985)

Gaia

The Gaia hypothesis, closely allied to 'deep' ecological thinking, and already referred to in Part II above, argues that the Earth can be regarded as if it were a single living organism (Lovelock, 1989). All parts help to regulate and balance the planet via feedback mechanisms, thus sustaining life as we know it. In this sense, only Earth is 'alive' because it is 'autopoietic', that is, self-renewing: it can repair its own 'body' and grow by processing materials. This happens neither by pure chance nor by outside design, but only by virtue of Earth's own make-up and laws (Sahtouris, 1989).

> It is the living organisms on Earth which process chemicals so as to produce a non-equilibrium atmosphere. Living things themselves produce the conditions most conducive to their thriving. So they are not passive: they manipulate and radically change environments in ways most favourable to their future development. This makes the whole planet a self-sustaining system: a discrete entity able to maintain its own integrity by responding appropriately to changes via feedback mechanisms. Life and non-life are complementary and collaborating.
>
> (Pepper, 1996, pp. 21–22)

Inevitably, shortcomings have been articulated that relate to the appropriateness or usefulness of the 'deep' versus 'shallow' distinction. For example, Sylvan (1995) regards it as a false dichotomy that does not recognise crucial intermediate positions. Sylvan argues that most positions in environmentalism place serious human concerns first, but attribute value in their own right to higher animals. Rather than the 'sole value assumption' of shallow ecology, this shows a 'greater value assumption', saying that the rest of nature may have intrinsic value, but the value of humanity is higher. Vincent (1993) also refers to an intermediate position which he describes as 'weak anthropocentric'.

87

Weak anthropocentrics are prepared to extend what is clearly recognised as a human set of moral attitudes (not intrinsic in nature) towards the rest of nature.

Another shortcoming identified in the 'deep' versus 'shallow' dichotomy is the fact that the terms lack precise meaning: deep in relation to what?

> Marxists, for example, accuse 'deep' ecology of being in fact shallow because it does not place at the centre of its analysis the deep economic structures of society without which the workings of cultures and belief systems cannot be fully understood.
>
> (Pepper, 1996)

Ecocentrism and technocentrism

An alternative and more tightly defined set of distinctions and terms was developed by O'Riordan (1988), as shown in Table 3.1. His basic distinction is between 'ecocentrism' and 'technocentrism'. Ecocentrism sees humankind as part of a global ecosystem, subject to ecological laws. These and the demands of an ecologically based morality are seen to constrain human action, particularly through imposing limits to economic and population growth. Ecocentrics hold a strong sense of respect for nature in its own right, as well as for pragmatic reasons. The ecocentric position on technology is complex. Certainly it lacks faith in modern larger-scale technology. Rather, it advocates 'alternative', that is 'soft', 'intermediate' and 'appropriate', technologies, partly because they are considered environmentally benign, but also because they are potentially 'democratic'. In other words, unlike high technology they can be 'owned, understood, maintained and used by individuals and groups with little economic or political power' (Pepper, 1996).

> Technocentrism recognises environmental problems but believes either unreservedly that our current form of society will always solve them and achieve unlimited growth (the interventionist 'cornucopian' view) or, more cautiously, that by careful economic and environmental management they can be negotiated (the 'accommodators').
>
> (Pepper, 1996)

Both ways forward place considerable faith in the usefulness of classical science, technology and conventional economic reasoning, e.g. cost–benefit analysis.

A yet more complex classification is provided by Merchant (1992), as shown in Table 3.2. She contrasts 'egocentrism', which has a very mechanical view of nature as in cornucopian technocentrism, with ecocentrism, including deep and spiritual ecology, which views nature as an organism rather than a machine. Unlike O'Riordan, Merchant maps out middle ground between deep and shallow ecology perspectives. In between egocentrism and ecocentrism she places 'homocentrism', which draws on both mechanism and organicism.

88

Table 3.1 Contemporary trends in environmentalism
(European perspectives on environmental policies and resource management)

Ecocentrism		Technocentrism	
Gaianism	*Communalism*	*Accommodation*	*Intervention*
Faith in the rights of nature and of the essential need for co-evolution of human and natural ethics.	Faith in the co-operative capabilities of societies to establish self-reliant communities based on renewable resource use and appropriate technologies.	Faith in the adaptability of institutions and approaches to assessment and evaluation to accommodate environmental demands.	Faith in the application of science, market forces, and managerial ingenuity.
'Green' supporters; radical philosophers.	Radical socialists; committed youth; radical-liberal politicians; intellectual environmentalists.	Middle-ranking executives; environmental scientists; white-collar trade unions; liberal-socialist politicians.	Business and finance managers; skilled workers; self-employed; right-wing politicians; career-focused youth.
0.1–3 per cent of various opinion surveys.	5–10 per cent of various opinion surveys.	55–70 per cent of various opinion surveys.	10–35 per cent of various opinion surveys.
Demand for redistribution of power towards a decentralised, federated economy with more emphasis on informal economic and social transactions and the pursuit of participatory justice.		Belief in the retention of the status quo in the existing structure of political power, but a demand for more responsiveness and accountability in political, regulatory, planning and educational institutions.	

Source: O'Riordan (1988)

This does prioritise human values and desires, but its humanism does not lead to the destructive and short-sighted view of nature associated with egocentrism's aggressive and competitive individualism. Including social ecology and eco-socialism and most animal rights movements, homocentrism would steward nature in the attempt to maximise the sum of human happiness and welfare.

(Pepper, 1996)

Turner (1988) realigns the 'technocentrism–ecocentrism' dichotomy into four 'world views of modern environmentalism', reflecting the essence of the distinctions made by O'Riordan as set out in Table 3.1. The world views, as expressed by Turner, are:

Table 3.2 Three-fold classification of environmentalism – based on grounds for environmental ethics and showing antecedents in Western thought

	Self: egocentric		Society: homocentric		Cosmos: eocentric	
	Self-interest	**Religious**	**Utilitarian**	**Religious**	**Eco-scientific**	**Eco-religious**
	Thomas Hobbes John Locke Adam Smith Thomas Malthus Garrett Hardin	Judeo-Christian ethic Arminian 'heresy'	J. S. Mill Jeremy Bentham Gifford Pinchot Peter Singer Barry Commoner Murray Bookchin Social ecofeminists Left greens	John Ray William Derham René Dubos Robin Attfield	Aldo Leopold Rachel Carson Deep ecologists Restoration ecologists Biological control Sustainable agriculture	American Indian Buddhism Spiritual feminists Spiritual greens Process philosophers
Grounds for obligation	Maximisation of individual self-interest: what is good for each individual will benefit society as a whole Mutual coercion mutually agreed upon	Authority of God Genesis 1 Protestant ethic Individual salvation	Greatest good for the greatest number of people Social Justice Duty to other humans	Stewardship by humans as God's caretakers Golden Rule Genesis 2	Rational, scientific belief system based on laws of ecology Unity, stability, diversity, harmony of ecosystem Balance of nature or chaotic systems approach	Faith that all living and non-living things have value Duty to whole environment Human and cosmic survival
Metaphysics	Mechanism 1 Matter is composed of atomic parts 2 The whole is equal to the sum of the parts (law of identity) 3 Knowledge is context-independent 4 Change occurs by the rearrangement of parts 5 Dualism of mind and body, matter and spirit		Both mechanistic and holistic		Organicism (Holism) 1 Everything is connected to everything else 2 The whole is greater than the sum of the parts 3 Knowledge is context-dependent 4 The primacy of process over parts 5 The unity of humans and non-human nature	

Source: Merchant (1992)

- *'Cornucopia' technocentrism*: an exploitative position supportive of a growth ethic expressed in material terms (e.g. GNP); it is taken as axiomatic that the market mechanism in conjunction with technological innovation will ensure infinite substitution possibilities to mitigate long-run real resource scarcity;
- *'Accommodating' technocentrism*: a conservationist position, which rejects the axiom of infinite substitution and instead supports a 'sustainable growth' policy guided by resource management rules;
- *'Communalist' ecocentrism*: a preservationist position, which emphasises the need for prior macroenvironmental constraints on economic growth and favours a decentralised socio-economic system;
- *'Deep ecology' ecocentrism*: an extreme preservationist position, dominated by the intuitive acceptance of the notions of intrinsic (as opposed to instrumental) value in nature and rights for non-human species.

Two modes of sustainability

Another distinction in this complex array of definitions and classifications is that made between sustainable growth and sustainable development. Various authors comment on this distinction and the origins of the terms, e.g. Turner (1988) and O'Riordan (1988). Key elements of the two ideas are set out in Table 3.3 below, which show that sustainable development, unlike sustainable growth, should be both ecologically and socially sustainable.

O'Riordan (1988) shows that attempts to regulate the reproduction of the conditions of production are not new and describes how ways of reconciling development with nature conservation in the South have gradually evolved into the notion of sustainable livelihood development (Glaeser, 1984; Chambers, 1986). This also applies to northern nations, and involves the following principles:

Sustainable (Livelihood) Development –

- regards its fundamental OBJECTIVE as meeting people's BASIC NEEDS
- employs SUSTAINABLE RESOURCE USE as the MEANS of meeting needs
- makes use of APPROPRIATE TECHNOLOGY and encourages SELF-RELIANCE
- draws on ECO-DEVELOPMENT strategies to ensure CONTEXT (location/culture) specific variants of sustainable development
- generally requires STRUCTURAL TRANSFORMATION (DEMOCRATISATION) as an ENABLING CONDITION

    (Huckle, 1990, based on O'Riordan, 1988 and Swee-Hin, 1988)

O'Riordan also identifies four premises that underlie the concept of sustainability. These are:

1 *knowability*: the amount, rate and other characteristics of renewability are knowable and calculable;

2 *homeostasis*: renewable resource systems operate broadly around equilibria or can be manipulated to approximate steady states following human intervention – homeostasis is a preferred state of nature;

3 *internal bioethics*: the act of drawing upon a renewable resource even below some threshold of take has implications only for the tightly confined ecosystem that is that resource;

4 *external bioethics*: utilising a renewable resource up to the point of sustainable yield is morally justifiable even though that resource, below the threshold of optional 'take', may have other ecological values and functions.

(O'Riordan, 1988 in Huckle, 1990)

It will be seen that the first two premises are concerned with the scientific feasibility of sustainable resource use and apply to sustainability in the 'sustainable growth' mode. The third and fourth relate to ethical and political issues and are more relevant to the concept in the 'sustainable development' mode. A key

Table 3.3 Two modes of sustainability

Sustainable growth	Sustainable development
technocentrist	ecocentrist
essentially a technical concept	a broader concept embracing ethical norms, e.g. bioethics, inter/intragenerational justice
bound by formalistic rules of existing institutions	requires new institutions to deliver
social reform	social revolution
conservation one of several goals within an overall materials policy including waste recycling/reduction	conservation the sole basis for defining a criterion on which to judge policy/alternative allocations of resources
three basic elements of policy: resource recovery/recycling, residuals management, waste reduction	policy derived from theories of, e.g., zero growth, steady state economy, bioeconomic equilibrium, coevolutionary development
requires a modified economics	requires a new economics
requires attention to O'Riordan's premises (1) and (2) (see above)	requires attention to all four premises
core is reforming social systems to ensure reproduction of conditions of production	core is changing social systems to ensure popular control of livelihood or the conditions of production
is manageable and politically acceptable because it is safely ambiguous	is politically treacherous since it challenges the status quo
the 'greening of capitalism'	the 'greening of socialism'

Source: Based on Turner (1988) and O'Riordan (1988)

question for debate is the extent to which these principles are realistic, practicable or justifiable – about which O'Riordan expresses serious doubts.

PATHWAYS TO ENVIRONMENTAL IMPROVEMENT

Various typologies have been constructed to illuminate approaches to thinking about environmental improvement and means to achieving it. (See, for example, Devall and Sessions, 1985; Enzensberger, 1974; Fox, 1984; Huckle, 1983.) Stevenson (1987) comments that although these typologies often distinguish different emphases on a number of dimensions, one common and critical dimension is the political scenario through which environmental reform is to be enacted. Essentially, he claims, one of two broad scenarios is embraced (if not explicitly at least implicitly), with two variations on the type of approach adopted within each (Stevenson, 1987; representing an adaptation of the work of Enzensberger, 1974 and Huckle, 1983). These are:

1. Conservative reform (within the present system)

   (a) The *technical approach* is concerned with developing 'quick technological fixes' of environmental conflicts (Enzensberger, 1974) by injecting ecological principles and information into existing decision-making structures. Its adherents believe that scientific and technological expertise can provide the basis for resolving quality-of-life issues without the need for social and economic changes (O'Riordan, 1981). In this approach there is no place for non-professional or citizen participation in environmental planning.

   (b) The *political approach* involves working within the present political system to reduce the impact of human activity on the environment. These reformers foresee a need for improving legal, political, economic and technological decision-making, but without addressing the structure of our social and economic institutions. Typical concerns are the preservation of open space and wilderness areas and the siting of undesirable development projects (such as airports, freeways and factories): in other words, issues that impinge on the quality of life of the middle class who have the clout to use the conventional political process effectively.

   Both the technical and the political approaches, partly by supporting the primacy of economic growth, tend to maintain the status quo rather than transform the economic and political order.

2. Radical reform (of the present system)

   (a) The *socially critical approach* treats environmental crises as symptoms of a larger problem in our society (Huckle, 1983), namely the dominant role of economic considerations and the unequal distribution of resources. Radical reformers regard major economic reorganisation as the only way to rectify violations of both environmental quality and social justice. Most Marxists and neo-Marxists attribute the problem to capitalism (i.e. private ownership of the mode of production), while others point out the equally serious nature of environmental destruction in socialist countries (Enzensberger, 1974). Disagreement on the means of reform tends to be accompanied by the lack of a clear vision of an alternative economic and political system.

(b) The *alternative approach* rejects traditional forms of society and advocates a virtually pre-industrial lifestyle involving a close relationship with nature in small, self-sufficient (usually rural) communities. This Utopian alternative, which is presently feasible for very few people, includes reliance on soft or low-impact technologies. 'Deep' ecologists or environmentalists, who emphasise the intrinsic (rather than the instrumental) value of all of nature, often are included in this category (Huckle, 1983). However, many deep ecologists combine the cultivation of a personal environmental ethic with political activism by addressing public policy through the vehicle of the Green Party (Devall and Sessions, 1985). In this latter respect they have more in common with the socially critical reformers, but with less concern for social inequalities.

Both socially critical and alternative reformers argue that economic growth should be a subsidiary consideration to environmental quality.
(Stevenson, 1987)

Stevenson goes on to argue, and surely rightly, that the different ideologies associated with the environmental movement have two important implications for education. Firstly, by revealing the existence of substantively different perspectives of the root causes of environmental problems and of the appropriate means to effecting change, the implication is that students should examine all perspectives and judge their respective merits. Whilst some writers (e.g. Huckle, 1983) have implied that only the 'socially critical approach' to radical reform is consistent with the goals and principles of environmental education, and so students and teachers should be concerned with only this ideological position, surely

to be consistent with demographic principles students should be exposed to the plurality of environmental ideologies, and that through a process of inquiry, critique and reflection they can be assisted to develop and defend their own set of environmental beliefs and values. After engaging in this rational process of social inquiry and moral deliberation, it should be each student's choice to pursue actions deemed necessary and justifiable for achieving environmental reform in accordance with the ideological

94

position he or she supports. But students also need to be competent to implement or act on that choice. . . .

(Stevenson, 1987)

The development of this competence leads to the second implication for education, which is that if environmental reform is political, and if students are to be capable of acting on their choices and influencing environmental decision-making, then environmental education must incorporate the development of students' knowledge of the political-legal process and skills in political advocacy.

These implications are certainly consistent with recent widely acclaimed descriptions and the rhetoric of the environmental education process, as outlined in Part I of this text.

> The goals of environmental education include the intellectual task of critical appraisal of environmental (and political) situations and the formulation of a moral code concerning such issues, as well as the development of a commitment to act on one's values by providing opportunities to participate actively in environmental improvement.

(Stevenson, 1987)

Evidence in support of this statement is found in almost all of the influential and widely accepted documents, guidelines and policy statements on the subject. For example, *The Belgrade Charter* states that objectives for environmental education include 'fostering clear awareness of and concern about economic, social, political, and ecological inter-dependence . . . providing every person with opportunities to acquire the knowledge, values, attitudes, commitment and skills needed to protect and improve the environment . . .' (UNESCO, 1975); the *Tbilisi Report* recommendations (UNESCO, 1977) make clear that environmental education 'views the environment in its entirety including social, political, economic, technological, moral, aesthetic and spiritual aspects . . . emphasises active responsibility'; the *World Conservation Strategy* (IUCN, 1980) claims that 'environmental education has the task of transforming the attitudes and behaviour of entire societies if a new conservation ethic . . . is to become a reality'; *Caring for the Earth* (IUCN, UNEP, WWF, 1991) emphasises that environmental education teaching should be practical (action orientated) as well as theoretical; and *Agenda 21* states that

> education, including formal education, public awareness and training should be recognised as a process by which human beings and societies can reach their fullest potential. Education is critical for promoting sustainable development and improving the capacity of the people to address environment and development issues . . . it is also critical for achieving environmental and ethical awareness, values and attitudes, skills and behaviour consistent with sustainable development and for effective public participation in decision-making.

(Quarrie, 1992)

Whilst the educational implications of having varying perspectives on under-standing and addressing the root causes of environmental problems may well be consistent with the rhetoric of the 'recognised' influential documents in the field of environmental education, a critical question arises: to what extent are these implications and rhetoric consistent with present-day environmental education practice?

EDUCATIONAL PRACTICE: THE RHETORIC–REALITY GAP

Conflicts, inconsistencies and limitations

The question of match and mis-match between rhetoric and reality in environ-mental education is, like most issues addressed in this book, highly complex, and variable depending on location and circumstances. Yet reference to a number of substantiated generalisations will illuminate a range of conflicts, inconsistencies and limitations impeding the implementation of successful programmes of environmental education.

For Esland (1971) the introduction of environmental education into a school curriculum represents a fundamental challenge to the dominant conception, organisation and transmission of knowledge, creating for most teachers a conflict with their approach to teaching and learning. Other writers (see, for example, Robottom, 1982, 1983; Volk *et al.*, 1984) elaborate on the discrepancy between the acquisition of environmental knowledge and awareness in 'traditional' school programmes, and the action-orientated goals of the contemporary rhetoric of environmental education. Following on from these authors, Stevenson (1987) outlines a series of major contradictions between environmental education and schooling. In the first instance, he describes a situation in which the rhetoric of environmental education 'focuses on improving the quality of life of all humankind on our planet by finding ways to ensure that no nation should grow or develop at the expense of another nation and that the consumption of no individual should be increased at the expense of other individuals' (Belgrade Charter in Stevenson, 1987) and thus 'has the revolutionary purpose of trans-forming the values that underlie our decision-making, from the present ones which aid and abet environmental (and human) degradation to those which support a sustainable planet in which all people live in human dignity' (Tanner, 1974). This, according to Stevenson, provides the first major contradiction between environmental education and the traditional purpose of schools, which is to conserve the existing social order by reproducing the norms and values that currently dominate environmental decision-making.

Secondly, there are fundamental curriculum and pedagogical contradictions between environmental education and schooling. The goals, principles and guidelines of environmental education (see, for example, UNESCO, 1975, 1977; IUCN, UNEP, WWF, 1991) suggest a particular orientation of curriculum and pedagogical practices in which students engage individually or in groups in problem-solving, action-based activities. Inevitably such a focus on real environmental issues calls for inter-disciplinary and flexible inquiry. In contrast, however, school curricula tend to be discipline-based and emphasise abstract theoretical problems. 'The common curriculum emphasis can be described as the mastery of many fragmented facts, concepts and simple generalisations organised loosely within discrete bodies or fields of study. The predominant pedagogical process involves the teacher as dispenser of factual knowledge . . . ' (Stevenson, 1987, drawing upon the work of others, e.g. Goodlad, 1984; Sizer, 1984; Young, 1980). Furthermore,

> whereas a curriculum in environmental education is emergent and problematic in that the content arises as students are involved in specific environmental problems, most school curricula are predefined since they are designed to serve predetermined behaviourally specific ends (that is, ends whose attainment can be readily assessed). . . . While environmental education advocates learning that is holistic and co-operative, school learning tends to be atomistic and individual. . . . In environmental education rhetoric students are active thinkers and generators of knowledge, but in schools students are usually in the passive position of spectators and recipients of other people's knowledge and thinking.
>
> (Stevenson, 1987)

Such predominant practices and inconsistencies between environmental education and schooling, as described a decade or so ago, clearly hold true today, apparently throughout much of the world's formal education provision. Certainly, the introduction of the National Curriculum for Schools in the UK, following the Education Reform Act of 1988, together with its related assessment arrangements, led to increasing levels of prescription and specificity in the definition of a subject-based curriculum. For the first time, educators in England and Wales were provided with clear statements of pupil entitlement, targets and 'benchmark' standards for subjects, far removed (on paper at least) from the inter-disciplinary, flexible modes of inquiry and view of students as generators of knowledge portrayed in descriptions of environmental education.

The contradictions and inconsistencies outlined are inevitably linked to school and classroom organisation, and to the day-to-day practicalities of formal education. The style of learning implicit in descriptions of the environmental education process, involving, as it may, elements of difficulty, ambiguity, contradiction and autonomy, involves teachers in far more complex organisational methods and indeed in taking more 'risks' in relation to maintaining order and control than the style of learning associated with more traditional subject-knowledge acquisition tasks. It is reported (e.g. McNeil, 1983; Sedlak et al., 1986) that teachers' overall priority is maintaining order and control in their classrooms, and that in many classrooms teachers agree to make minimal work demands in return for good behaviour. For many teachers, a major criterion in deciding on pedagogical strategies and in selecting student tasks is that they are unlikely to create control problems (Doyle, 1983; Stevenson, 1987). It follows, then, that such teachers, perhaps the majority, are unlikely to take readily to the demands of implementing action-orientated, open-ended inquiry into environmental issues. Furthermore, even given the motivation and commitment to take on this challenge, the vast majority of teachers would cite lack of time and resources, and pressure to prioritise other things as valid reasons for declining to do so. The research study cited in Part I of this text (p. 25, Tomlins and Froud, 1994) identified lack of timetable time – because of the need to meet the statutory requirements – and lack of resources as the two major constraints to delivering environmental education in schools in the UK (alongside lack of staff expertise and lack of staff motivation).

Another great mis-match between the rhetoric and reality of environmental education, which may best be described as a substantial limitation of the reality, relates to its breadth of coverage or primary location in a subject-based curriculum. The accepted policy and guidelines expect environmental teaching and learning to be truly cross-curricular. For example, the *Tbilisi Report* sees environmental education as 'inter-disciplinary and holistic in nature and application ... an approach to education rather than a subject' (UNESCO, 1977) and *Our Common Future* states that 'Education should provide comprehensive knowledge, encompassing and cutting across the social and natural sciences and the humanities, thus providing insights on the interaction between natural and human resources, between development and environment' (WCED, 1987). Yet in reality we see a very strong emphasis on the grounding of environmental education within the scientific domain. A primary location is often science courses, and, often at best, environmental issues are seriously addressed within science and geography. This situation is very apparent in many locations around the world, including the UK, where the most recent government publication on *Teaching Environmental Matters Through the National Curriculum* (SCAA, 1996) makes it quite clear that

> It is for schools to decide how to teach environmental matters through the National Curriculum and how far to go beyond statutory obligations. In some National Curriculum subjects, notably geography and science, the programmes of study ensure that environmental matters are taught. . . .
>
> Environmental matters may also feature in other National Curriculum subjects, not because they are required, but because schools choose to take up opportunities to include an environmental dimension.
>
> (SCAA, 1996)

In other words, environmental education will extend beyond geography and science only if the whims, enthusiasms and motivation of individual teachers and schools so decide ... hardly a recipe for successful implementation of internationally accepted guidelines, when teachers already have overburdened timetables because of the need to fulfil statutory requirements. This question of the primary location of environmental education within the scientific domain will be returned to within the discussion of trends in research in the field on p. 102 below, and in Part IV. At this stage, suffice to say that it represents a major limitation to its success, which, together with other serious inconsistencies and conflicts, as outlined, give an overall picture of a wide rhetoric–reality gap.

A question of paradigm shift?

Perhaps the solutions to such inconsistencies, conflicts and limitations lie in the development and adoption of substantial changes in approaches to environmental education (indeed education), involving what some writers describe as major paradigm shifts.

Gough (1987), for example, argues the desirability of shifting from the materialistic and atomistic world view and epistemological paradigm that dominates formal education towards an ecological paradigm for education. His paper is rich with examples and references, and only a brief and oversimplified account of it can be provided here. It is suggested that from time to time we should examine the underlying structures and paradigms of education with a view to reconstruction, and indeed that our present system of education has been built upon understandings of reality, nature and human nature that can no longer be taken for granted:

> The social construction of reality that once provided a certain coherence to western society has been unravelling for decades. It was a worldview that valued progress, economic efficiency, science and technology – and saw a world composed of separate entities such as atoms, individuals, . . . nations.
>
> (Michael J. Anderson in Gough, 1987, p. 15)

This materialistic world view continues to dominate formal education, whilst in Western society generally one can observe some movement towards the strengthening of ecological, humane and spiritual values and away from scientific materialism. In developing countries we see a parallel shift from Western materialism towards a reassertion of native cultural values and beliefs (based on Harman, 1985).

For Gough, environmental education is a product of both the 'order' and emerging world views,

> and to some extent reflects the contradictions and conflicts that accompany a new paradigm shift. For example, most environmental educators would claim to hold 'ecological' and 'humane' values, but many are also suspicious of 'spiritual' values and cling to the 'confident scientific materialism' of the past.
>
> (Gough, 1987, p. 52)

From this position, it is argued that environmental educators should capitalise on one feature of the changing world view that is likely to prevail – i.e. its holistic (rather than fragmented) emphasis – and encourage the shift away from an epistemological paradigm for education (based on Western society's dominant form of theorising, namely positive empirical science) towards an ecological paradigm. The term 'ecological paradigm' is acknowledged as deriving from the work of Emery (1981), whose use of it is linked to studies in human perception. Emery challenges the fact that for 200 years most of our educational practices have been based on the empiricist theories of perception and knowledge that were put forward by several eighteenth-century philosophers, including Locke, Berkeley and Hume.

> Education practice since the onrush of positivist science has not valued an individual's perceptions as a source of knowledge. It is held that the meaning of perceptions emerges from intellectual processes of analytic abstraction and logical inference (hence the now taken-for-granted separation of perception from cognition) and that the prime task of education is to distribute the socially validated knowledge that has been so gained.
>
> (Gough, 1987, p. 55)

Emery's ecological theories of perception, by way of contrast, suggest that we can access information that is present in our personal, social and physical environments through an 'education of the senses', i.e. a learning process within our environments. 'It is an education in searching with our own perceptual systems not an education in how to someday research in the accumulated pile of so-called social knowledge' (Emery, 1981, p. 7). Teaching, according to ecological theories of perception, focuses on promoting inter-relationships between learners and environments, rather than on imparting knowledge in traditional teacher–learner hierarchical relationship.

Gough advances ecological theories of perception as one of three compelling sources of support for an ecological paradigm for education (the others being the historical roots of an ecological paradigm, and the significance of Earth Education). Such a paradigm is characterised by reality-centred projects (rather than textbooks or standardised procedures), co-operation rather than competition between learners, pupils learning together and from each other (rather than in teacher–pupil relationships), and learning that takes place in community settings rather than school classrooms. The object of learning includes discovery of universals in particulars in learners' environments and perception of invariants, rather than the transmission of existing knowledge and the abstraction of generic concepts (Gough, 1987, p. 63, adapted from Emery, 1981, p. 15). In short, a major shift towards an ecological paradigm involves rethinking all of education – not merely environmental education – according to an ecological world view.

Other writers (see, for example, Fien, 1992; Elliot, 1991; Robottom and Hart, 1993) similarly challenge the dominant scientific paradigm. For Robottom and Hart (1993), the field of formal education is characterised by the materialistic

Western world view that developed from the scientific revolution and replaced intrinsic values with instrumental values. It is a world view that sees the human species apart from nature and having the ethical right to manipulate nature for its own purposes. Positivistic approaches share a basically applied science approach to educational inquiry, seeking to apply standards and methods of the natural sciences to the problems of education. 'They have a strong empiricist quality which assumes that the only valid knowledge is that which is obtained through the scientific method and that this method is the only rational avenue to knowledge that is objective, rational and true' (Codd, 1982 in Robottom and Hart, 1993, p. 29). The dominant scientific world view appears to have had an overwhelmingly powerful influence not only on education and educational inquiry in general, but also on the development of the research field in environmental education, a matter that will be returned to on p. 102. In their lengthy, complex critique of the dominant paradigm, Robottom and Hart make quite clear that, in their view, such instrumental research that has dominated the literature in the 1980s and 1990s is inadequate for the task of improving environmental education

> precisely because in such research the ideological appropriateness of the goals (their value in every sense) is taken for granted . . . in the absence of appraisal of the goals themselves, such instrumental measures actually tell us nothing about the value of an environmental education programme, for instance, in addressing and responding to particular environmental issues in particular environmental and social settings in ways that are just and equitable for the stakeholders involved in that issue.
>
> (Robottom and Hart, 1993, p. 38)

Aside from the reified status ascribed to its goals, the dominant approach to environmental education and its research is critiqued on a number of other grounds in this monograph, including its behaviourist, deterministic ideology; its individualistic interpretation of environmentalism; and the tension between its determinism and the idea of critical thinking in environmental education. The authors are also critical of the way this paradigm has the effect of imposing the social values of the researcher on to environmental education in ways that disempower teachers and learners. In short, they view forms of inquiry deriving from this paradigm as inappropriate and inadequate for application to the political, value-laden and social world encompassed by environmental education. In response to the critique, more coherent and appropriate approaches to environmental education and its research are called for, essentially ones deriving from an emerging 'environmental' world view. Skolimowski (1981) describes this emerging world view as an ecophilosophy which is about the resurrection of intrinsic values, and the reuniting of knowledge with values. Ecophilosophy is characterised by a fundamental reorientation of perception wherein the natural world becomes vested with the same value as the human world and leads to notions of stewardship. It is

101

life orientated, committed to human values and to nature, comprehensive and global (reality is more than description or scientific explanation), concerned with wisdom (exercises judgement based on qualitative criteria), ecologically conscious (human values seen as part of a larger spectrum in which nature participates and codefines), aligned with an economics of the quality of life, politically aware (human actions have political consequences), tolerant of transphysical phenomena, vitally concerned with society's well-being, and about individual responsibility.
(Robottom and Hart, 1993, p. 48, based on Skolimowski, 1981)

Aligned with this ecophilosophy, or emerging new world view, is what has been termed 'new paradigm research' (Reason, 1988). This includes a move to 'participatory and holistic knowing based on participative and dialogic relationship with the world'. It seeks what could be described as 'deep inquiry', or deeper understanding of phenomena, which is a parallel to 'deep ecology', as previously discussed. It is

essentially a socially critical approach to environmental education inquiry, which fosters the development of independent critical and creative thinking in relation to environmental issues . . . this approach entails involving all participants (in participatory action research) in three ways of knowing: propositional knowing (knowing 'about' ideas, propositions and theories), practical knowing (knowledge of skills and abilities) and experiential knowing (knowledge by encounter which is tacit, intuitive and holistic).
(Robottom and Hart, 1993, based on Reason, 1988)

For these authors, the notion of participatory inquiry in education is appropriate to environmental education because the world views that underpin both this form of inquiry and environmental education are virtually the same.

TRENDS IN ENVIRONMENTAL EDUCATION RESEARCH

Positivist tradition

As suggested in the previous part of this book, the scientific research paradigm has tended to dominate the relatively young and evolving body of environmental education research. This is hardly surprising, given the academic background of early and influential researchers in the field. It was in the United States that the development of an environmental education research agenda gained momentum during the late 1970s and the 1980s. Studies reported in the *Journal of Environmental Education* were then dominated by researchers at the University of Southern Illinois (Hungerford *et al.*, 1980, 1983; Hungerford and Volk, 1990), and their work had significant impact upon Australian, European and Asian environmental education curriculum development and research. The Illinois team, alongside other influential researchers active at that time (see, for example,

Fensham, 1978; Lucas, 1979; Stapp *et al.*, 1980), were trained scientists whose quantitative approaches dominated developments and published research outcomes. Marcinkowski (1990) provides an overview of the characteristics of this dominant 'quantitative paradigm' in environmental education research as follows:

- presents results in numerical, and more specifically, in statistical form;
- derived from the natural and physical sciences, and reflects the tradition of scientific inquiry;
- takes a 'logical' positivist view, which assumes that there are social facts with a single objective reality apart from individuals' beliefs;
- takes the position that 'truth' consists of observable and verifiable (or objective) facts, and not of internal conditions, such as personal dispositions or values. This gives rise to a 'fact–value' dichotomy;
- seeks to establish patterns of, relationships between, and causes of social phenomena (Description, Prediction and Explanation);
- recognised procedures have been established for generating questions and designs before the study begins (i.e. a priori);
- prototypical designs (are) Survey, Correlational and Experimental Designs;
- researcher remains detached from the setting to avoid bias, and tends to rely upon instruments as an intermediary device for data collection purposes;
- validity and reliability are seen as characteristics of measurement devices. Estimates are obtained using known analysis procedures.

(Marcinkowski, 1990, pp. 10–11)

The majority of research studies published in the 1970s and 1980s in the *Journal of Environmental Education* (the then leading research journal in the field) reflect these characteristics, being concerned with 'ascertaining the congruence between outcomes and assumed goals and seeking empirically (objectively) to derive generalisations (theory) and hence legitimate scientific knowledge' (Robottom and Hart, 1993). Many studies of this period were concerned with the identification, prediction and control of the variables that are believed to be the critical cognitive and affective determinants of responsible environmental behaviour (see, for example, Ramsey and Hungerford, 1989; Hungerford and Volk, 1990). Iozzi (1981) reports that 90–92 per cent of research studies in environmental education at this time were quantitative.

As previously mentioned, such quantitative approaches align with the positivist (empiricist) paradigm, wherein

a distinction has to be made between phenomena which can be carefully observed, accurately recorded and classified and those interpretations of human phenomena which focus on feelings, understandings and mean-ings. Doubt and ambiguity are to be removed and objectivity asserted.

Thus, in research terms, there is an emphasis on continually improving those methods which enable social phenomena to be directly observed, described and measured.

(Williams, 1996)

It would seem that two decades after positivism and the quantitative tradition steered the definition and development of a research base for environmental education, their characteristics continue to be an extremely powerful influence today. The call for a broadening of paradigms, as discussed above, certainly applies as much to the realm of research as it does to that of curriculum development. Readers interested in pursuing debate on the roots, characteristics and articulated limitations of the positivist tradition in relation to environmental education will find further references to overviews and critiques in Williams (1996) and Robottom and Hart (1990, 1993).

Two further points must be emphasised before moving away from a focus on criticisms of quantitative, experimental and quasi-experimental research designs. Firstly, there most certainly *has* been a reduction in the dominance of such approaches in recent years and a very real shift towards the use of more humanistic and interpretive lines of inquiry by environmental educationists. To these modes, attention shortly turns. Secondly, despite the criticisms levelled at the quantitative tradition, we must not ignore the contribution that studies aligned to it have so far made to the field, and indeed their on-going role and significance. As Williams (1996) rightly points out:

> Quantitative studies have a role in eclectic investigations. The collection of quantitative data is often a significant preliminary stage, which helps to shape up inquiry, opening up avenues for exploration, indicating hypotheses worth testing and closing off areas not worth investigation further. In the gathering of factual data . . . the use of carefully designed tests is important. So is the use of objective questions in studies which employ interviews and questionnaires to gather data in order to construct patterns of behaviour. There is no doubt that valuable cognitive, affective and behavioural data can be gathered using these techniques. There is also no doubt that in some circumstances such data can be validated and made more reliable through the use of supplementary qualitative studies.

(Williams, 1996, p. 9)

So this section is concluded with reference to an example taken from the scientific, empiricist school of research which has, without doubt, served as an influential study in its own right, and has stimulated further work which employs a variety of forms of inquiry.

'Changing Learner Behaviour Through Environmental Education'

This paper by Hungerford and Volk (1990) of the Southern Illinois University challenges traditional approaches to practice. 'Responsible citizenship can be developed through environmental education. The strategies are known. The tools are available. The real challenge lies in a willingness to do things differently than we have in the past' (Hungerford and Volk, 1990, p. 18). The authors argue that research into environmental behaviour does not bear out the validity of linear models for changing behaviour, i.e. that increased knowledge about the environment and its associated issues leads to favourable attitudes . . . which in turn lead to action promoting better environmental quality. They comment that whilst numerous researchers have investigated a variety of variables hypothesised to be associated with responsible environmental behaviour, notably in correlational studies that cannot claim 'cause and effect' relationships, the research field as a whole has revealed important findings. They cite, for example, Hines *et al.* (1986/87) who published a meta-analysis of the behaviour research literature in environmental education which involved the analysis of 128 studies

> which had been reported since 1971 . . . which assessed variables in association with responsible environmental behaviour and which reported empirical data on this relationship. . . . An analysis of data (from these studies) resulted in the emergence of a number of major categories of variables which had been investigated in association with responsible environmental behaviour. . . . In the end, fifteen separate variables were meta-analysed in an effort to determine the strength of their association with environmental behaviour.
>
> (Hines et al., 1986/87, pp. 1–8)

From this scientific analysis, a model of responsible environmental behaviour was constructed (Hines *et al.*, 1986/87) and the following inferences drawn from it:

- An individual who expresses an intention to take action will be more likely to engage in the action than will an individual who expresses no such intention. . . . However, it appears that intention to act is merely an artifact of a number of other variables acting in combination (e.g. cognitive knowledge, cognitive skills, and personality factors).

- Before an individual can intentionally act on a particular environmental problem, that individual must be cognizant of the existence of the issue. Thus knowledge of the issue appears to be a prerequisite to action.

- An individual must also possess knowledge of those courses of action which are available and which will be most effective in a given situation.

- Another critical component . . . is skill in appropriately applying this knowledge (i.e. knowledge of action strategies) to a given issue.

- In addition, an individual must possess a desire to act. One's desire to act appears to be affected by a host of personality factors . . . locus of control, attitudes (toward the environment and toward taking action), and personal responsibility toward the environment.

105

- Situational factors, such as economic constraints, social pressures and opportunities to choose different actions may ... serve to either counteract or to strengthen the variables in the model.

(Hungerford and Volk, 1990)

Their own work and other related studies (e.g. Ramsey and Hungerford, 1989; Sia *et al.*, 1985) led the authors to conclude that there are probably three major categories of variables that contribute to environmentally responsible behaviour, and operate in a 'more or less' linear fashion. These are 'entry-level variables', including the development of environmental sensitivity; 'ownership variables', including having in-depth knowledge about issues and personal investment in issues and the environment; and 'empowerment variables', including having knowledge of and skill in using environmental action strategies, the locus of control (expectancy of reinforcement) and the intention to act.

This analysis leads to the identification of a number of critical components of an educational programme that seeks to change learners' behaviour. These include:

- the teaching of environmentally-significant ecological concepts and the environmental interrelationships that exist within and between these concepts;
- the provision of carefully designed and in-depth opportunities for learners to achieve some level of environmental sensitivity which will promote a desire to behave in appropriate ways;
- the provision of a curriculum that will result in an in-depth knowledge of issues;
- the provision of a curriculum that will teach learners the skills of issue analysis and investigation as well as provide the time needed for the application of these skills;
- the provision of a curriculum that will teach learners the citizenship skills needed for issue remediation as well as the time needed for the application of these skills;
- the provision of an instructional setting which increases learners' expectancy of reinforcement for acting in responsible ways, i.e. attempts to develop an internal locus of control in learners.

(Hungerford and Volk, 1990)

Amongst their key conclusions are the facts that the majority of instructional materials in environmental education fails to develop skills associated with investigating and evaluating issues, or with responsible citizenship participation; and that too few environmental education programmes incorporate serious attempts to develop ownership and empowerment in learners.

Critics of the approach employed by these researchers argue that it is strongly behaviourist in nature, with its focus on understanding, predicting and

106

modifying 'responsible behaviour', with its view that the ultimate achievement of research is perceived as a situation in which it is possible fully to predict environmental behaviour and with teachers and pupils seen as manipulable by researchers.

> It is considered proper to apply behavioural intervention strategies and to manipulate situational factors in order to produce desired behavioural changes, even if the individuals (whom it must be remembered are members of a democracy interested in independent critical thinking) do not necessarily want to change in this way.
>
> (Robottom and Hart, 1993, p. 36)

Advocates of this undoubtedly behaviourist, deterministic approach clearly defend the position that

> in situations in which individuals do not possess those personality characteristics which would lead to the development of a desire to help alleviate environmental problems, these individuals may be enticed into behaving responsibly toward the environment by the application of behavioural intervention strategies
>
> (Hines *et al.*, 1986/87, p. 7)

on the grounds that 'the acquisition of responsible environmental behaviour has long been recognised as the ultimate goal of environmental education' (Sia *et al.*, 1985, p. 31) and that 'responsible environmental behaviour is a learned response/action . . . it is contingent on several variables interacting with one another' (p. 32). Whatever the 'rights and wrongs' of their approach, these researchers have provided valuable insights into our understanding of the development of people's environmental awareness, concern and actions – a fundamental topic that will be returned to later in the text.

Interpretivist and critical paradigms

Let us now turn to two further paradigms upon which research methodology is based, which, along with the positivist paradigm, form the three key approaches that characterise research and understanding in environmental education. The three provide the contextual or theoretical background against which any individual research studies or developments in the field can be interpreted.

Interpretive approaches

The interpretivist (constructivist) research paradigm has developed from critique of, and with very different underlying assumptions of, the positivist (empiricist) paradigm. Whilst positivism sees reality as external to the individual, interpretivism sees it as internally constructed. Schwandt writes that the goal of interpretive research is:

an abiding concern for the life world, . . . for understanding meaning, for grasping an actor's definition of a situation. . . . The world of lived reality and situation-specific meanings that constitute the general object of investigation is thought to be constructed by social actors . . . particular actors, at particular times, fashion meaning out of events and phenomena through prolonged, complex processes of social interaction involving history, language and action.

(Schwandt, 1994)

The central endeavour in the context of this paradigm is to understand the subjective world of human experience. To retain the integrity of the phenomena being investigated, efforts are made to get inside the person and to understand from within. The imposition of external form and structure is resisted, since this reflects the viewpoint of the observer as opposed to that of the actor directly involved (Cohen and Manion, 1989). Interpretivists do not believe that positivist research is as value-free as is claimed; neither do they believe that research can establish theories of human behaviour that can be abstracted and used for general prediction purposes.

Researchers in the interpretive tradition argue that human behaviour is too diverse and complex to be described through generalisations and theories. Interpretivists maintain that human behaviour is situation-specific and that any attempt to systematise human behaviour will give rise to incomplete and unreliable knowledge.

(Fien and Hillcoat, 1996)

Interpretive understanding does not rely on abstraction of variables, hypotheses and statistical techniques. Rather it is grounded in interactive, field-based inductive methodology, which in turn is embedded in practice and within a context. The inquirer seeks the perspectives and meanings of participants, both propositional and tacit, and aims to construct holistic patterns or webs of influence (Green, 1990 in Robottom and Hart, 1993).

The implications for educational research are that interpretive methods cannot be preordinate but are emergent and, hence, are problematic in the eyes of the traditional scientific methodologies . . . [they] assume that human actions can be understood only in relation to the meanings in terms of which the human actors make those actions intelligible. In other words, actions can be understood only in terms of meanings, and it is the task of interpretive approaches to explicate those actions and meanings.

(Robottom and Hart, 1993, p. 10)

Researchers in this field rely on the transferability of principles and themes, rather than replicability and generalisability. Research questions that may be explored through interpretive modes of inquiry (e.g. case studies, participant observation, semi-structured interviews, discourse analysis, connoisseurship and criticism, etc.) include investigations of how students and teachers understand or conceptualise the environment and related issues, studies of how people develop meaning of environmental concepts, studies of individuals' reflections and experiences relating to the environment, and studies of the use of discourse or language in environmental teaching and learning.

For some researchers, the term 'constructivism' is used synonymously with or alongside 'interpretivism' in descriptions of essentially qualitative research along the lines described. Robertson (1994) provides a review of theoretical aspects of science education research of this type, and argues for the development of constructivist-based research in environmental education. According to Robertson, only three research reports published in the *Journal of Environmental Education* between 1989 and 1994 were styled in constructivist terms (see Brody 1990/91; Brody and Koch, 1989/90; Lisowski and Disinger, 1992); and the study of Wals (1992) was one of few explicitly constructivist studies published at all in the environmental education literature of the time. He points out that many research endeavours in science education are framed within a post-positivist constructivist epistemology, wherein learning is considered to involve an interaction between meaningful concepts in the learner's 'conceptual framework' (Driver and Erickson, 1983). As one researcher explains,

> Because students have experienced and thought about the world, they enter learning situations with a complex cluster of ideas, beliefs, values and emotions ... and it is the potential match between these existing cognitive commitments and the new information which determines how the student will respond to the instructional inputs.
>
> (Snively, 1986 in Robertson, 1994)

Constructivism rejects the idea of an objective base of observations against which the validity of theories about the world can be measured or checked. For Driver, 'Science as public knowledge is not so much a discovery as a carefully checked "construction". In our attempts to represent the world, we construct theoretical entities (magnetic fields, genes, orbitals ...) which in turn take on a "reality"' (Driver, 1987 in Robertson, 1994). The term 'construct' emphasises the understanding that these categories exist in an individual's thinking because they have been constructed or framed in meaning as discrete entities; so it is an 'intellectual device by means of which one construes events. It is a means of organising experiences into categories' (see Cherryholmes, 1988). As Robertson points out, research eliciting students' personal conceptualising and under-standings of scientific principles and natural phenomena builds on earlier work by Piaget and Ausubel (see Novak and Gowin, 1984), and the work of other current researchers in the field, e.g. Driver (1989) and Millar (1989). For example, a core concept in Ausubel's learning theory central to constructivist approaches is that of meaningful learning (as contrasted with rote learning) in which individuals relate new knowledge to relevant concepts and propositions that are already known. This view of learning assumes that young children actually know a good deal as and when they enter schooling and that education is a process of re-education: 'reconstructing what they already know and value into new patterns. Formal schooling begins in mid-stream' (Gowin, 1981). One key goal of constructivist research in science education has been to investigate pupils' existing knowledge that they bring to learning situations, so that it can be made explicit and characterised. In line with Ausubel's belief that 'the most important single factor influencing learning is what the learner already knows' (in Novak and Gowin, 1984, p. 40), it is understood that learning will inevitably be more successful if teachers can relate to and build upon pupils' existing understandings of whatever concept or phenomenon is being addressed. Robertson cites studies in various domains that probe students' understandings of phenomena commonly studied in science classrooms and their interpretation of scientific principles (see, for example, Driver, 1989; Driver and Erickson, 1983; Hewson and Hamlyn, 1983; Shipstone *et al.*, 1989), and discusses definitions of and distinctions between a variety of constructs that have been used to frame the outcomes of such studies, including 'concept', 'conception', 'preconceptions', 'misconceptions', 'alternate conceptions', 'prior conceptions', 'naive conceptions', etc. All of these terms (and others) refer to ideas that individuals develop about natural phenomena (Driver, 1987). Most of the studies in constructivist research in science education that aim to elicit and interpret students' understanding of concepts and their explanations of particular phenomena used methodologies employing interview techniques, in which the researcher allows the interviewee as much freedom as possible in the expression of responses.

Robertson (1994) concludes his account of on-going constructivist work in the domain of science education by drawing attention to the fact that 'environment' is not something that has a reality separate from ourselves, but is a social construct that should be understood 'as the conceptual interactions between our physical surroundings and the social, political and economic forces that organise us in the context of these surroundings' (Di Chiro, 1987). Environmental problems likewise are socially constructed in terms of their conceptualised effects on human individuals, groups, and other living things and systems. There is, however, little research literature to inform our understanding of how others conceptualise environment, environmental issues and human–environment relationships (Robertson, 1993; Wals, 1992).

> Thus, research based on constructivist principles is worthy of attention in environmental education, largely because these principles provide a coherent framework in which to theorise about learning, on the one hand, and ways in which we understand these socially constructed categories and issues, including knowledge, on the other.
>
> (Robertson, 1994)

Certainly at the time of Robertson's call for constructivism to receive attention in environmental education research, the interpretive research paradigm in this field was in its infancy. His paper contributed to the growing number of statements supporting the promotion of a more broadly based view of research in environmental education that were published in the late 1980s and early 1990s (see, for example, Jickling, 1991a; Posch, 1993b; Robottom and Hart, 1993). Several years beyond this time, one can report without doubt an upsurge of interest in interpretive research (see p. 119), although many would argue that there is still a long way to go.

The example that follows is a brief overview of research conducted in the constructivist mode, deriving from the author's own multi-faceted international project on the development of individuals' environmental thinking, awareness and concern.

Emergent understanding of environmental concepts

Palmer (1993, 1995) describes aspects of the preliminary data analysis of a research project entitled 'Emergent Environmentalism', which is concerned in part with the nature and development of children's early knowledge and awareness of environmental issues. The project uses autobiographical, qualitative analysis to investigate the acquisition of environmental subject knowledge and concern for the environment, and the development of this during children's first three years in school, i.e. aged 5–7 years. It aims

- to investigate the acquisition of environmental subject knowledge in preschool children (aged 4 years), in particular to examine the way in which scientific knowledge may underpin children's knowledge of the environment;
- to monitor the development of environmental knowledge and concern during children's first three years in school – and in particular to ascertain how incomplete or stereotypical knowledge may constrain their subsequent understanding of environmental issues.

In the first phase of this work, 124 children aged between 4.0 and 5.0 years were interviewed, 62 in California, USA, and 62 in the north-east of England. All were attending nursery schools at the time of data collection. In line with a constructivist framework for aiming to elicit and interpret pupils' understandings of concepts and their explanations of particular issues and phenomena, a semi-structured interview/discussion approach was utilised to find out as much as possible about the children's knowledge of and concern for certain environmental issues. Attention focused on four well-known issues of concern to environmentalists today, namely tropical rainforests, deforestation/endangered species, global warming and management of waste materials. Each child was interviewed individually and discussion was promoted with the help of a series of photographs relating to the issues. The same photographs, format and 'lead' questions were utilised in all interviews in order to maximise reliability as far as is possible in qualitative, interpretive research of this kind. The interviews were audio-taped and subsequently transcribed for analysis.

111

Three categories of information emerged from the wealth of data provided by the conversations:

- details of the children's knowledge and understanding about people, places and environmental issues – their emerging concepts and characterisation of these – their accurate understandings, gaps in knowledge, and erroneous thinking (preconceptions or misconceptions). Such details provided substantial insight into the development of key environmental concepts upon which teaching in the early years of schooling may build;
- insights into the children's levels of awareness and concern for the world in which they are growing up, and problems that affect our planet;
- insights into the origins and sources of knowledge and concern in these pre-school children who had received no formal educational instruction.

A 'snapshot' of the fascinating findings now presented confirms the view promoted by Ausubel (Novak and Gowin, 1984) that young children do indeed possess a great deal of prior knowledge when they come into formal schooling.

In the first instance, data were analysed to establish elements of accurate subject knowledge relating to each issue. A concept map was constructed for each subject, recording the network of linked concepts referred to, explained and apparently understood. A minimum concept map contained no elaboration on the basic concept under discussion – here, global warming will be used as the example. Thirteen subjects who could provide no elaboration or explanation of the theme of what would happen if snow became warmer are in this category. The remaining subjects in the sample provided some degree of elaboration of understanding, ranging from a score of one accurate concept to a score of five. Taking the sample as a whole, the subjects between them articulated 'core' extension concepts, as outlined in Figure 3.1. It should be noted that, for the purpose of this example, only core concepts are shown in the diagram; clearly these are linked in various patterns or networks with other related ideas discussed by individuals. There are, of course, also patterns of misconceptions or preconceptions that can be linked to the nets of accurate concepts.

Significant confirmation of the hypothesis that pre-school children know a good deal about the physical world in which they are growing up was provided by the fact that some 90 per cent of the whole sample could provide an elaboration of the basic idea of global warming, expressed in terms of what would happen if the poles became warmer. In each case this involved an explanation of the fact that if snow gets warmer it disappears. Seventy-seven per cent of the sample could explain that the snow goes because it melts; 38 per cent could articulate the fact that melting snow produces water; and 8 per cent of the sample could demonstrate still higher levels of understanding by going on to articulate conceptual links between melting snow, increase in water in rivers and oceans, effects of these processes on living things and, in some cases, subsequent flooding of the land (Palmer, 1993). As far as preconceptions, misconceptions or gaps in knowledge are concerned, many of the same wrong or incomplete

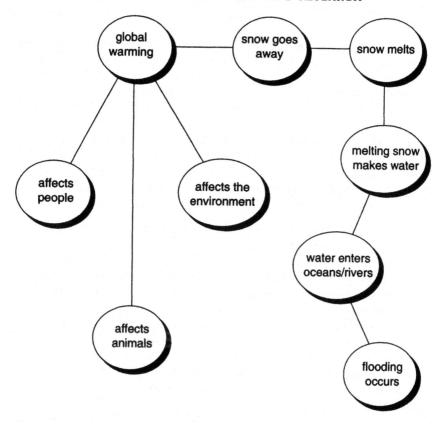

Figure 3.1 Global warming: related core concepts identified and understood by subjects

answers and explanations were given by a substantial proportion of the subjects, thus illuminating areas of knowledge and understanding that teachers in the early years of schooling need to know about and pay attention to. For example, common answers to the question 'where does the melting snow go?' were 'under the ground' (with no further explanation), 'up into the air' or 'it evaporates', suggesting preconceptions that represent a good start towards more accurate and complete understanding that can be addressed. Other incorrect answers to this question, such as 'to Santa Claus's house' or 'to heaven' are clearly illuminative of existing pre-knowledge bases that at an appropriate stage must be built upon.

Data collection and analysis on a much larger international scale in this project as a whole continues (see, for example, Palmer *et al.*, 1996). It is providing, through interpretive means, important insights into the links between knowledge in the early years and the development of understanding about environmental issues.

The critical tradition in research

A second post positivist perspective on research, which has emerged from and shares the interpretivist critique of the positivist paradigm, is 'critical theory'. Critical researchers are supportive of interpretivism in so far as they agree that interpretive methods provide knowledge that promotes understanding and meaningful dialogue. However, advocates of the critical paradigm argue that the interpretive paradigm does not take into account the fact that our subjective views are not only internally constructed but are also influenced by persuasive social forces. Individuals or groups cannot be considered separately from their societal context (Fien and Hillcoat, 1996). Critical theory has been described as ideologically orientated inquiry (Guba, 1990). Robottom and Hart (1993), drawing upon the work of Green (1990) and Carr and Kemmis (1983), state:

> Becoming critical means exposing one's ideological bases, penetrating one's ideological assumptions, through critique. Whereas 'critical' can mean internal criticism from the perspective of analytical questioning of argument and method, it can also mean developing a conception of reality that ties ideas, thought and language to social and historical conditions; that is, social criticism based on notions of power and control. These meanings [can be combined] so that becoming critical means developing an analytic posture towards arguments, procedures and language using a lens related to issues of power and control in relationships, and developing an action-orientated commitment to common welfare . . . critical theory has an emancipatory action-constitutive interest (improving the quality of human existence).
>
> (Robottom and Hart, 1993, p. 11)

The approach has an explicit commitment to social justice, and is therefore value centred. Research 'employs a practical form of reasoning (like that of interpretive research) which at the same time is critical; it is shaped by the emancipatory intent to transform educational practices through, ultimately, ideology critique' (Kemmis, 1988 in Hart, 1993). Researchers use critical reflection or reflexivity to be openly ideological in their approach. This provides means by which the status quo can be questioned. The critical paradigm is the only research methodology that seeks to transform the dominant social paradigm (Fien and Hillcoat, 1996).

Robottom and Hart (1993, pp. 23–25) provide a useful account of the 'socially critical' approach to environmental education. In their opinion, environmental education should ideally involve students, teachers and community agencies in collaborative investigations of real environmental issues in their local environments. The investigations should be socially critical in that they seek to uncover and make explicit the values and vested interests of the individuals and groups who adopt positions with respect to the issue. This form of environmental education gains its authority from the strongly educative process of collaborative, critical self-reflection within particular practical situations. It encourages participants at all levels to adopt a research stance towards their own environmental education activities. It is necessarily community based and should be a collaborative endeavour.

An approach of this kind clearly involves a great challenge to traditional pedagogy and curriculum organisation, a challenge that, for a variety of reasons, few may feel able or willing to rise to – as discussed above. It involves, to a greater extent than interpretivism does, new roles and relationships for and among pupils, teachers and curriculum developers. It seriously challenges the status quo in subject-based curricula, in initial teacher education and continuing professional development, and in research.

Robottom and Hart provide examples of the kind of questions that a critical approach to research in environmental education should address, for example:

- What are the sources of environmental knowledge acquired by students in schools, and what are the sources of knowledge about environmental education acquired by educators in professional associations?
- What impact do schools and professional associations have on students and educators in environmental education?
- Whose interests are being served by the perspectives and values immanent in the policies, organisation and practices of schools and professional associations active in environmental education?
- How can students and practitioners in environmental education be moved toward greater liberation, equity and social justice?

(Robottom and Hart, 1993, p. 25)

Various forms of data collection and analysis techniques are employed by educational researchers in the critical tradition, three key approaches being discourse analysis, critical ethnography and action research. A useful introduction to these is provided by Fien and Hillcoat (1996) who see that the differences between them may be identified by the relative emphasis given to the three tasks of understanding, critique and action, these being the three tasks of the critical educational researcher. 'The focus of discourse analysis is critique and involves the sustained deconstruction of ideas, educational materials and pedagogical actions. The focus of critical ethnography is both understanding and critique. Action research is characterised by a focus on all three tasks' (Fien and Hillcoat, 1996, p. 35). Williams (1996) contains chapters outlining the characteristics, methods and issues associated with forms of critical inquiry; see Bennett (1996) on discourse analysis and Hillcoat (1996) on action research.

Here, a little more will be said about action research by way of an example to illustrate the critical tradition. The type of action research referred to is that based on the socially critical paradigm. It is 'emancipatory' or 'participatory', and, according to Tesch:

[E]mancipatory action research is a form of self-reflective inquiry undertaken by participants in social situations in order to improve the rationality

PERSPECTIVES ON THEORY AND RESEARCH

and justice of their own practices, their understandings of these practices, and the situations in which the practices are carried out.

(Tesch, 1990, p. 49)

The presence of emancipatory and participatory qualities distinguishes it from 'technical action research' of the positivist paradigm 'whose aim is efficient and effective practice judged by reference to criteria which may not themselves be analysed in the course of the action research process' (Tesch, 1990, p. 49). Cohen and Manion (1989) define socially critical action research as 'a small-scale intervention in the functioning of the real world and a close examination of such intervention'. According to their definition, it is

situational – it is concerned with diagnosing a problem in a specific context and attempting to solve it in that context. It is usually collabora-tive – teams of researchers and practitioners work together on a project; it is participatory – team members themselves take part directly or indirectly in implementing the research, and it is self-evaluative – modifications are continuously evaluated within the ongoing situation.

(Cohen and Manion, 1989, p. 217)

As with the other approaches to research described above, an example follows in order to illustrate the application of these principles in practice.

The OECD 'Environment and School Initiatives Project'

The Organisation for Economic Co-operation and Development (OECD) was instrumental in taking a leading role in supporting action research-based approaches to professional development within a context of community-focused environmental education. In particular, it sponsored a substantial 'Environment and School Initiatives Project', involving various countries in Europe and beyond, each with a national co-ordinator and several participating schools (Posch, 1988, 1990, 1993a; Elliot, 1991). As a whole the project set out to accomplish two key objectives or principles:

1 that selected schools demonstrate (if at varying degrees of intensity) environmental education curriculum activities characterised by the adoption of a research perspective:

⇒ personal involvement of students and emotional commitment;
⇒ interdisciplinary learning and research;
⇒ reflective action to improve environmental conditions;
⇒ involvement of students, at least partially, in decision-making on problem-finding, on procedures and on monitoring their work;

2 that participating teachers adopt a research perspective in respect to their own teaching and curriculum activities:

⇒ the participating teachers were asked to . . . systematically reflect on their own activities in order to improve them and in order to contribute to their own and other people's knowledge of environmental education. In other words: they should involve themselves in action research.

(Posch, 1990)

Thus this project is distinctive in two ways, placing it firmly within the socially critical action research framework: it argues both for an environmental education that is community based and action orientated and for a higher professional role for teachers – that of teachers-as-researchers. Rather than confining teachers to the role of technical implementers of the curricula designed by others, the project encourages teachers to participate in research of their own, conducted in their own classrooms, and addressing environmental education issues of interest and concern to themselves (Robottom, 1990). From the point of view of the pupils themselves, they are involved in environmental issues at three levels – personal experience and emotional commitment; inter-disciplinary learning and research (the generation of 'local knowledge'); and socially important action (Posch, 1993a).

Within the Environment and School Initiative (ENSI) Project framework, various individual action research projects were established. One based in Australia, for example, reported in fuller detail in Robottom and Hart (1993, pp. 56–57) and also in Posch (1988) and Elliot (1991), aims:

1 to explore the relationship between recent state and national education policies and current and emerging school initiatives in environmental education;

2 to explore the relationship between current approaches to professional development and emerging school initiatives in environmental education; and

3 to develop a series of case studies of school initiatives and professional development in environmental education – case studies that present contextualised descriptions of the relationships among policy, curriculum development practices and professional development in environmental education.

Personal interviews, professional diaries, document analysis and analysis of the archive of published teacher-prepared material are used as the means for data collection to inform the research agenda and preparation of case studies. Issues addressed in the case studies include consideration of alternatives to the traditional view of curriculum content or knowledge that are evident in community-based environmental education curricula; and teacher justification for involvement in community-based environmental education curriculum development.

The ENSI action research projects as a whole have given rise to many extremely worthwhile case studies and examples of innovative practice in the field; yet it seems fair to say that the approach is not entirely unproblematic.

The projects co-ordinator himself reports that teachers found it difficult to enact the role of teacher-as-researcher (Posch, 1988). He attributes this difficulty to a lack of necessary support and training in the time available, and to the fact that the idea that teachers themselves can generate worthwhile theoretical knowledge about their practice was so new to them. They found it easy to produce descriptive reports of their professional activities, but far more difficult to identify and explicate educational issues associated with the activities. That issue aside, it is evident that the ENSI projects are serving a critical function in the on-going exploration of an alternative role for research in environmental education.

Validity in the critical paradigm

The question of validity of data and outcomes of such projects applies across the whole spectrum of approaches to socially critical research. This major issue is addressed in relation to specific projects by the researchers concerned (see, for example, Posch, 1988, 1990, 1993b; Elliot, 1991) and in general terms relating to emancipatory action research by Hillcoat (1996). For Hillcoat, critical research requires validation within its specific context, so that the researcher does not misconstrue the evidence due to personal bias. Without validation, the research process ceases and subjective pondering begins (Hillcoat, 1996, p. 153). He identifies and describes four major means to validate the research, namely triangulation (the use of two or more methods and/or sources of data collection to establish the researchers' observations and findings); face validity (involving the research participants reviewing the findings and giving their reactions to the researcher); construct validity (which exists when the experiences of the people involved in the research validate or extend the theory); and catalytic validity (which is present if the research process results in the participants changing behaviours, and is vital to the emancipatory effectiveness of an action research project).

Recent trends and initiatives

It would seem then that the evolution of environmental education research has involved a slow yet steady movement away from its roots in the scientific paradigm towards a broader base of postpositivist methodologies. For many researchers actively developing projects in the field today, this evolutionary trend has been far too slow to develop – see, for example, the accounts by Ho, Hart and Robottom in Part V of this book.

So what *are* the characteristics of, and trends in, the field of environmental education research 30 years on from its origins? Evidence from a variety of sources (see below) suggests that

- The field is dynamic, and expanding at a rapid pace around the world. Many more educationists are developing a research perspective in their work, and more researchers and research students are working full time in the field than ever before.

- Quantitative research studies are still dominant in the field.
- The number of qualitative (including interpretive and socially critical) research studies has increased considerably during the 1990s. Some of these are exemplary, but all too many appear to be based on methodologies that are either lacking in rigour or poorly articulated, which raise serious questions relating to reliability and validity. There is still a great deal to be done in terms of developing the field's qualitative research base, broadening the research base in general, and critically appraising the role of research.
- There is an increasing number of major funded research studies being commissioned around the world, also of collaborative studies involving partnerships between individuals and research teams at both national and international levels.
- There is an ever-widening range of themes pursued by environmental education researchers, with increasing emphasis being placed on the links between empirical research and the improvement of practice.

Evidence for the above statement of trends derives from a variety of sources – as now detailed – which serve as guideline references for readers wishing to pursue this topic in greater depth.

1 The increasing number and size of international conferences devoted to environmental education research. The largest annual conference in the field is that of the North American Association for Environmental Education (NAAEE), which in 1996 attracted some 1,400 delegates from over 20 nations.

2 The increasing number and global readership of refereed academic journals devoted to the field.

The founding journal, and indeed the most influential for a large number of years, was *The Journal of Environmental Education (JEE)* established in 1970. This is published quarterly by Heldref Publications, 1319 Eighteenth Street NW, Washington, DC 20036–1802. The large team of international consultant editors is never short of manuscripts to review. It has previously been mentioned that this journal promoted large numbers of quantitative research studies, many in the behaviourist tradition, in the 1970s and 1980s. Analysis of its contents today shows a continuing though not all-pervading trend for the publication of quantitative materials. The stated editorial policy is that manuscripts from all research perspectives are equally welcome; the explanation for the continuing dominance of quantitative studies is that, in general, more of these are 'publishable' according to the academic criteria for review, i.e. they have more clearly articulated and defended methodologies.

The *Australian Journal of Environmental Education*, like *JEE*, despite its all-embracing title, publishes rigorous, refereed academic papers, many of which focus on empirical research. Founded in 1985, it is published in one volume a year, based at AAEE, PO Box 64, Norton Summit, SA 5136, Australia. It has an international editorial board and welcomes papers with an international perspective and those with a focus on qualitative methodologies.

In 1992, *International Research in Geographical and Environmental Education* was established and has three issues per year. Its editors are based at the Centre for Applied Environmental Research, Queensland University of Technology, Locked Bag No. 2, Red Hill, Brisbane, Queensland 4059, Australia. As the title suggests, this journal publishes papers in the field of geographical education, including those with an environmental slant, but welcomes contributions on all aspects of environmental education research with international dimensions.

1995 saw the launch of *Environmental Education Research*, based in the UK. This is published by Carfax, and the editor is based at the School of Education, University of Bath, Bath BA2 7AY, England. The international editorial board aims to achieve a balance between qualitative and quantitative papers on research and development activities. It carries papers on pure research, and also more diverse contents including conference reviews, retrospective analyses of activities in a particular field, commentaries on policy issues, comparative aspects of an environmental education issue and critical reviews of environmental education provision in a particular country or region. The journal is published three times a year, but the number of papers received by the editors has led to on-going consideration of quarterly publication. There need have been little speculation about the potential market for another journal in the field.

Indeed, yet another journal aimed at an international readership was launched in 1996 – the *Canadian Journal of Environmental Education*, published once a year and based at Yukon College, Box 2799, Whitehorse, Yukon, Canada Y1A 5K4.

The five journals cited, which have a specific emphasis on research and on international developments, play a leading role in the dissemination of environmental education research findings on a global scale. Together with national associations for environmental education journals and professionally orientated newsletters in a number of other countries, they form an extensive and ever-expanding literature base on environmental education research and practice.

3 An ever-widening range of themes being pursued by researchers. In the United Kingdom, the National Foundation for Educational Research has compiled a Directory of environmental education research centres (Tomlins and Evans, 1995) in order to facilitate liaison between researchers in this field. The Directory is based on information made available by research centres in the UK focusing on environmental education for 5–18 year olds. It contains details for each research centre, a brief summary of the research being undertaken, and a list of associated publications. The document contains a thematic index, as summarised below, but regrettably the entries

for each centre do not contain sufficient information about their research methodologies and findings for comment to be made here about these. Readers may wish to obtain a copy of the Directory and follow up individual themes and indexed items. There now follows a list of the themes identified by research centres, together with the number of centres pursuing work in each theme in brackets.

- Implementing environmental education across the curriculum (22)
- Development of curriculum resources (18)
- Initial teacher training/youth worker training (16)
- Pupils' values concerning and attitudes towards the environment (16)
- INSET teacher education/professional development (14)
- Pupils' knowledge and appreciation of international environmental issues (14)
- Teaching about the environment through the science and/or geography curriculum (13)
- Using the 'outdoor classroom'/nature areas/fieldwork (11)
- Influencing pupils'/teachers' behaviour (8)
- 'Greening' issues/institutional responsibility (7)
- Effectiveness of teaching styles (5)
- Teacher attitudes towards the environment (5)
- Global issues in environmental education (2)
- Culture, media and the environment (1)
- Environmental monitoring (1)
- Information technology and environmental education (1)
- Landscaping in special schools (1)
- National environmental education policies (1)
- Participative environmental design with children (1)
- Teaching of controversial environmental issues (1)

An examination of programmes of various national and international conferences suggests that this range of themes from the UK, with its clear emphasis on the implementation of environmental education across the curriculum and the development of curriculum resources, seems an accurate reflection of what is going on around the world. Four key, overarching themes that appear to dominate global effort in the field are the location of environmental education in the curriculum, the development of resources, models for teacher education, and the development of environmentally responsible behaviour.

Key reference works for those interested in the range and scope of environmental education research themes and in following up particular lines of inquiry are the NAAEE's *Research in Environmental Education 1971–1980* and *Research in Environmental Education 1981–1990* (R. Marcinkowski and R. Mrazek, eds) available from NAAEE Publications Office, PO Box 400, Troy, Ohio 45373, United States of America.

4 The academic justification by individual researchers for a shift in emphasis in the research field, or at least a broadening of its base. Robottom and Hart (1993, p. 65) suggest that there is a need to engage the debate about the relative adequacy of different (competing) approaches to research in environmental education, so that their respective epistemologies, political theories and assumptions about the role of research itself are made explicit and critically appraised (see also O'Donoghue and McNaught, 1991). The case is made for sustaining and theorising about such research as:

- philosophical research (e.g. Jickling, 1991b)
- feminist critique (e.g. Di Chiro, 1987)
- narrative inquiry (e.g. Gough, 1991)
- interpretive/historical research (e.g. Greenall, 1987)
- case study research (e.g. Monroe and Kaplan, 1988)
- action research (e.g. Muhlebach and Robottom, 1990)

Palmer (1988) provides an argument based on research evidence for a shift in emphasis in the field of environmental education theory and practice, to incorporate greater understanding of the role of aesthetic and spiritual experiences in the development of individuals' environmental awareness and concern.

5 Reports from around the world (see Part V) confirm an increasing recognition of the importance of environmental education research, and engagement with it. These reports, together with international conference proceedings (e.g. of NAAEE and of the Association of Teacher Education in Europe – Environmental Education Working Group) and journal articles, reveal a wealth of collaborative studies involving partnerships between individuals and research teams at both national and international levels. There has also been a recent increase in substantial funded research projects, for example the OECD-ENSI project in Europe, involving some 20 countries; Palmer's 'Emergent Environmentalism' project based at Durham, England, involving 12 countries and funded by the Economic and Social Research Council in the UK, the European Commission and the British Council in Slovenia and Greece; and the funded projects referred to by Pei-Jen Chen, Hart and Robottom (see Part V, pp. 217, 173 and 169).

The European Commission has dedicated substantial funding to the promotion of environmental education in recent years, and a list of grant holders and their projects, some of which incorporate a research element, is available from the EC in Brussels: Rue de la Loi 200, B-1049 Brussels, Belgium.

REFERENCES

Adams, W.M. (1990) *Green Development: Environment and Sustainability in the Third World*, London: Routledge.

Barbier, E. (1989) *Economics, Natural Resources, Scarcity and Development*, London: Earthscan Publications.

Barde, J.-P. and Pearce, D. (1991) *Valuing the Environment*, London: Earthscan Publications.

Bennett, S. (1996) 'Discourse Analysis: A Method for Deconstruction', in Williams, M. (ed.) *Understanding Geographical and Environmental Education*, London: Cassell.

Brody, M.M. (1990/91) 'Understanding of Pollution Among 4th, 8th and 11th Grade Students', *Journal of Environmental Education*, 22 (1) 24–33.

Brody, M.M. and Koch, H. (1989/90) 'An Assessment of 4th, 8th and 11th Grade Students' Knowledge Related to Marine Science and Natural Resource Issues', *Journal of Environmental Education*, 21 (2) 16–26.

Carr, W. and Kemmis, S. (1983) *Becoming Critical*, London: Falmer.

Chambers, R. (1986) *Sustainable Livelihoods: An Opportunity for the World Commission on Environment and Development*, Brighton: Institute for Development Studies, University of Sussex.

Cherryholmes, C. H. (1988) *Power and Criticism: Post-Structural Investigations in Education*, New York: Teachers College Press.

Codd, J. (1982) 'Epistemology and the Politics of Educational Evaluation', in Deakin University, *Curriculum Evaluation: Philosophical and Procedural Dilemmas*, ECS 801 Curriculum Evaluation, Geelong, Victoria: Deakin University Press.

Cohen, L. and Manion, L. (1989) *Research Methods in Education*, London: Routledge.

Devall, W. and Sessions, G. (1985) *Deep Ecology: Living as if Nature Mattered*, Salt Lake City, Utah: Gibbs M. Smith.

Di Chiro, G. (1987) 'Environmental Education and the Question of Gender: A Feminist Critique', in Robottom, I. (ed.) *Environmental Education: Practice and Possibility*, Geelong, Victoria: Deakin University Press.

Doyle, W. (1983) 'Academic Work', *Review of Educational Research*, 53 (2) 159–199.

Driver, R. (1987) *Changing Conceptions, Adolescent Development and School Science*, International Seminar, King's College, London.

Driver, R. (1989) 'Students' Conceptions and the Learning of Science', *International Journal of Science Education*, I 481–490.

Driver, R. and Erickson, G. (1983) 'Theories-in-Action: Some Theoretical and Empirical Issues in the Study of Students' Conceptual Frameworks in Science', *Studies in Science Education*, 10 37–60.

Elliot, J. (1991) *Developing Community-focused Environmental Education Through Action-research* Mimeograph. Norwich: Centre for Applied Research in Education, School of Education, University of East Anglia.

Emery, F. (1981) 'Educational Paradigms', *Human Futures*, Spring, 1–17.

Enzensberger, H.M. (1974) 'A Critique of Political Ecology', *New Left Review*, 84 3.31.

Esland, G. (1971) 'Teaching and Learning as the Organisation of Knowledge', in Young, M.F.D. (ed.) *Knowledge and Control: New Directions for the Sociology of Education*, London: Collier-Macmillan.

Fensham, P. (1978) 'Stockholm to Tbilisi – the Evolution of Environmental Education', *Prospects*, 8 (4) 446–455.

Fien, J. (1992) *Education for the Environment: A Critical Ethnography*, Brisbane: University of Queensland.

Fien, J. and Hillcoat, J. (1996) 'The Critical Tradition in Research in Geographical and Environmental Education Research', in Williams, M. (ed.) *Understanding Geographical and Environmental Education*, London: Cassell.

Fox, W. (1984) 'Towards a Deeper Ecology?', *Habitat Australia*, 13 (4) 26–28.

Glaeser, B. (ed.) (1984) *Ecodevelopment: Concepts, Projects, Strategies*, Oxford: Pergamon.

Goodlad, J.I. (1984) *A Place Called School*, New York: McGraw-Hill.

Gough, N. (1987) 'Learning with Environments', in Robottom, I. (ed.) *Environmental Education: Practice and Possibility*, Geelong, Victoria: Deakin University Press.

Gough, N. (1991) 'Narrative and Nature: Unsustainable Fictions in Environmental Education', *Australian Journal of Environmental Education*, 7 31–42.

Gowin, D.B. (1981) *Educating*, Ithaca: Cornell University Press.

Green, J. (1990) 'Multiple Perspectives: Issues and Directions', paper presented at the Conference on Multidisciplinary Perspectives on Literacy Research, National Conference on Research in English, Chicago.

Greenall, A. (1987) 'A Political History of Environmental Education in Australia: Snakes and Ladders', in Robottom, I. (ed.) *Environmental Education: Practice and Possibility*, Geelong, Victoria: Deakin University Press.

Guba, E.G. (1990) 'The Alternative Paradigm Dialog', in *The Paradigm Dialog*, Newbury Park, California: Sage.

Harman, W.W. (1985) 'Colour the Future Green?: The Uncertain Significance of Global Green Politics', *Futures* 17 (4) 318–330.

Hart, P. (1993) 'Alternative Perspectives in Environmental Education Research: Paradigm of Critically Reflective Inquiry', in Mrazek, R. (ed.) *Alternative Paradigms in Environmental Education Research*, Troy, Ohio: NAAEE.

Hewson, M. and Hamlyn, D. (1983) 'The Influence of Intellectual Environment on Conceptions of Heat', paper presented at the annual meeting of the American Educational Research Association, Montreal, Quebec.

Hillcoat, J. (1996) 'Action Research', in Williams, M. (ed.) *Understanding Geographical and Environmental Education*, London: Cassell.

Hines, J., Hungerford, H. and Tomera, A. (1986/87) 'Analysis and Synthesis of Research on Responsible Environmental Behaviour: A Meta-analysis', *Journal of Environmental Education*, 18 (2) 1–8.

Huckle, J. (1983) 'Environmental Education', in *Geographical Education: Reflection and Action*, Oxford: Oxford University Press.

Huckle, J. (1990) 'Education for Sustainability: Assessing Pathways to the Future', in Blight, S., Sautter, R., Sibley, J. and Smith, R. (eds) *Our Common Future – Pathways for Environmental Education*, Proceedings of the Australian Association for Environmental Education International Conference, Adelaide, South Australia, September 1990.

Hungerford, H. and Volk, T. (1990) 'Changing Learner Behaviour Through Environmental Education', paper prepared for the Round Table on Environment and Education at the World Conference on Education for All (UNESCO, UNICEF), Jomtien, Thailand, March 1990. In *Journal of Environmental Education*, 21 (3) 8–21.

Hungerford, H., Peyton, R. and Wilkie, R. (1980) 'Goals for Curriculum Development in Environmental Education', *Journal of Environmental Education*, 2 (3) 42–47.

Hungerford, H., Peyton, R. and Wilkie, R. (1983) 'Editorial – Yes EE Does Have a Definition and Structure', *Journal of Environmental Education*, 14 (3) 1–2.

ICCE (with IUCN, UNEP) (1984) *Planning for Survival*, Cheltenham, UK.

Iozzi, L. (1981) *Research in Environmental Education 1971–1980*, Columbus, OH: ERIC/SMEAC.

IUCN (1980) *World Conservation Strategy*, Gland, Switzerland: IUCN.

IUCN, UNEP, WWF (1991) *Caring for the Earth: a Strategy for Sustainable Living*, Gland, Switzerland: IUCN.

Jickling, B. (1991a) 'Environmental Education, Problem-Solving and Some Humility Please', in Simmons, D., Knapp, C. and Young, C. (eds) *Setting the Agenda for the 1990s*. Proceedings of the 19th Annual Conference of the NAAEE, Troy, OH: NAAEE.

Jickling, B. (1991b) 'Thinking Environmentally: Considerations for Education and Curriculum in the Yukon', PhD Thesis, Simon Fraser University, Vancouver, Canada.

Lisowski, M. and Disinger, J. F. (1992) 'The Effect of Field-based Instruction on Students' Understandings of Ecological Concepts', *Journal of Environmental Education*, 23 (1) 19–23.

Lovelock, J. (1989) *The Ages of Gaia: A Biography of Our Living Earth*, Oxford: Oxford University Press.

Lucas, A.M. (1979) *Environment and Environmental Education: Conceptual Issues and Curriculum Interpretations*, Kew, Victoria: Australia International Press and Publications.

Mannion, A.M. and Bowlby, S.R. (1992) *Environmental Issues in the 1990s*, Chichester: Wiley & Sons.

Marcinkowski, T. (1990) 'A Contextual Review of the "Quantitative Paradigm" in EE Research', paper presented at a symposium entitled 'Contesting Paradigms in Environmental Education Research', *Annual Conference of the North American Association for Environmental Education*, San Antonio, Texas, 1990.

McNeil, L.M. (1983) 'Defensive Teaching and Classroom Control', in Apple, M.W. and Weis, J.L. (eds) *Ideology and Practice in Schools*, Philadelphia, PA: Temple University Press.

Merchant, C. (1992) *Radical Ecology*, New York: Routledge.

Michael, D.N. and Anderson, W.T. (1986) 'Norms in Conflict and Confusion', in Didsbury, H.F. Jr (ed.) *Challenges and Opportunities: From Now to 2001*, Bethesda, MD: World Future Society.

Millar, R. (1989) 'Constructive Criticisms', *International Journal of Science Education*, 2 587–596.

Moffat, I. (1992) 'The Evolution of the Sustainable Development Concept: a Perspective from Australia', *Australian Geographical Studies*, 30 (1) 27–42.

Moffat, I. (1996) 'Sustainable Development Principles', in *Analysis and Policies*, London: Parthenon.

Monroe, M. and Kaplan, S. (1988) 'When Words Speak Louder than Actions: Environmental Problem Solving in Classrooms', *Journal of Environmental Education*, 19 (3) 38–41.

Muhlebach, R. and Robottom, I. (eds) (1990) *Supporting Community-Based Environmental Education: Report of the Environmental Education and Computer Conference Project*, Deakin Institute for Studies in Education, Geelong, Victoria: Deakin University Press..

Naess, A. (1973) 'The Shallow and the Deep, Long-Range Ecology Movement: A Summary', *Inquiry*, 16 95–100.

Naess, A. (1988) 'The Basics of Deep Ecology', *Resurgence*, 126 4–7.

Novak, J.D. and Gowin, D.B. (1984) *Learning How to Learn*, Cambridge: Cambridge University Press.

O'Connor, J. (1989) 'Uneven and Combined Development and Ecological Crisis: a Theoretical Introduction', *Race and Class*, 30.3.

O'Donoghue, R. and McNaught, C. (1991) 'Environmental Education: The Development of a Curriculum Through "Grass-Roots" Reconstructive Action', *International Journal of Science Education*, 13 (4) 391–404.

O'Riordan, T. (1981) 'Environmental Issues', *Progress in Human Geography*, 5 (3) 393–407.

O'Riordan, T. (1988) 'The Politics of Sustainability', in Turner, R. (ed.) *Sustainable Environmental Management: Principles and Practice*, London: Belhaven.

O'Riordan, T. (1989) 'The Challenge for Environmentalism', in Peet, R. and Thrift, N. (eds) *New Models in Geography*, London: Unwin Hyman.

Palmer, J.A. (1988) 'Spiritual Ideas, Environmental Concerns and Educational Practice', in Cooper, D.E. and Palmer, J.A. (eds) *Spirit of the Environment*, London: Routledge.

Palmer, J.A. (1993) 'From Santa Claus to Sustainability: Emergent Understanding of Concepts and Issues in Environmental Science', *International Journal of Science Education*, 15 (5) 487–495.

Palmer, J.A. (1995) 'Environmental Thinking in the Early Years: Understanding and Misunderstanding of Concepts Relating to Waste Management', *Environmental Education Research*, 1 (1) 35–47.

Palmer, J.A., Suggate, J. and Matthews, J. (1996) 'Environmental Cognition: Early Ideas and Misconceptions at the Ages of Four and Six', *Environmental Education Research*, 2 (3) 301–330.

Pearce, D., Markandya, A. and Barbier, E. (1989) *Blueprint for a Green Economy*, London: Earthscan Publications.

Pepper, D. (1996) *Modern Environmentalism: An Introduction*, London: Routledge.

Posch, P. (1988) 'The Project Environment and School Initiatives', in OECD (ed.) *Environment and School Initiatives: International Conference, Linz, Austria, September 1988*, Paris: OECD.

Posch, P. (1990) 'Educational Dimensions of Environmental School Initiatives', *Australian Journal of Environmental Education* 6.

Posch, P. (1993a) 'I: Action Research in Environmental Education', *Educational Action Research*, 1 (3) 447–455.

Posch, P. (1993b) 'Research Issues in Environmental Education', *Studies in Science Education*, 21 21–48.

Quarrie, J. (ed.) (1992) *Earth Summit 1992*, London: The Regency Press.

Ramsey, J. and Hungerford, H. (1989) 'The Effects of Issue Investigation and Action Training on Environmental Behaviour in Seventh Grade Students', *Journal of Environmental Education*, 20 (4) 29–34.

Reason, P. (ed.) (1988) *Human Inquiry in Action*, London: Sage.

Redclift, M. (1987) *Sustainable Development*, London: Methuen.

Riddell, R. (1981) *Ecodevelopment: Economics, Ecology and Development; an Alternative to Growth Imperative Models*, Farnborough: Gower.

Robertson, A. (1994) 'Toward Constructivist Research in Environmental Education', *Journal of Environmental Education*, 25 (2) 21–31.

Robertson, A. S. (1993) 'Eliciting Students' Understandings: Necessary Steps in Environmental Education', *Australian Journal of Environmental Education*, 9 95–114.

Robottom, I.M. (1982) 'What Is: Environmental Education as Education about the Environment', paper presented at the Second National Conference of the Australian Association for Environmental Education, Brisbane.

Robottom, I.M. (1983) *The Environmental Education Project Evaluation Report*, Curriculum Development Centre, Canberra/Deakin University, Victoria.

Robottom, I. (1990) 'EE Pathways Through the 90s: Some Alternative Ways to Go', in Blight, S., Sautter, R., Sibly, J. and Smith, R. (eds) *Our Common Future: Pathways For Environmental Education*. Proceedings of the Australian Association for Environmental Education International Conference, Adelaide, September 1990, Australian Association for Environmental Education.

Robottom, I. and Hart, P. (1990) 'Beyond Behaviourism: Making Environmental Education Research Educational', paper presented at symposium on 'Contesting Paradigms in Environmental Education Research', *Annual Conference of the North American Association For Environmental Education*, San Antonio, Texas, 1990.

Robottom, I. and Hart, P. (1993) *Research in Environmental Education: Engaging the Debate*, Geelong, Victoria: Deakin University Press.

Sahtouris, E. (1989) 'The Gaia Controversy: A Case for the Earth as a Living Planet', in Bunyard, P. and Goldsmith, E. (eds) *Gaia and Evolution: The Second Wadebridge Ecological Centre Symposium*, Camelford, Cornwall: Wadebridge Ecological Centre.

Sarre, P. (ed.) (1991) *Environment, Population and Development*, London: Hodder & Stoughton.

SCAA (1996) *Teaching Environmental Matters Through the National Curriculum*, London: SCAA.

Schwandt, T.A. (1994) 'Constructivist, Interpretivist Approaches to Human Inquiry', in Denzin, N.K. and Lincoln, Y.S. (eds) *Handbook of Qualitative Research*, London: Sage.

Sedlak, M.W., Wheeler, C.W., Pullin, D.C. and Cusick, P.A. (1986) *Selling Students Short*, New York: Teachers College Press.

Shipstone, D.M., Rhoneck, C.V., Jung, W., Karrqvist, C., Dupin, J.J., Joshua, S. and Licht, P. (1989) 'A Study of Students' Understanding of Electricity in Five European Countries', *International Journal of Science Education*, 10 303–316.

Sia, A., Hungerford, H. and Tomera, A. (1985) 'Selected Predictors of Responsible Environmental Behaviour: An Analysis', *Journal of Environmental Education*, 17 (2) 31–40.

Sizer, T.R. (1984) *Horace's Compromise: The Dilemma of the American High School*, Boston, Mass.: Houghton Mifflin.

Skolimowski, H. (1981) *Eco-Philosophy: Designing New Tactics for Living*, Boston, Mass.: Marion Boyars.

Snively, G.J. (1986) *Sea of Images: A Study of the Relationships Amongst Students' Orientations, Beliefs and Science Instruction*. Unpublished doctoral thesis, University of British Columbia, Vancouver, BC.

Stapp, W., Caduto, M., Mann, L. and Nowail, P. (1980) 'Analysis of Pre-service Environmental Education of Teachers in Europe and an Instructional Model for Furthering this Education', *Journal of Environmental Education*, 12 (2) 3–10.

Stevenson, R.B. (1987) 'Schooling and Environmental Education: Contradictions in Purpose and Practice', in Robottom, I. (ed.) *Environmental Education: Practice and Possibility*, Geelong, Victoria: Deakin University Press.

Swee-Hin, T. (1988) 'Third World Studies: Conscientisation in the Geography Classroom', in Fien, J. and Gerber, R. (eds) *Teaching Geography for a Better World*, Edinburgh: Oliver & Boyd.

Sylvan, R. (1995) 'A Critique of Deep Ecology, part 1', *Radical Philosophy*, 40 2–12.

Tanner, R.T. (1974) *Ecology, Environment and Education*, Lincoln, Nebraska: Professional Educators Publications.

Tesch, R. (1990) *Qualitative Research: Analysis Types and Software Tools*, Lewes: Falmer.

Tomlins, B. and Evans, A. (eds) (1995) *Environmental Education Research Centres Directory*, Slough: National Foundation for Educational Research.

Tomlins, B. and Froud, K. (1994) *Environmental Education: Teaching Approaches and Students' Attitudes: A Briefing Paper*, Slough: NFER.

Turner, R. (1988) 'Sustainability, Resource Management and Pollution Control: An Overview', in Turner, R. (ed.) *Sustainable Environmental Management: Principles and Practice*, London: Belhaven.

Turner, R. (ed.) (1988) *Sustainable Environmental Management: Principles and Practice*, London: Belhaven.

UNESCO (1975) *The International Workshop on Environmental Education Final Report* (The Belgrade Charter), Belgrade, Yugoslavia. Paris: UNESCO/UNEP.

UNESCO (1977) *First Intergovernmental Conference on Environmental Education. Final Report*, Tbilisi, USSR. Paris: UNESCO.

Vincent, A. (1993) 'The Character of Ecology', *Environmental Politics*, 2 (2) 248–276.

Volk, T.L., Hungerford, H.R. and Tomera, A.N. (1984) 'A National Survey of Curriculum Needs as Perceived by Professional Environmental Educators', *The Journal of Environmental Education*, 16 (1) 10–19.

Wallace, I. (1990) *The Global Economic System*, London: Unwin Hyman.

Wals, A. (1992) 'Young Adolescents' Perceptions of Environmental Issues: Implications for Environmental Education in Urban Settings', *Australian Journal of Environmental Education*, 8 45–58.

WCED (1987) *Our Common Future*, Oxford: Oxford University Press.

Williams, M. (1996) 'Positivism and the Quantitative Tradition in Geographical and Environmental Education Research', in Williams, M. (ed.) *Understanding Geographical and Environmental Education*, London: Cassell.

Young, R.E. (1980) 'The Controlling Curriculum and the Practical Ideology of Teachers', *The Australian and New Zealand Journal of Sociology*, 16 (2) 62–70.

Part IV

ENVIRONMENTAL EDUCATION: STRUCTURE AND PRACTICE

DOES ENVIRONMENTAL EDUCATION MATTER?

One key question that has been running throughout this text so far is the extent to which environmental education is currently incorporated into formal education policies and programmes in a planned and strategic manner – or whether it remains a servant of individual commitment and enthusiasm. A related question concerns the actual impact of environmental education in formal settings on people's lives – does it actually make a difference to environmental awareness, attitudes and behaviour? So, before moving on from a focus on aspects of theory and research trends in the field to a closer look at the translation of its structure into practice, research evidence will be presented that sheds some light on these two related and extremely important questions. Three studies will be referred to in which the present author is engaged.

The first research study, on the development of concern for the environment and influences and experiences affecting the pro-environmental behaviour of educators, forms part of the overall 'Emergent Environmentalism' project discussed on p. 111. The particular study within the project of relevance here examines the relative importance of various categories of influence and formative life experiences on the development of environmental educators' knowledge of and concern for the environment (Palmer, 1993b; Palmer and Suggate, 1996). The motivation for this study was the belief that if a fundamental aim of education is to help children and students understand, appreciate and care for the environment, then those responsible for teaching and designing programmes in this curriculum area should be familiar with the types of learning experiences that help to develop active and informed minds.

In the first instance, the study was distributed to the membership of the NAEE, and later to various international destinations. Subjects were asked to provide their approximate age, gender, details of their demonstration of practical concern for the environment and an autobiographical statement identifying those experiences and formative influences that led to this concern. The participants were also asked to state what they considered to be their most significant life experiences, and to write a statement indicating which, if any, of the years

131

of their lives were particularly memorable in the development of positive attitudes towards the environment. As the outlines and proformas gave only the aims and purposes of the research, the participants were able to provide original responses unbiased by any examples. In order to confirm the sample as a group of active and informed citizens who know about and care for the environment in their adult life, a list of seven possible activities relating to pro-environmental behaviours was provided, and the subjects were asked to indicate those in which they regularly engaged.

Two hundred and thirty-two responses were returned in the UK sample (102 male, 130 female). Fifty-five of the respondents were in the under 30 age group; 124 in the 30–50 years group, and 53 in the over 50 years group. Without doubt the sample was confirmed as a group of people committed to practical actions in relation to environmental concerns. Over 90 per cent of the sample participated in some of the activities listed and 62 per cent or more participated in all but one category. For example, around 90 per cent of respondents read about environmental issues and made positive attempts to lead a 'green' lifestyle; over 80 per cent regularly engaged in voluntary recycling of materials and so on (Palmer and Suggate, 1996).

The core interpretive data for the study, namely the autobiographical statements giving details of formative influences and significant life experiences leading to a commitment to environmental concerns, were analysed and the results were coded into categories of response. Thirty preliminary categories were derived in the initial analysis, which were then refined into 13 categories, incorporating various sub-categories from the original list of 30. The number of subjects identifying with each major category of response is shown in Table 4.1. The category 'outdoors' includes three substantial sub-categories: childhood outdoors (97 respondents), outdoor activities (90 respondents) and wilderness/solitude (24 respondents). 'Education courses' refers to two sub-categories:

Table 4.1 Significant life experiences: categories of response

Category of influence	No. (n = 232)	%
Outdoors	211	91
Education courses	136	59
Parents/close relatives	88	38
Organisations	83	36
Television/media	53	23
Friends/other individuals	49	21
Travel abroad	44	19
Disasters/negative issues	41	18
Books	35	15
Becoming a parent	20	9
Keeping pets/animals	14	6
Religion/God	13	6
Others	35	15

higher education or other courses taken as an adult (85 respondents) and school courses (51 respondents). Details of the data analysis and conclusions drawn will be found elsewhere – of both the initial analysis (Palmer, 1993b) and of a more fine-grained analysis which looks not only at patterns of influence across the whole sample, but also by age group (Palmer and Suggate, 1996). The relevance of this study here is to show the relative influence of education courses, compared to other dimensions of people's lives. By far the most significant category of response overall was experiences 'outdoors', and in particular subjects talked of the great significance of experiences outdoors in early childhood – experiences *in* the world of nature. 'Education' – meaning courses in the formal sense – was the second most significant category, though a very long way behind 'outdoors' in terms of numbers mentioning it.

As mentioned above, responses relating to education were divided into two sub-categories: higher education or other courses taken as an adult (85 respondents) and school courses (51 respondents). The apparent impact of secondary school and higher education courses on environmental matters is very encouraging – of the seven subjects who cited education as being the single most important influence on their environmental thinking and practice, five wrote about degree level courses and two about A level courses. Of the 51 respondents citing school-based work as a significant influence (though not necessarily the single most important), 38 referred to A level courses and related fieldwork. The data also revealed some worryingly negative aspects: 23 individuals (10 per cent of the sample) chose to report that school programmes had had no influence on them at all, and there was not one reference to a school course below A level as a single most important influence. The many accounts of early and mid-childhood commonly referred to such things as outdoor activities and experiences; the influence of friends, parents, grandparents; watching television, etc. – with hardly any references to primary school teachers and courses. This project has more recently been extended to include data from a range of other locations, including both developed and developing nations. Preliminary data analysis (ongoing) suggests firm confirmation of the fact that people's personal experiences in and with the natural world are by far the most significant influences on environmental thinking and awareness.

Two other ongoing research projects provide further evidence of critical influences on the development of people's concern for the environment. Firstly, a project on 'The Global Environment and the Expanding Moral Circle' aims to investigate recent changes in attitudes and feelings of responsibility towards the environment, animals and future generations. As part of the study, individual subjects from the local community (n = 182) filled in questionnaires that probed their views and attitudes relating to the research agenda. In response to a question 'What would you identify as the single most important influence or experience that has affected your attitude to our responsibility towards (a) animals and (b) the environment?', only 9 out of 182 subjects (5 per cent) cited education as the single most important influence affecting their attitudes and sense of responsibility towards animals, and 25 subjects (13 per cent) cited it as the single most important influence affecting attitudes and responsibility towards the environment in general. Another question asked subjects to provide an assessment on a scale from 0 (not at all important) to 5 (very important), of the influence of certain things (e.g. media images, television documentaries, books, intellectual argument, education, parents, friends, travel, etc.) on their attitude to responsibility towards animals and the environment. Figures relating to subjects' perceptions of the influence of education are shown in Table 4.2 (average score 2.7).

Analysis of the assessment of influence question as a whole shows television documentaries to be the most significant influence (average score 4.02). The five most important influences overall are, in rank order: television documentaries, media images, personal experience with animals and nature, nature and wildlife films, and intellectual argument (linked to media coverage). Higher education courses came sixth in the ranking, and school level courses ninth, out of 14 categories of influence.

Secondly, a project on 'Subject and Community Knowledge in Environmental Education' (Palmer and Suggate, publication in preparation) aims to investigate various forms of knowledge and awareness of environmental issues possessed by 50 undergraduate students of education. Each subject was interviewed individually and asked questions relating to the student's own level of understanding of environmental issues, views on what an environmental education programme for school pupils should address, how knowledge about the environment should be conveyed to pupils, experiences that have helped prepare the student for effective teaching in this area, and sources of environmental knowledge and ideas. Responses to questions probing sources of students' knowledge were divided into two main groups: 'formal' sources, including school, higher education courses, books, television, media, etc.; and 'community or informal' sources, leading to knowledge acquired by living and interacting with people in a community or locality and so absorbing facts, ideas and attitudes from these experiences. Only 19 of the subjects (38 per cent) said that formal education, as opposed to knowledge acquired informally by living and interacting within a community, was the most significant way in which they had acquired environmental knowledge and concern. This seems a surprisingly low number given, firstly, that 'formal education' included books, television and media in this instance which

Table 4.2 Subjects' assessment of the influence of education courses on environmental responsibility

| Influence | Assessment | | | | | |
	0	1	2	3	4	5
School level courses	9	43	34	34	32	18
Higher level courses	6	36	28	36	34	30

presumably would account for some people's response, thus reducing the apparent impact of school-based education even further; and secondly, the background of subjects in this sample – all are university undergraduates who have a record of success in formal education.

The overall picture emerging from these various projects is interesting and important; it suggests that programmes of environmental education in the formal education service – in certain locations at least – are indeed playing a significant role both in the development of people's knowledge and understanding of the environment and in their formulation of attitudes and feelings of responsibility towards it. Yet the influence of environmental education is certainly not as dominant or successful as it ought to be. Clearly this is for two reasons. The first has already been addressed – there are various conflicts, inconsistencies and practical limitations leading to a substantial gap between the rhetoric and the reality of the implementation of environmental education policy and practice. The second reason is well illustrated by empirical research as discussed – even where well-designed and successful programmes of environmental education do exist, their impact on long-term thinking and action is not as great as that of other significant experiences and formative influences in people's lives. This central theme, and the obvious core issue arising from it, i.e. how can the impact of environmental education be enhanced?, will be the focus of attention in the text's final section. Firstly, however, we turn to a closer look at what environmental education actually *is*. Preceding sections of text have provided an overview of developments in the field, a justification of why we need concern ourselves with it at all, and a glimpse at some of its theoretical and research perspectives. Yet very little has so far been said about how one might describe its structure, and translate it into practice at various levels.

STRUCTURAL ELEMENTS

The whole

As a result of the various international initiatives described in Part I, a broad consensus has emerged on the principles, goals and objectives of environmental education, even though, as has already been acknowledged, some writers argue that the ideological appropriateness of them is taken for granted and that the accepted goals should be challenged (see, for example, Robottom and Hart, 1993, p. 38). Despite the passing of time and pleas for challenge and reform, the generally accepted principles largely reflect the outcomes of the Tbilisi Conference of 1977, whose Final Report set out the three 'goals' of environmental education, repeated here as an *aide-mémoire*:

1 To foster clear awareness of, and concern about, economic, social, political and ecological inter-dependence in urban and rural areas;

2 To provide every person with opportunities to acquire the knowledge,

values, attitudes, commitment and skills needed to protect and improve the environment;

3 To create new patterns of behaviour of individuals, groups and society as a whole towards the environment.

(UNESCO, 1977)

Beyond any agreed goals, defining the precise content of environmental education is inevitably problematic. Since the environment is all-embracing, then it must to some extent at least be considered in its totality to include aspects that are urban and rural, technological, political, economic, social, aesthetic and ethical. Page 98 of this book cites various keynote policy statements and documents that emphasise the inter-disciplinary holistic nature of environmental education. The very eclectic nature of its content may be regarded as one of its greatest strengths – it 'fits everywhere' – but surely it is also a weakness. Either environmental education becomes equated with the whole of education, thus essentially losing its identity, or else selected features of it need to be singled out at any one time to become a focus for teaching and learning. In either of these extremes, crucial elements of environmental education are highly likely to be overlooked or given scant attention. Indeed, one of the criticisms of the place of environmental education in the revised National Curriculum for Schools in England (elaborated upon on p. 26) is that whilst geographical and scientific emphases of it are likely to be well covered, other fundamental elements of it may well fall by the wayside – leading to a completely unbalanced or biased approach to complex, multi-faceted issues. The traditional response to this problem, or commonly suggested way of overcoming it, is to recognise that an environmental dimension can be found in most aspects of education, and thus environmental education may be considered to be an *approach* to education that incorporates considerations of the environment, rather than being a separate part of education. It does, however, have a discrete 'content' that must be recognised and deliberately incorporated in a progressive fashion into teaching and learning tasks. This approach sounds very laudable and straightforward, yet in practice is seemingly complex and difficult to implement with any degree of certainty and success.

The many students of environmental education with whom I have worked have appreciated an attempt to 'disintegrate' the structure of it, to break it down into various structural elements that together entwine to form an extremely complex whole. Perhaps in this way we can find starting points for debate on how such an eclectic entity can be tackled within the imposing time and resource constraints of many educational situations of the world today.

Threads of a theme

It has been generally accepted since the 1970s (though not without constructive challenge, as has been mentioned and which will be returned to in the final section) that education related to the environment comprises three core 'threads'. This three-fold structure was first formalised and published in the UK Schools' Council's *Project Environment* (1974) whilst it had been included in a doctoral thesis of 1972, published seven years later (Lucas, 1979). According to *Project Environment*, there are three threads that have contributed to our present ideas and it has become almost commonplace nowadays to characterise these as education either *about*, *from* or *for* the environment.

> ... education *about* the environment seeks to discover the nature of the area under study often through investigatory and discovery approaches; the objectives are chiefly cognitive ones in that the aim is to amass information;
>
> ... in educating *from* the environment, teachers must have sought to forward the general education of the child by using the environment as a resource in two main ways; firstly as a medium for enquiry and discovery which may lead to the enhancement of the learning process, the most important aspect being learning how to learn; secondly, as a source of material for realistic activities in language, mathematics, science and craft;
>
> ... to be education *for* the environment ... is education which is environmental in style with emphasis on developing an informed concern for the environment. The objectives go beyond the acquisition of skills and knowledge and require the development of involvement to the extent that values are formed which affect behaviour. . . . Thus the aim is to develop attitudes and levels of understanding which lead to a personal environmental ethic; that is, to educate pupils so that their actions and influences on collective action will be positively for the benefit of the earthly environment.
>
> (Schools' Council, 1974)

In more recent years, alongside world-wide acceptance of the need for sustainable development, and education for sustainability, there has been an ever-increasing focus in the environmental education literature on the crucial importance of education *for* the environment in particular. This trend parallels the call for movement from an empiricist to an ecological paradigm in education, and for a shift from positivist to socially critical approaches to teaching and research in the field. Of the many examples that could be cited, attention is drawn to Huckle (1991), who defines nine components of education for the environment, summarised below, and Sterling/EDET (1992) who define the nature of education for sustainability as also indicated.

The Nine Components of Education for the Environment

1 Knowledge of the Natural Environment and its Potential for Human Use (including knowledge of major ecological systems, processes which sustain them, carrying capacity and vulnerability to human modification. Science and geography should develop appropriate knowledge and

together with the arts, should cultivate a sense of the sacredness of nature).

2 A Theoretical and Practical Grasp of Appropriate Technology (the development of technology in different societies and its impact on nature and the environment . . . development of a theoretical and practical understanding of appropriate technologies and their role in sustainable development).

3 A Sense of History and a Knowledge of the Impact of Changing Social Formations on the Natural World (developing understanding of changing social formations and their use of nature . . . how human environments are socially constructed . . . how social relations shape environmental relations. Pupils should . . . recognise the value of indigenous knowledge and technology in promoting sustainability in the past . . . develop a basic understanding of the history and nature of a global society . . . explain why dominant forms of development and underdevelopment are not sustainable).

4 An Awareness of Class Conflict and Social Movements (. . . pupils should be aware that the costs and benefits derived from using nature are shared unequally in most societies . . . should focus on the struggle of the labour and environmental movements to lessen economic exploitation, to improve people's environmental well-being, and realise sustainable development . . . should study a range of environment and development issues around the world which illustrate the nature of environmental politics in societies variously located within the world system).

5 Political Literacy (political education should develop pupils' political literacy so that they are able to understand and participate in environmental politics. Appropriate knowledge, skills and attitudes, should be developed through real or simulated involvement with environment and development issues at all scales . . . due attention should be given to the social use of nature and environmental politics in societies organised on different principles from their own . . . they should critically explore the limits to political action imposed by the dominant mode of production or world economy).

6 An Awareness of Alternative Social and Environmental Futures and the Political Strategies Whereby They are Likely to be Realised (social education should encourage pupils to consider a range of social and environmental futures and the ideologies and utopias which these reflect. They should recognise the need for sustainable development and the contradictions such development raises within the present world system . . .).

7 An Understanding of Ideology and Consumerism (media and communication studies should help pupils to interpret the images, beliefs and values about nature and the environment transmitted by popular culture ... pupils should develop a basic understanding of the main environmental ideologies and utopias ... an ability to detect and handle bias in the news media ... an understanding of the politics of consumerism and the limits to green consumerism).

8 Involvement in Real Issues (pupils should be encouraged to identify for themselves practical ways in which they can work for a more sustainable relationship with the natural world ... schools should be fully integrated in the life of the community and engaged in projects which promote sustainability).

9 Tentativeness and Optimism (we lack total knowledge of environmental systems and often make decisions under conditions of great uncertainty ... environmental education needs to be tentative in its assertions and combine humanistic and rational approaches to knowledge ... teachers should avoid indoctrination but should be committed to justice, rationality and democracy ... if they are not to overwhelm pupils with the world's problems, teachers should also teach in a spirit of optimism ... successful examples of sustainable development should be built into the curriculum ... they should develop awareness of sources of hope).

(Huckle, 1991, pp. 53–57)

Education for sustainability

- enables people to understand the inter-dependence of all life on this planet, and the repercussions that their actions and decisions may have both now and in the future on resources, on the global community as well as their local one, and on the total environment;
- increases people's awareness of the economic, political, social, cultural, technological and environmental forces which foster or impede sustainable development;
- develops people's awareness, competence, attitudes and values, enabling them to be effectively involved in sustainable development at local, national and international level, and helping them to work towards a more equitable and sustainable future. In particular, it enables people to integrate environmental and economic decision-making;
- affirms the validity of the different approaches contributed by environmental education, and development education and the need for the further development and integration of the concepts of sustainability in these and other related cross-disciplinary educational approaches, as well as other established disciplines.

(Sterling/EDET, 1992, p. 2)

The dimensions of learning

Inextricably woven with the three threads of learning about, from (often recorded as in or through) and for the environment, are the three dimensions of the learning process: knowledge and understanding, skills and attitudes. Once again, these have been referred to and elaborated upon in a variety of documents that attempt to define the aims and content of environmental education. As an example, the content of the National Curriculum for Schools in England will be outlined (NCC, 1990), i.e. its stated range of knowledge and understanding, skills and attitudes. It is stressed that this is used for illustrative purposes, and the issue of defining an appropriate range of curriculum content will be returned to.

Knowledge and understanding

As a basis for making informed judgements about the environment, pupils should develop knowledge and understanding of:

- the natural processes which take place in the environment
- the impact of human activities on the environment
- different environments, both past and present
- environmental issues such as the greenhouse effect, acid rain, air pollution
- local, national and international legislative controls to protect and manage the environment; how policies and decisions are made about the environment
- the environmental inter-dependence of individuals, groups, communities and nations
- how human lives and livelihood are dependent on the environment
- the conflicts that can arise about environmental issues
- how the environment has been affected by past decisions and actions
- the importance of planning, design and aesthetic considerations
- the importance of effective action to protect and manage the environment

Skills

- communication skills
- numeracy skills
- study skills
- problem-solving skills
- personal and social skills
- information technology skills

Attitudes

Promoting positive attitudes to the environment is essential if pupils are to value it and understand their role in safeguarding it for the future. Encouraging the development of the attitudes and personal qualities below will contribute to this process:

- appreciation of and care and concern for the environment and for other living things
- independence of thought on environmental issues
- a respect for the beliefs and opinions of others
- a respect for evidence and rational argument
- tolerance and open-mindedness

Seven areas of knowledge and understanding are identified that may form the basis for the development of worthwhile topics or subject-based interpretation. These are:

- climate
- soils, rocks and minerals
- water
- materials and resources, including energy
- plants and animals
- people and their communities
- buildings, industrialisation and work

Note: The above is based on the National Curriculum's stated aims (NCC, 1990), as quoted in Part I of this text.

Elements of the curriculum/learning processes

To complicate the scene even further, subsumed within the environmental education curriculum are various 'elements'. These have been referred to and expressed in different ways in a number of documents and curriculum statements. Here, the report by HM Inspectors of Schools in Scotland (Scottish Education Department, 1974) is cited since it states that a programme of environmental education should disseminate the views (of educating from, about and for the environment) of *Project Environment*. Whilst not the most recent of reports, its description of curriculum elements is helpful and still entirely relevant to the delivery of environmental education programmes. This report details four elements of the environmental curriculum:

1 *The empirical element* This is concerned with those aspects of the environment that lend themselves to objective demonstration, measurement and analysis ... the main priority is to ensure that all pupils have as many opportunities as possible of making direct contact with the environment through observation and by measuring, recording, interpreting and discussing what has been observed.
2 *The synoptic element* Pupils need to be made aware of the complex nature of the environment. The aim of synoptic studies is to help pupils realise the

141

complexity of such issues and to introduce them to the inseparable nature of the various components of the environment and to the inter-relations of these. Method is as important as content in achieving this.

3 *The aesthetic element* Of the many aspects of the environment, perhaps the most important are qualitative rather than quantitative. . . . The aesthetic elements . . . can help a pupil to realise that there is no right or wrong answer in absolute terms to aesthetic questions and that the answer to environmental issues is frequently a compromise.

4 *The ethical element* A programme of environmental education aims at introducing pupils to the idea of personal responsibility for the environment and the concept of stewardship. It trains pupils to ask if the criteria of proposed actions are based on morally justifiable values.

These four elements are useful in that they help make the link between the three 'threads' of environmental education and the dimensions of learning. When all of these aspects are fused together, they form an approach to planning teaching and learning tasks that reflects the 'three-fold' structure of environmental education and the expectations of this, i.e.

- education about the environment, which is basic knowledge of and understanding the environment and our complex relationships with it, reflecting the synoptic element;
- education in or from the environment, that is using the environment as a resource with emphasis both on planned inquiry and investigations and also on providing opportunities for pupils to engage in first-hand personal experiences within it, reflecting the empirical and aesthetic elements;
- education for the environment, concerned with values, attitudes and positive actions, reflecting the ethical element.

Having disintegrated environmental education into its various structural parts, an attempt will now be made to reconstruct it. Effective environmental education, at whatever level, can take place only as a result of effective planning, and surely an integral part of planning for the inclusion of environmental education in the curriculum must be the need to develop an understanding of the inter-relationship between the various structural components. It cannot be left to chance that any of the various components of it will be incorporated into any learning situation if it is to be effective. So we now turn to a diagrammatic model of environmental education which attempts to explain the relationship between the components of its structure, and some ideas on how this might be used as a basis for practical planning and inclusion of environmental education in the curriculum. The first stage of this model (Figure 4.2) was first published in *Environmental Education* (Palmer, 1993a) and since has been reproduced in various sources (see, for example, Palmer and Neal, 1994). The subsequent elaboration of this is published here for the first time (Part VI), and is intended to further enhance the practical usefulness and impact of the theoretical model.

142

INTEGRATED MODEL FOR STRUCTURING ENVIRONMENTAL EDUCATION

We have seen that environmental education should provide experiences of problem-solving, decision-making and participation, with considerations based on ecological, political, economic, social, aesthetic and ethical aspects. It is also about promoting changes in attitudes and behaviour that will help to solve existing problems relating to the environment and to avoid the generation of new ones. The ultimate aim is for every citizen to have formulated for him or herself a responsible attitude towards the sustainable development of the Earth, an appreciation of its resources and beauty, and an assumption of an environmental ethic. Furthermore, it has been suggested on a wide global scale that in order to achieve this aim, every educational institution needs adequate arrangements for planning and implementing coherent and progressive programmes of work with appropriate teaching and learning tasks.

If one is to adopt an approach to planning based on the three recognised 'threads' of education about, in/from and for the environment, then it will be necessary to analyse their inter-relatedness and recognise that all are essential components of planning at every level of education. In schools, this means at levels ranging from whole institution and year group planning to more specific plans for programmes of study, integrated topics, subject-based curricula, and tasks applicable to a whole class, group of learners or an individual. This terminology can of course be adapted to appropriate levels in any educational setting. So, an integral part of the planning process must be a consideration of the inter-relationships that exist among the three threads. Perhaps the best way of achieving this is to analyse the core *content* of environmental knowledge and understanding that one wishes to address, as well as the desired development of related *skills* and *attitudes*. Then, by planning a range of complementary learning processes and ensuring coverage of various curriculum *elements* (e.g. ensuring some practical problem-solving, investigatory activities, qualitative tasks, personal reflections, consideration of responsibilities, etc.) it will be apparent that the dimensions of concepts (knowledge), skills and attitudes are inter-linked with the three core structural components (threads) or overall framework of the educative process. Figure 4.1 represents these various components of environmental education in diagrammatic form. Let us consider some examples of the inter-relationships between the components identified:

- The acquisition of knowledge and understanding *about* the environment will enable pupils not just to hold a store of relevant concepts, facts and figures, but also to critically evaluate issues and situations in the light of informed understanding. Knowledge will also inevitably encourage the appreciation and promotion of desired *values* and *attitudes*, especially if that knowledge is gained as a result of addressing real issues and problems that have a reference point in the learners' own lives.

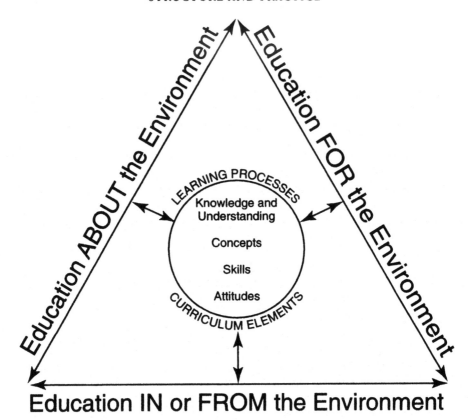

Figure 4.1 Inter-related components of environmental education

- Personal experiences, investigations and problem-solving *in* the environment enable reflection and the development of critical awareness and concern. Working in or through the environment leads to the acquisition of a great deal of *knowledge* and *understanding* as a result of first-hand experiences, as well as to the refinement of *skills* such as those needed for investigation, communication, negotiation and problem-solving.
- When pupils are encouraged to explore their personal response to and relationship *with* the environment and environmental issues, it is likely that this will help them to develop a personal ethic *for* the world. Knowledge becomes more than 'facts to be learned'. Learning and reflection 'on behalf of' the environment is likely to be of an issue-based, action-orientated, problem-solving nature. Such learning will clearly link with the development of *attitudes* and *values*, including elements of and reflections on human understanding and behaviour necessary for the development of sustainable living patterns and caring use of the planet and its resources.

144

Three critical words have been introduced into the above examples of natural linkages in the learning process that do not appear on Figure 4.1, since that focused essentially on structural elements. These are 'experience', 'concern' and 'action'. Without these components, no environmental learning can be truly meaningful and worthwhile. So let us now extend Figure 4.1 into an overall model for teaching and learning, as shown in Figure 4.2. The various components of this suggested model are those to be incorporated into the task of planning a policy for the inclusion of environmental education in any school or other educational institution, and indeed into the task of planning the teaching and learning experiences themselves.

The model expands upon the three-fold framework that underpins planning as shown in Figure 4.1. Educational experiences should be provided that enable

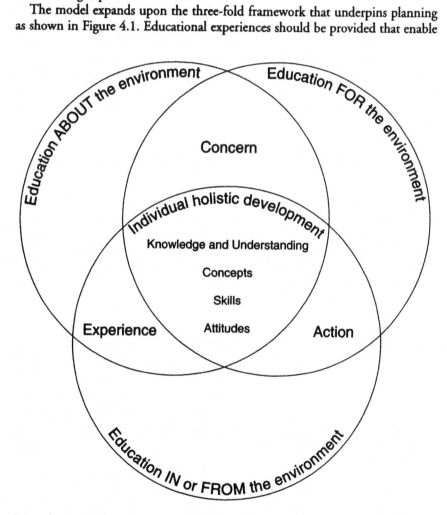

Figure 4.2 Model for teaching and learning in environmental education: components of the planning task (1)

pupils to acquire an appropriate range of knowledge, understanding and concepts about the environment, so that critical judgements can be made concerning people's inter-relationships with it. Investigatory tasks and opportunities for sensory experiences and reflection in the environment should be planned for, allowing for the acquisition and refinement of environmentally focused skills, the gaining of further relevant knowledge, and the development of appropriate attitudes and environmental awareness. Specific tasks should focus on educating for the environment, perhaps of a problem-solving, action-orientated nature, fostering the development of understanding, attitudes and values. Within this basic framework, the crucial components of extending personal *experiences*, developing personal *concerns* and promoting personal *actions* are inevitably incorporated. *Successful programmes of environmental education will take account of the inclusion of all of these elements, by providing appropriate tasks and experiences.*

Before considering the question of what this might actually look like in practice, it is perhaps interesting to consider the structure of this integrated model alongside various 'visions' of environmental education described earlier in this text.

A QUESTION OF EMPHASIS: INTEGRATED MODEL OR DISTINCT VISIONS?

The model portrayed in Figure 4.2 suggests that the three-fold framework of education about, in/from and for the environment can operate in some form of planned 'integrated whole' approach, where the three aspects are relatively balanced in terms of emphasis placed upon them. This viewpoint raises the key question of whether such an approach is incompatible with the notion that there are three very distinct visions of environmental education, each involving a specific emphasis on one or other of the 'about', 'in', 'for' modes of learning. As previous parts of this text have indicated, the positivist view of environmental education tends to see its purpose as learning 'about the environment', with externally imposed, taken-as-read goals. The interpretive view sees the goals as externally derived, but often negotiated, and places emphasis on activities 'in the environment'. The critical view focuses on critique of goals, a socially critical purpose and the undertaking of action 'for the environment'. The views and positions of these three images of environmental education are well summarised by Robottom and Hart (1993, pp. 26–27), as shown in Table 4.3.

The integrated model and the three-fold distinction of Table 4.3 seemingly portray very different messages. More often than not, the approach displayed in the model (Figure 4.2) has been discussed alongside the traditional (if negotiated) goals of environmental education, and indeed the overview of it presented here refers to a body of knowledge, concepts, skills and attitudes as defined within national documentation deriving out of the recommendations of Belgrade

Table 4.3 Three images of environmental education

	Positivist	Interpretivist	Critical
Purposes			
view of environmental education	knowledge 'about the environment'	activities 'in the environment'	action 'for the environment'
educational purpose	vocational	liberal/progressive	socially critical
learning theory	sometimes behaviourist	constructivist	reconstructivist
Roles			
role of goals of environmental education	externally imposed taken-for-granted	externally derived but often negotiated	critiqued (seen as icons of ideology)
teachers' role	authority-in-knowledge	organiser of experiences in the environment	collaborative participant/inquirer
students' role	passive recipients of disciplinary knowledge	active learners through environmental experiences	active generators of new knowledge
curriculum supporters	disseminators of prepared solutions to environmental problems	external interpreters of the learners' environments	participants in new problem-solving networks
role of texts	pre-existing source of authoritative knowledge about the environment	pre-existing source of guidance about environmental experiences	emergent reports of outcomes of critical environmental inquiries
Knowledge and power			
view of knowledge	preordinate commodity systematic personal objective derived from experts	intuitive semi-structured personal subjective derived from experience	generative/emergent opportunistic collaborative dialectical derived from inquiry
organising principles (source of authority)	disciplines	personal experience	environmental issues
power relationships (PR)	reinforces PR	ambivalent about PR	challenges PR
View of research			
research is	an applied science objectivist instrumental quantitative acontextual/ individualistic deterministic	interpretivist subjectivist constructivist qualitative contextual/ individualist illuminative	critical social science dialectical reconstructivist qualitative contextual/ collaborative emancipatory

Table 4.3 continued

	Positivist	*Interpretivist*	*Critical*
research design	preordinate/fixed	preordinate/ responsive	negotiated/ emergent
researchers are	external experts	external experts	internal participants
prime example	Hungerford, Peyton and Wilkie (1983)	Van Matre (1972)	Elliot (1991)

Source: Robottom and Hart (1993, p. 26)

and Tbilisi. Table 4.3 on the other hand reveals substantial philosophical and practical differences separating 'traditionalists' and those who seek to promote education 'for' the environment.

Rather than emphasising such differences, I wish in this text to interpret them as a question of where emphasis falls in their understanding and application. This matter will be returned to in Part VI, where the model will be elaborated upon. At this stage, suffice to say that the authors of Table 4.3 at no stage suggest in their account that one paradigm or image can or should exist with total disregard for the others; rather they see that in education about the environment, the intention is to provide the student with a systematic coverage of subject matter, whereas in education for the environment, the intention is to investigate an issue (so content will be drawn upon opportunistically). Thus the environmental issue is the organising principle. Education about the environment can go alongside a socially critical approach, but, more importantly, it goes within it. My own view, which does not radically disagree with their basic interpretation, is that whilst the integrated model may be associated with 'traditional' (including interpretive) approaches, it can actually be applied to any context. The components it embraces reflect the true complexity of thinking and learning in relation to the environment. Inevitably, individual contexts will warrant a greater or lesser emphasis being placed on each of the elements within the whole. The key thing is that they are all represented, inter-linked and mutually supportive. No aspect of the model can be left to chance or opportunistic coverage.

Let us now turn to the applications of this model to practical educational situations.

THE MODEL IN PRACTICE

The final section of this part illustrates by way of four very different case studies of good practice how environmental education may be structured, organised and delivered. In other words, it shows how the model is being achieved in practice in various locations.

Firstly, from England, we have an example of a school policy document for environmental education. This is a statement of the aims, principles and strategies for the teaching and learning of environmental education at an infant school located in Cleveland county in the north-east of the country. This clear outline statement is available for all members of the school community and is augmented with specific 'theme' plans and schemes of work in geography and science. At Newtown Infant School, environmental education is not left to chance; it is co-ordinated at whole school level and the organising principles derive from subject knowledge.

Secondly, from Scotland, we have a splendid example of environmental education in practice in a primary school where environmental issues themselves are the organising principle. Beancross Primary School has a written policy to promote and co-ordinate environmental education; it utilises the basic three-fold framework of education 'about', 'in and through' and 'for' the environment; but places considerable emphasis on a whole school approach to curriculum and community involvement in educating 'for' the environment. Environmental education in this school is approached through issues-based teaching, with a distinct focus on developing values and attitudes as well as knowledge.

Thirdly, we have an example of organisation, structure and delivery of environmental education at a national level, involving 16 Latvian schools, the Ministry of Education and the University of Latvia, collaborating with the Norwegian Ministry and National Education Office. In this excellent example of both international and inter-disciplinary co-operation, teams of teachers play an active role in establishing, developing and evaluating project-based approaches to learning. The organising principle on which the various projects are designed is that of inter-disciplinary, action-orientated exploration of issues in the local environment.

Finally, an example from Greece illustrates how community involvement can successfully be harnessed as a result of a problem-solving, action-orientated approach to teaching and learning about local environmental issues.

POLICY FOR ENVIRONMENTAL EDUCATION, NEWTOWN INFANT SCHOOL

BY CAROLE GOODCHILD

Introduction

- This document is a statement of the aims, principles and strategies for the teaching and learning of environmental education at Newtown Infant School.
- It was developed during the autumn of 1996 through a process of consultation with the teaching staff.
- It was approved by the governing body during 1996.
- This policy will be reviewed in 1999.

What is Environmental Education?

Environmental Education is the relationship between children and their environment and the influence they are able to bring to bear upon it.

Aims

Our aims in teaching Environmental Education are that all children will

- develop the knowledge, understanding and skills necessary to discuss environmental issues;
- understand the world and the part natural resources play and the possibilities of protecting and managing environments;
- examine and interpret the environment from a wide variety of perspectives;
- be aware and curious about their environment and become actively involved in resolving environmental problems.

Principles of teaching and learning of Environmental Education

- it is a body of knowledge essential to our understanding of sustainable solutions to environmental problems;
- the skills and knowledge of Environmental Education are applicable to everyday life;
- it is enjoyable, interesting and rewarding to be environmentally aware.

Environmental Education is not a statutory subject of the National Curriculum. Although Environmental Education can be covered in all subject areas, it is mainly implicit with the geography and science programmes of study. Guidance has been issued to all schools on the teaching of environmental matters. The guidance is contained within a booklet entitled 'Teaching Environmental Matters through the National Curriculum' by SCAA.

Strategies for the teaching of Environmental Education

Environmental Education is taught on a topic basis wherein it is integrated into the yearly programme of topics followed throughout the school.

In addition to this integrated programme the following extra activities are carried out:

- using resources displayed in classroom;
- carrying out tasks asked in assemblies;
- being involved in projects organised by outside agencies, e.g. British Trust for Conservation Volunteers, Cleveland Wildlife Trust, *Evening Gazette*.

The predominant mode of working in Environmental Education is co-operative group work, although individual work and class teaching are used where appropriate within this structure.

- Groups are usually of mixed/matched ability.
- Relevant discussion is encouraged.
- Groups are encouraged to communicate their findings in a variety of ways.
- *There is no specialist teaching in Environmental Education*, it is taught by class teachers.
- *Classroom helpers are used in Environmental Education* to assist in:

  1 supporting group activities
  2 reading stories with an environmental content
  3 providing extra help for children with particular needs
  4 accompanying and supervising groups during outside activities
  5 accompanying and supervising groups during fieldwork outside the school grounds

- *Commercially available packs* for Environmental Education are not used in school.
- *Pupils with special needs* have the same Environmental Education entitlement as all other pupils and are offered the same curriculum.
- *Homework* is used to support Environmental Education through tasks such as:

  1 finding answers to questions posed in school through the use of books and interviews
  2 answering questions posed in assembly

- Excellence in Environmental Education is celebrated in display and performance including:

  1 the mounting of pictures/written findings/graphs/computer print-outs of the results of an enquiry into an environmental question
  2 group/class/whole school assemblies or gatherings highlighting environmental activities

Strategies for ensuring progress and continuity

Planning in Environmental Education is a process in which all teachers are involved wherein:

- the foundation for curricular planning is the school development plan, developed through a process of collaboration between staff and approved by governors
- there is no individual scheme of work for Environmental Education; it is incorporated within the science and geography schemes of work
- the science and geography co-ordinators developed the schemes of work in collaboration with the whole staff and they are integrated into the school topic plan

- medium-term plans are drawn up by year group teams for each half term and are monitored by the Headteacher
- daily lesson plans are written by individual teachers

The role of the Environmental Education Co-ordinator is shared jointly between the science and geography co-ordinators. Their roles are to:

- take the lead in policy development and the production of schemes of work designed to ensure progress and continuity in Environmental Education throughout the school
- support colleagues in the development of detailed work plans, their implementation of the scheme of work and in assessment and record keeping activities
- monitor progress in Environmental Education and advise the Headteacher on action needed
- take responsibility for the purchase and organisation of central resources for Environmental Education
- keep up to date with developments in information to colleagues as appropriate

Feedback to pupils about their own progress in Environmental Education is usually done whilst a task is being carried out through discussion between the child and the teacher, and through the marking of work. Effective marking

- aims to be encouraging and supportive
- is often done whilst a task is being carried out, through discussion between child and teacher
- includes ticks and written comments that aim to be positive and constructive

Formative assessment is used to guide the progress of individual pupils in Environmental Education. It involves identifying each child's progress, determining what each child has learned and what therefore should be the next stage in his/her learning. Formative assessment is mostly carried out informally by teachers in the course of their teaching. Suitable tasks for assessment include:

- small group discussions perhaps in the context of a practical task
- specific assignments for individual pupils
- individual discussions in which children are encouraged to appraise their own work and progress
- class circle activities where children offer suggestions and answers to teacher-led tasks

Strategies for recording and reporting

Records of progress are not kept specifically for Environmental Education as they are implicit with the science and geography records, which contain:

- a yearly report of progress to parents through a written report

- a portfolio of work, dated and annotated with teacher comments and containing exceptional items of achievement and progress
- comments made in individual teachers' daily record books

Reporting to parents is done twice a year through interviews and annually through a written report. Exceptional work is brought to parents' notice when appropriate.

Strategies for the use of resources

Classroom and central resources for Environmental Education are kept with the science and geography resources. There is also a selection of story books that have explicit environmental themes. These are housed in the staffroom with the teachers' reference books.

External resources include:

- a senses garden in the main playground
- two inner courtyard wildlife areas
- the local area

Information Technology is a resource that is used in Environmental Education for

- written work
- illustrations
- handling information

Health and safety issues in Environmental Education are the same as for science and geography:

Science

Guidelines are provided on:

- appropriate handling of equipment and materials
- appropriate storage of equipment and materials

Geography

Guidelines are provided on:

- wearing gloves when picking litter
- wearing gloves when gardening
- handling garden tools as taught
- being aware of school policy on using outside areas within school grounds for activities

- being aware of school policy on visits and excursions to places within and outside the county

Carole Goodchild is Headteacher of Newtown Infant School, Durham Road, Stockton on Tees, Cleveland TS19 0DE

TAKING ACTION FOR THE ENVIRONMENT IN SCOTLAND

BY MOIRA LAING

Beancross Primary School is a suburban school in Grangemouth, Scotland's main oil-refining town. In common with other Scottish primary schools, Beancross staff are now very engaged in designing appropriate and coherent programmes in environmental studies, which occupies 25 per cent of the 5 to 14 primary curriculum in Scottish schools and encompasses science, technology, social subjects, health education and IT. Traditionally, environmental studies is a Scottish concept where the emphasis has always been on the knowledge and understanding dimension and the acquisition of inquiry-based skills. In other words, it has always had a focus upon learning 'about' the environment, 'in' and 'through' the environment. But the 5 to 14 guidelines have given a new prominence to environmental education and charged teachers with giving a priority to the 'development of informed attitudes' in their pupils, with the essential messages for schools that while environmental studies gives pupils

> the knowledge and skills to understand and interpret environment . . .
> it should go further . . . by encouraging and providing opportunities
> for developing informed attitudes . . . related to the need to care for the
> environment in its immediate, local and global contexts and to the desir-
> ability of taking an informed position on topical and important issues.
>
> (SOED, 1993)

With this background of expectations, Beancross school decided to formulate a written policy to promote environmental education effectively through a whole school approach to grounds, community involvement and curriculum. Already, Beancross exemplified a number of good practices in helping children to learn to care *for* the environment. For a number of years, pupils and staff have been instrumental in planning and negotiating community expertise to develop a series of gardens and play areas for pupils. The Headteacher charts the evolving elements of the school's landscape as a time-line in the school's development plans. At the present point on the time-line crucial deployment of community personnel is required to reshape a demolished wall into a landscape of hills and valleys including a bog garden, working with the pupils' and architects' plans and following the expert advice of the local Jupiter Project, a Zeneca-funded nature project for schools, on the selection of plants and a progressive schedule for the maintenance of gardens and planted areas.

Such networking of the school and its community has paid dividends in creating an outdoor classroom where the pupils can learn about the living environment and enjoy experiences that develop their sensitivity to the environment, that first essential step towards developing a custodial concern for the environment. The pupils have been key participants in several innovative practices and are obviously proud that they can help effect such changes. Members of the school feel that their sense of pride and ownership have contributed to a gradual decrease in vandalism and graffiti.

An obvious and tangible characteristic of Beancross Primary School is its explicit ethos of caring. Responding to the needs of the pupils, school policy ensures that there is a paramount emphasis on health education, on building confidence and self-esteem, on showing respect and concern for other people. Caring for the environment and showing how this contributes a quality to life is a natural extension of this ethos. The school provides a sound role model in promoting Healthy Eating and Recycling Weeks and Stewardship Campaign at regular intervals, and pupils have again felt that they can take some action by persuading parents and shopkeepers to review their own practices and act in more sustainable ways.

Despite such effective practices, however, the school management and staff felt that something more was needed. There was some evidence that while the pupils were confident and competent about effecting changes within the school and its grounds, they were far more diffident, even frightened, about their ability to act in wider community issues. What was needed was some kind of process that would set targets for effective environmental education practices and engage the whole staff in creating experiences within the curriculum that would consciously focus upon 'developing informed attitudes' in pupils and, in so doing, increase their confidence and commitment to act and give them the skills and strategies to take action.

To start the whole school process the staff were asked to respond to these questions:

'Which environmental values should a school try to promote?'

and

'What can a school (and an individual teacher) *do* to promote such values?'

Their responses identified values very closely related to the needs of their pupils in their particular environment, namely conservation and care of their local environment, a respect for community and property, an awareness of the need to balance development with conservation, working with others to discourage pollution, litter and vandalism and making a personal sacrifice sometimes in the interests of others. Above all, they wished their pupils to realise that they could confidently communicate their views and take some action to change things for the better. 'What a school could do' is

- have a written policy so that everyone is clear about the values being pursued;
- ensure that these values are explored and developed across the formal curriculum;
- show everyone (pupils, parents and community) that the school does try to practise what it preaches;
- be alert to pupils' ideas and use resources and community contacts to support them;
- promote practical actions, co-operate in community projects and provide the structures to see them through.

In addition to being an effective role model, an individual teacher could set the right kind of atmosphere to help pupils work out what they think and where they stand and take time to raise awareness and understanding of issues in ways meaningful to their pupils' life experiences.

The teachers reviewed their collective responses, then ranked them in priority, formulating a set of aims to promote environmental understanding and action competence in their pupils, which they all genuinely shared. The most highly ranked aims in the new written policy were:

- to help the pupils to develop positive values and attitudes by raising their awareness and developing self-respect, consideration, honesty and self-discipline;
- to develop the pupils' respect towards property, other people and living things and encourage them to see things from other viewpoints;
- to develop the pupils' appreciation and awareness of the total environment in which we all live and their responsibilities for events and consequences;
- to help the pupils realise that everyone is important and can play a very positive role in changing things for the better.

The next phase in the implementation of a whole school approach to environmental education focused upon the controversial nature of environmental issues and the handling of issues-based learning and teaching in the classroom. The Beancross staff were attracted to the Action Competence Model (Jensen, 1995) because it provided a useful process through which they could try to develop their pupils' action competence by ensuring that

- their pupils have adequate knowledge and understanding of an issue;
- they are given time and opportunities to work out their values and take up a stance;
- they are encouraged to 'vision' what the future could be like;
- they are exposed to some alternative action strategies relevant to the issue, which they can explore and evaluate.

Table 1 Action Competence Model

Knowledge/Insight	What is this issue about?
	Why is it important to us?
	What caused it?
	How have things changed as a result of it?
	How can we better find out about it?
	What solutions do experts offer?
Commitment	What's my position on this?
	What do I think should happen?
	What could be difficult for me – even frightening?
	Nevertheless, what I intend to say/do is . . .
Visions	How could this issue affect the future quality of life – for me and others?
	What type of lifestyle/environment do we want?
	What could/should happen in ten years' time?
Action Experiences	What could I do to change things for the better?
	What are the difficulties/barriers to changing things?
	What is a workable range of possibilities?
	I have decided to take *this* action . . .

Source: Jensen (1995)

Table 1 illustrates how this model provided a structure enabling the teachers to effectively address the teaching of issues in their classrooms, the key questions identifying the essential personal focus for the pupil. In addition, the teachers participated in a workshop session that explored a variety of techniques to enable pupils to raise a range of questions around an issue (pollution, housing, safety), to vision and predict changes, rank preferences and empathise with varying points of view. That issues-based learning calls for changes in teaching styles and in the roles of both pupils and teachers was recognised, discussed and analysed. Through subsequent reflection by the staff, Table 2 shows how the staff are interpreting pupil skills and teachers' strategies.

The Beancross staff were encouraged to contextualise and implement issues-based teaching wherever and whenever they judged it most appropriate. Environmental education is not, after all, another curriculum element to find a space for but a way of learning and teaching with the reality, *and* the imagery, of social and natural issues as the focus. Consequently, issues-based learning could be implemented as a key element in a cross-curricular topic study, as a related issue emerging from a historical, technological or religious/moral study and as a context for creative responses in art, drama, music and movement. Staff and

Table 2 Action Competence Model continued: pupil skills and teacher strategies

Action Competence Model	Pupil skills	Teachers' strategies (roles?)
Knowledge/ Insight	identify the issue as a conflict of values analyse issue and recognise 'players' in the conflict identify research questions use research sources detect bias/opinion learn to sample, survey and record data share information with others analyse alternative solutions to issue evaluate 'completeness' of evidence	clarify, by most appropriate means, the context of the issue provide/evaluate experiences for co-operative working ensure ability in 5–14 skills so that pupils can select and justify the best mode of enquiry provide sources of information be provocative, challenging views, solutions, strategies be an active 'heckler' in the audience
Commitment and Vision	use evidence draw conclusions listen, compare a range of solutions make inferences formulate recommendations communicate personal position/view state and justify personal decision	pose the challenge of 'making up your own mind' about . . . provide appropriate techniques to probe perceptions/values, to justify, predict, explore 'what if . . .' alternatives consider how best to participate facilitate discussion, debate, decision-making and decision-taking reassure challenge
Action Experiences	analyse effective action to make a change evaluate the feasibility of success (consider failure) persuade others about chosen solution(s) decide on best way forward act alone and in a group	facilitate reflection on action plan, i.e. ask awkward questions, ask to check, etc. cause to think ahead and predict ask to evaluate 'right' and 'wrong' challenge 'ideas/strategies' evaluate strategy

Source: Jensen (1995)

pupils enjoyed their experiences and were gratified and proud of the quality and variety of responses. One class wrote the script and enacted a music-drama interpretation of the state of Planet Earth entitled 'Close to Home' for the Edinburgh Environment Festival.

The process continues to be reviewed and refined. In order to ensure that proper emphasis should continue to be given to environmental education within any context, a forward planner was negotiated asking the teachers to state the attitudes being targeted, the central issues that could be raised, and to indicate techniques to be used to enable their pupils to work out their values and evaluate alternative viewpoints and solutions.

The work to consolidate and effect a whole school approach to environmental education will continue to evolve, but Beancross staff feel that they have collaborated to develop a system that ensures that all pupils will have action-orientated experiences that will help them to 'gradually develop positive attitudes towards the environment and a personal code of environmental values' (SOED, 1993).

References

Jensen, B.B. (1995) *Concepts and Models in a Democratic Health Education: Research in Environmental Health Education*, Copenhagen: Royal Danish School of Studies.
Scottish Office Education Department (1993) *Environmental Studies 5 to 14*, Edinburgh: HMSO.

Moira Laing is a Senior Lecturer in Primary Education, Programme Co-ordinator for Environment (BEd) and Course Director for the Certificate in Environmental Studies at the University of Strathclyde, Jordanhill Campus, 76 Southbrae Drive, Glasgow G13 1PP.

With thanks to Margaret Sharp, Headteacher, Beancross Primary School, Grangemouth, Falkirk (Falkirk Regional Council, Scotland).

NORWEGIAN–LATVIAN PROJECT ON ENVIRONMENTAL EDUCATION IN LATVIA: THE INTEGRATION OF ENVIRONMENTAL EDUCATION INTO SCHOOL SUBJECTS DEVELOPING A MULTIDISCIPLINARY TEAM PROJECT METHOD

BY R. ERNSTEINS, D. STELMAHERE AND D. SHULGA

Overview

This project aims to promote the introduction of environmental education into the school system and curriculum in Latvia. It is a joint venture between the Ministries of Education in Norway and Latvia, directed by the National Education Office in Vest-Agder county in Norway and the Centre for Environmental Sciences and Management Studies at the University of Latvia (UL CESAMS). Sixteen schools (elementary, primary and secondary) are involved in different regions of Latvia. Within them, staff focus on inter-disciplinary project-orientated teaching relating to environmental matters. The school and class projects are based on local, natural, historic and cultural environments. Each

159

school has a teaching team, composed of specialists from the natural sciences, social sciences and humanities, which is led by a teacher co-ordinator. These leaders together form a group of 16 resource teachers or teacher trainers able to undertake consultancy work on environmental education across the country. In-service training courses for the co-ordinators themselves are organised regularly and led by trainers from both Latvia and Norway. Knowledge and skills gained are then shared at seminars with team members in the schools.

Each school team discussed and agreed the project issue to be developed in its particular location. A wide variety of fascinating issue-based studies emerged, examples of which are described below.

Projects are evaluated by the teaching teams within their own schools, and desired changes and adaptations are made. It is planned to publish teaching resource materials based on the schools' work and to disseminate their collective experience into the Latvian school system through teacher seminars around the country.

Background

This project derived from a foundation of work begun in the late 1980s by UL CESAMS which focused on different approaches and methods that are appropriate for the realisation of sound environmental education in schools. Methods believed to be appropriate, particularly in the light of the experience of Norwegian schools, include the project approach and, in particular, multidisciplinary projects taught by teams of teachers from varying backgrounds.

The work of the Norwegian–Latvian project (NORTIM), supported both financially and professionally by Norway, as mentioned above, commenced in 1994, at the time when 'The Concept of Environmental Education for General-Education Schools of Latvia', worked out in co-operation between the Children Environment School and the University of Latvia Ecological Centre, was the only official document recognised by the Latvian Ministry of Education as a guideline for environmental education (see also pp. 194–197).

Thus, for some time, UL CESAMS had recognised the necessity of an integrated approach to environmental education, whilst also acknowledging barriers to this – notably professional and psychological barriers of monodisciplinary trained teachers who were not used to inter-disciplinary co-operation. The NORTIM project set out with the intention of developing new multidisciplinary subjects (e.g. environmental studies), both inter-disciplinary in contents and interactive by nature.

Aims of the NORTIM project

1 To select, develop and implement inter-disciplinary local environment class/school projects supervised by the multidisciplinary team of teachers – including teachers not only of natural sciences but also of humanities.

2 To work out proposals for the integration of the inter-disciplinary themes in the formal monodisciplinary curricula, i.e the integration of environmental projects into the lessons of particular traditional subjects.
3 To prepare a set of educational materials for each project and appropriate teacher courses, as well as to train teachers in the methodology and help them overcome the psychological and professional barriers involved in co-operation.
4 To raise public awareness about such changes in both the educational system as a whole and in environmental education in particular, and the impact of these changes at local (school), regional and national levels.

As mentioned above, within each of the 16 project schools in Riga, Liepaja, Ogre, Cesis, Jekabpils, Kuldiga, Tukums and Daugavpils districts, a team of between four and six teachers have worked together on the choice and implementation of a project that can engage pupils in thinking and learning from a variety of disciplines in the natural sciences and humanities. The project teaching then leads into wider dissemination of the methodology and results through teacher education (consultancy work and in-service training seminars), and thorough testing and evaluation of the developed projects both by in-school teaching teams and by outside 'experts'.

The projects: examples

*   Life at the Lake – Liepaja Ezerkrasta Elementary School
    Concerned with acquainting pupils with the processes of the natural world, as influenced by the nearby city and human activities. Pupils are personally involved in identifying and acknowledging environmental problems and in finding resolutions to them. The project introduces other schools of the city and students of the Liepaja Pedagogical University to its resource materials and to the techniques of action-orientated out-of-class activities.

*   My Town on the Banks of the Daugava River – Jekabpils High School
    This project focuses on the town as a cultural and social environment. Pupils are involved in personal investigations and appreciation of aspects of the townscape, and teachers aim to generate within them the deliberate and spontaneous desire to preserve, respect and care for the local environment.

*   Nature Trails in Augszeme – Ilukste Secondary School No. 1, Daugavpils District
    Focuses on the development of innovatory, action-orientated study trails. This work involves the creation of a complex net of trails, the development of methodology for designing and using trails, and co-operation between school, higher education establishment and the local authority.

*   Rainbow – Four Schools of Jurmala: Pumpuri Secondary School, Sloka Primary School, Majori Primary School, Kemeri Secondary School
    These four schools are working on independent but linked sub-projects:

161

'Environment Developing a Personality', 'The Development of Sloka Cultural Environment', 'The Way to my School' and 'Kemeri – The Unique Part of Jurmala City'. These sub-projects are united by the common objective of developing teaching and learning strategies through which the environment itself acquires the role of primary teaching aid. Pupils learn in, from and through the environment, developing a harmonious and balanced relationship with it, and the desire to take action 'for' it.

- <u>Self-awareness in the Environment – Engure Secondary School, Tukums District</u>
  Sets the individual at the heart of environmental thinking and understanding by considering 'I' and 'We' in the environment. The project aims to develop ideas about what the environment is, beginning with an individual's inner environment, then investigating local and more distant environments. It develops understanding of the links between the environment and man, of inter-relations among living things, and of the impact of human life on the natural world. Pupils follow an investigatory, action-orientated, problem-solving approach, and cover elements of subject knowledge deriving from the disciplines of history, geography, chemistry, biology and psychology.

Outcomes

Evaluations have shown the methods used to be much more effective than traditional methods of organising out-of-school courses, because more teachers are involved and because the pupils see more clearly the relevance of and links between various forms of subject knowledge. Another very positive outcome is the teacher-training aspect and the success of regional seminars. When the materials are published, this will further enhance the dissemination of acquired collective experience of environmental education within the educational system in Latvia.

Also, besides the realisation of the projects and their objectives, the participants will be responsible for teaching aids and hand-out materials for each of the projects, which will be published and disseminated through teachers' seminars.

Furthermore, these will be promoted through a methodological newsletter 'Vides Lapa Skolai' (Environment Page for School) for wider dissemination nationally; and CESAMS aims to develop an 'Environmental Education Strategy Action Plan for Schools' resulting from the projects. Participating school co-ordinators will be awarded a qualification: a certificate of 'Teacher-Trainer of Environmental Education' from the University of Latvia.

In conclusion, it is believed that this project has enabled wide opportunities both for the content of learning in environmental education and also for the diversification of the knowledge and ability of teachers. Future outcomes will include in-service training for environmental education leadership, aimed at head teachers, regional school boards and the Ministry of Education, and hopefully promoting the necessary conditions for positive improvements in integrative and disciplinary realisation of environmental education in Latvia at all levels in the education system.

R. Ernsteins PhD is Director of UL CESAMS where D. Stelmahere MSc and D. Shulga also teach and research. Address: Centre for Environmental Science and Management Studies, University of Latvia, Raina Blvd. 19, Riga, LV-1586, Latvia. (D. Shulga is also Head of the Environmental Education Department at the University of Latvia Ecological Centre. This Centre and UL CESAMS are separate yet complementary in their running of several partnership programmes. See also pp. 194–197).

COMMUNITY INVOLVEMENT IN GREECE

BY ELISSAVET TSALIKI

In the county of Trikala, an agricultural area situated in the central part of Greece, one can see how some of the developments that the Ministry of Education has promoted have had an impact on the development of environmental education in the area. The two enthusiastic advisers, one for primary and one for secondary, encourage the teachers to carry out environmental education projects both by their personal help and by the training courses they organise. Importantly, they co-operate very well together, and both deeply believe in the importance of engaging teachers and pupils in learning situations where the learner is valued. This belief they transfer through their advisory practice and in the courses they organise. The result is that very interesting school projects have emerged.

One such project was that undertaken by 8–9 year olds of the 17th primary school of Trikala town, which took as its content the river that passes by their school and their community. The teacher was aware that the children had a relationship with the river through, for example, stories told to them by parents and grandparents. Wanting to build upon this knowledge and interest, she designed a project the aims of which were to:

- understand that the river is a source of life
- learn about the flora and fauna of the river
- discover how the jobs of local people (crop and animal farming, mills, etc.) are related to the presence of the river
- find out about how the pollution (rubbish, pesticides, waste from small-scale factories) affects the life of the river
- find out about the other rivers of the county
- propose solutions for the protection of the river

The way they worked involved discussions with the local people to acquire information about the river (its sources, where it goes, how it was in the past,

163

where mills were located, etc.). They learned the stories and the fairy tales related to the river. The children walked by the river, and during this investigation they photographed it, drew it, recorded the flora and fauna, took note of the amount and type of rubbish, and listed the type of human activities done there (intensive agriculture evidenced by the presence of greenhouses, animal stables, etc.). Back at school in the period following their on-site investigation, the children worked hard through a variety of tasks to make sense of what they had seen. An unavoidable conclusion for the children was that a major factor in the decline of the health of the river and its immediate environs was human activity.

Perhaps many projects would have stopped at this 'awareness' stage, but far from thinking that they had done their work, the children and their teacher now moved into overdrive! They decided to take action. They wrote to the mayor asking him to arrange for the river to be cleaned, and to put signs in place forbidding the dumping of rubbish. In co-operation with the municipality, the children organised the placing of a large panel designed and created by themselves next to the road near the river bridge informing people about the importance of the river and inviting them to protect it. They decided to be river watchers/caretakers themselves, and that they would work hard trying to raise the awareness of other people. The project, in its formal phase, ended with a presentation of all their findings to the local community.

Elissavet Tsaliki is based at an urban environmental education centre in Thessaloniki (see also pp. 188–190).

The crucial topic of planning for and organising good practice, such as is illustrated by these four splendid examples, will be returned to in the final part. First, however, attention turns to a more general and wide-ranging overview of progress and practice in environmental education at a global level.

REFERENCES

Elliot, J. (1991) *Developing Community-focused Environmental Education Through Action-research*. Monograph. Norwich: Centre for Applied Research in Education, School of Education, University of East Anglia.

Huckle, J. (1991) 'Education for Sustainability: Assessing Pathways to the Future', *Australian Journal of Environmental Education*, 7 43–62.

Hungerford, H., Peyton, R. and Wilkie, R. (1983) 'Editorial – Yes EE Does Have a Definition and Structure', *Journal of Environmental Education*, 14 (3) 1–2.

Lucas, A.M. (1979) *Environment and Education: Conceptual Issues and Curriculum Implications*, Melbourne: Australian International Press and Publications.

NCC (1990) *Curriculum Guidance 7: Environmental Education*, York: NCC.

Palmer, J.A. (1993a) 'A Model for Teaching and Learning in Environmental Education: Components of the Planning Task', *Environmental Education*, 43 12.

Palmer, J.A. (1993b) 'Development of Concern for the Environment and Formative Experiences of Educators', *Environmental Education*, 24 (3) 26–31.

Palmer, J.A. and Neal, P.D. (1994) *Handbook of Environmental Education*, London: Routledge.

Palmer, J.A. and Suggate, J. (1996) 'Influences and Experiences Affecting the Pro-Environmental Behaviour of Educators', *Environmental Education Research*, 2 (1) 109–122.

Robottom, I. and Hart, P. (1993) *Research in Environmental Education: Engaging the Debate*, Geelong, Victoria: Deakin University Press.

Schools' Council (1974) *Project Environment*, Harlow: Longman.

Scottish Education Department (1974) *Environmental Education: Inspectors of Schools* (Scotland), Edinburgh: HMSO.

Sterling, S./EDET Group (1992) *Good Earth-Keeping: Education, Training and Awareness for the Sustainable Future*, London: Environmental Development Education and Training Group, London: UNEP-UK.

UNESCO (1977) *First Intergovernmental Conference on Environmental Education, Final Report*, Tbilisi, USSR. Paris: UNESCO.

Van Matre, S. (1972) *Acclimatization: A Sensory and Conceptual Approach to Ecological Involvement*, Martinsville, Ind.: American Camping Association.

Part V

THE GLOBAL SCENE

What then *is* actually happening around the world in the field of environmental education? This part of the text is devoted to descriptions by invited contributors, all experienced researchers and educators, of developments in their own countries. The accounts that follow provide a fascinating overview of progress, potential and prospects on a global scale. It should perhaps be mentioned that the countries included in this chapter were selected neither randomly nor as the world's '15 best practice locations'. It is fully acknowledged that many other nations are doing outstanding things. An attempt was made to give some reasonably comprehensive coverage of the world – the 15 locations derive from six continents – and, most importantly, there is a wealth of good practice going on within them all.

As a whole, the descriptions provide numerous avenues for debate that readers may wish to bear in mind: for example, on whether countries around the world share common goals, strategies and priorities for environmental education; whether progress and achievements appear to be 'even' around the world; whether priorities in developed and developing countries are the same; on organisational differences between countries; on whether the 'rhetoric–reality gap' appears to be a world-wide phenomenon; and, perhaps most importantly, on whether the contributors provide insights into priorities for environmental education in the twenty-first century.

AUSTRALIA

BY IAN R. ROBOTTOM

Overview of origins of environmental education in Australia

While environmental education undoubtedly took place prior to 1975, and indeed some of the key players in the field for the next 20 years were active in the early 1970s, the field came to prominence in Australia with the organisation in Melbourne of the 1975 UNESCO seminar *Education and the Human Environment*. The organiser of this conference was Peter Fensham, who was also the Australian representative at the important conferences of the UNESCO–UNEP International Programme in Environmental Education (Stockholm in 1972; Belgrade in 1975; Tbilisi in 1977). The role played by Fensham and other 'founders' of the field of environmental education in Australia is traced by Greenall Gough (1993).

While environmental education in Australia was arguably shaped by international developments during the 1970s, the field became more highly organised internally in 1980 with the formation of its own national professional association which has gone from strength to strength with a significant presence in each state and territory.

Environmental education in the formal educational system

Historically, environmental education in Australia has been teacher-based and school-based. Interested teachers have had the opportunity to develop curricula based on investigation of environmental issues within the school's own community. In the last three or four years, however, the development of national curriculum statements and states' and territories' derivatives of these has resulted in a greater centralisation of environmental education curriculum. The effect of this centralisation of curriculum on the strongly contextual, community-based nature of environmental education is still being worked through.

While there is obviously a great diversity in environmental education across Australia (Andrew and Robottom, 1995), perhaps the defining characteristic of environmental education is its interest in addressing philosophical questions as well as empirical questions relating to the environment. It is a form of education interested in exploring and understanding the cultural, social, political, ethical, moral, emotional and economic dimensions of environmental issues as well as their 'scientific' dimension. Environmental education recognises that educating about environmental issues entails considerations of not only what is the case, but also what should/ought to be the case.

Higher education and community levels

Formal award-bearing courses that examine educational issues concerning policy, organisation and practice in environmental education are relatively rare; for example, there are course work Masters' degrees in environmental education at perhaps three universities only. The Deakin–Griffith Environmental Education Project, involving Deakin University in Victoria and Griffith University in Queensland, offers jointly developed distance education units in environmental education enabling mid-career teachers from all over the country to undertake postgraduate studies towards a Master of Education degree in environmental education. Many more tertiary institutions offer environmental studies and environmental science courses with an emphasis on environmental issues. In the period 1994–1996, under the auspices of the National Professional Development

Program funded by the Commonwealth Department of Employment, Education and Training, partnerships of universities, educational systems and professional associations collaborated in the presentation of mid-career professional development courses in environmental education; these courses have been undertaken by thousands of teachers at all levels of education. In terms of community environmental education, perhaps the best known is the National Landcare Program, in which groups of landowners can apply for funds from the federal government to support their own localised projects in animal and land management, thereby carrying out a research-based educative role in their respective communities. There is also important work being carried out supporting educators' direct linkage with community-based Landcare, with the 'Landcare for Teachers' programme (Stadler, 1995).

Who is responsible for environmental education?

The national professional association, the Australian Association for Environmental Education, was founded in 1980 and currently has a membership of over 500. The association sponsors an annual professional journal, a quarterly newsletter and biennial national conferences. The association is also a partner in a national professional development programme offering significant support for teachers. While the association offers significant support to teachers of environmental education, and the Commonwealth and state/territory government provide policies that provide 'official' legitimation for environmental education, environmental education tends to remain an activity for the enthusiast. Certainly most teachers of environmental education are able to evince a strong commitment to environmentalism that shapes and sustains their educational activities. Even with the legitimation accruing from the inclusion of studies of the environment within the national curriculum, systemic resources for environmental education remain low relative to other key learning areas. There are many instances in Australian environmental education where teachers and learners have formed strong working relationships with a range of community agencies and groups, no doubt in part with a view to attracting human and financial resources from these non-systemic sectors (Robottom, 1996).

Significant research programmes

There is an increasing tide of research being conducted in Australian environmental education – too much to describe adequately here. At the time of writing, three projects in environmental education are currently funded by the Australian Research Council, the most prestigious national research funding agency:

• John Fien of Griffith University and David Yencken of the University of Melbourne are chief investigators in a three-year project titled 'Young People and the Environment: An International Study';

171

- Roy Ballantyne of Queensland University of Technology and John Fien are chief investigators in a three-year project entitled 'Transgenerational Learning and the Environment';
- Ian Robottom and Rob Walker of Deakin University are chief investigators in a three-year project entitled 'Contestation over "National" and "Community" Interests in the Development of Environmental Education' which examines the effects of the introduction of newly centralised curriculum on environmental education in Australia.

An increasing number of doctoral studies are also being undertaken in environmental education, on such topics as feminism and environmental education (Gough, 1995; Barron, 1995), teacher education (Walker, 1995), ontology and critical discourse (Payne, 1995), and community-based environmental education (Malone, 1995; Andrew, 1996).

In addition to this formal, university-based research in environmental education, a considerable number of case studies of environmental education have been prepared by partnerships of universities, educational systems/departments and professional associations in connection with the National Professional Development Program funded by the Commonwealth Government (see, for example, Andrew and Robottom, 1995). These case studies represent an increasing archive of descriptive data relating to the experiences of schools and communities engaged in environmental education within a policy context of increasing centralisation of control over curriculum.

Prospects

The prospects for environmental education in Australia remain bright. A consistent feature of successful environmental education is a commitment to environmentalism on the part of teachers; teachers find a way of engaging in environmental education even in circumstances where this is 'against the grain'. Notwithstanding a clear continuation of this commitment, the foregoing brief account of environmental education in Australia suggests that there are at least two trends that are shaping the future prospects for the field:

1 There is a movement towards centralisation of control over curriculum. The development of the national curriculum statements and the various states' and territories' versions of these, together with their likely attendant of state-wide testing, represent a change from the historically teacher-based and school-based form of curriculum development. This will have implications for environmental education as a form of education that derives its content and, increasingly, its resources from explorations of environmental issues in local communities;
2 In Australia's national curriculum and its state and territory derivatives, environmental education is explicitly conjoined with social education. This represents a shift from the more traditional view of environmental education

as a stepchild of science education. Environmental education now has an explicit social agenda, with the national statement on Studies of Society and Environment recommending the values of democratic process, social justice and ecological sustainability. To the extent that these policies are influential, they provide a legitimation for examining environmental issues from a social perspective more empathetic to dealing with philosophical questions and not just empirical questions.

The prospects of environmental education will in part depend on how the implications of these two trends are worked out in the theory and practice of curriculum development, professional development and educational research in the field of environmental education.

References

Andrew, J. and Robottom, I. (1995) *Environmental Education Across Australia*, Geelong, Victoria: Deakin University Press.

Barron, D. (1995) 'Gendering Environmental Education Reform: Identifying the Constitutive Power of Environmental Discourses', *Australian Journal of Environmental Education*, 11 107–120.

Greenall Gough, A. (1993) *Founders in Environmental Education*, Geelong, Victoria: Deakin University Press.

Payne, P. (1995) 'Ontology and the Critical Discourse of Environmental Education', *Australian Journal of Environmental Education*, 11 83–106.

Robottom, I. (1996) 'Permanently Peripheral? Opportunities and Constraints in Australian Environmental Education', *Southern African Journal of Environmental Education*, 16 44–56.

Stadler, T. (1995) 'The Landcare for Teachers Program: Learning and Teaching for the Environment', *Australian Journal of Environmental Education*, 11 27–38.

Walker, K. (1995) 'The Teaching and Learning of Environmental Education in NSW Primary Schools', *Australian Journal of Environmental Education*, 11 121–130.

Ian Robottom PhD is Associate Professor at the Faculty of Education, Deakin University, Victoria 3217, Australia.

CANADA

BY PAUL HART

Environmental education is increasingly recognised by Canadian educators as an important emphasis within public education. Since the late 1960s, when environmental issues became a focus for public attention, educators, often with a background in areas such as nature study or natural history, conservation education and outdoor education, have worked to construct the emerging area of environmental education. During the 1970s, several world conferences, including Stockholm (1972), Belgrade (1975) and Tbilisi (1977), were important in assisting local educational organisations to broaden their mandate to include an environmental emphasis. However, despite an attempt in 1975 in the province of Saskatchewan to bring together environmental educators, Canadians, with the exception of a small UNESCO–Canada MABNET group, seemed content to associate through the North American Association for Environmental Education in the United States. It was not until the 1990s that a Canadian network was established: the Canadian Network for Environmental Education and Communication (EECOM).

Given this North American focus, Canadian activity in environmental education has been regional and is difficult to describe concisely. Key educators, typically with some ability to influence many others through university courses or curriculum development, have been instrumental in introducing environmental education to thousands of Canadians (Hart, 1990). And somehow as a result of this persistent activity and the growing concern, amplified by scientists such as David Suzuki and by the Canadian media, about serious threats to our own Canadian environment in areas such as forests and fisheries, environmental education has evolved through the 1980s to become everyone's concern in the 1990s.

Within the last ten years several federal and provincial government initiatives have emerged to reflect the Canadian public's growing concern for local, national and global environments. For example, many education-related programmes have resulted from Canada's Green Plan (Government of Canada, 1990), a comprehensive national commitment to clean up and protect Canada's environment. Other federal initiatives, such as the establishment of National and Provincial Roundtables on the Economy and the Environment (NRTEE, 1993), have resulted in considerable provincial activity, including the development of conservation strategies. Several of those provincial conservation strategies provide policy directives that focus on environmental education specifically, although there seems to be a tendency since the World Conservation Strategy, the Brundtland Commission Report and the Rio Earth Summit to supplant the words 'environmental education' with 'sustainable development education'. The Environmental Citizenship programme (Government of Canada, 1993) and the Learning for a Sustainable Future programme for elementary and secondary schools are examples of federal/provincial government support for at least the concepts of environmental education and/or sustainable development.

Federal and provincial co-operation in educational development is significant within Canada, because our national constitution defines education as a provincial mandate. Each province and territory has unique features that reflect differences in political and cultural backgrounds as well as geography and resources. Diversity within this country also stems from Canadian adherence to policies of bilingualism, multiculturalism and religious pluralism. Thus, issues confronting the introduction of innovations such as environmental education within Canadian education systems cannot be understood without considering the complex social and educational conditions that influence the development of any educational innovation.

Despite this complexity, Canada has one of the least politicised comprehensive public education systems in the world (OECD, 1976). Most Canadian provinces have adopted similar models of curriculum development where policies are developed at the provincial level and educational decision-making is limited within teaching to curriculum implementation. In essence, each of Canada's provinces has a 'national' curriculum. It should not be surprising then that innovations such as environmental education remain almost invisible within mainstream educational practice unless individual teachers are somehow personally convinced that they are crucial to basic public education (Hart, 1990).

Where is environmental education in Canada today? Many provincial science curriculum documents and guides now actively promote environment-related school activity. A growing number of provinces provide guidelines for integrating environmental education concepts into existing subjects (e.g. Government of British Columbia, 1995), or have developed education strategies for sustainable development (Government of Saskatchewan, 1992). In contrast to our past tendency to adopt and adapt American materials, new Canadian materials and resources are increasingly available to teachers. The Alberta-based SEEDS Foundation's Learners in Action programme, which challenges elementary schools to become 'Green' or even Jade, Emerald or Earth schools, is immediately obvious in classroom and hallway displays in thousands of Canadian elementary schools. Local materials on a variety of topics from water resources and forestry to more generic materials on sustainable living and environmental citizenship are a visible feature of many Canadian schools.

A key difference today when compared to 20 years ago is the general attitude of the public and the government towards environmental education curriculum development and research. At the grass roots level, from elementary schools to universities, environmental education activity is not only recognised as an acceptable curriculum emphasis, it is actively promoted by core people in academic as well as administrative positions. Recent research into the environment-related practices and thinking among Canadian elementary school teachers confirms the breadth of environmental education-related activity within Canadian schools (Hart, 1996a).

Despite a recent shift in government priorities and grassroots teacher concern about lack of support from local and provincial sources, environmental education courses and programmes within Canadian universities are expanding in the face of restraint. Most Canadian universities have education faculty members whose main interest is in environmental education. With universities such as the University of Toronto advertising for environmental education faculty positions, Canadian research and curriculum activity should increase. Government people who have survived recent cuts are active and working to be better co-ordinated through organisations such as EECOM, which in 1996 initiated the *Canadian Journal of Environmental Education*.

Other groups and non-profit organisations such as ECOSCOPE and the

Evergreen Foundation seem to be proliferating. In short, the number of people actively promoting environmental education-related activity is more visible to the public and to a growing number of teachers who need support in order to sustain their efforts.

If there is any doubt about the level of environmental education-related activity in Canada, I would suggest a visit to one of thousands of elementary schools from British Columbia to Newfoundland where environmental education is the focus of one or more dedicated teachers. In fact environmental education is a priority for so many teachers in Canadian elementary schools that one wonders what the next generation will demand of our elected officials. Throughout Canada, teachers and children are actively restoring school grounds, parks, even wetlands; recycling; fund-raising for rainforests and whales as well as the local zoo; planting trees, and writing to elected officials about local issues. This activity is the result of teachers passionately committed to doing something for the environment based on fundamental principles and values such as care, respect and responsibility which they extend from individual relationships to people–environment relationships (Hart, 1996b).

What does all of this environmental education-related activity mean? There is evidence to support the notion that environmental education-related activity is thriving within Canadian elementary schools (Hart, 1996b). Increasing numbers of people, mainly teachers, have come to recognise that environmental problems are everyone's concern and that they have a responsibility to promote respect for the environment as they do for individuals and for society. Ingrained as this attitude appears to be within Canadian consciousness, environmental education can be characterised as a still small part of public education which is expanding in a time of economic restraint. The explanation for this apparent anomaly seems to be that the drive comes from personal belief and commitment. Those who have come to adopt an ethic that includes the environment, as so many teachers of Canadian young people have, have transformed their thinking about how the world works and are transforming the consciousness of the next generation. What then?

References

Government of British Columbia (1995) *Environmental Concepts in the Classroom*, Victoria, BC: Ministry of Education.

Government of Canada (1990) *Canada's Green Plan for a Healthy Environment*, Ottawa: Minister of Supply and Services Canada.

Government of Canada (1993) *A Primer on Environmental Citizenship*, Ottawa: Minister of Supply and Services Canada.

Government of Saskatchewan (1992) *An Educational Strategy for Sustainable Development in Saskatchewan*, Regina, SK: Department of Environment and Resource Management.

Hart, P. (1990) 'Environmental Education in Canada: Contemporary Issues and Future Possibilities', *Australian Journal of Environmental Education*, 6 45–66.

Hart, P. (1996a) 'Problematising Enquiry in Environmental Education: Issues of

Method in a Study of Teacher Thinking and Practice', *Canadian Journal of Environmental Education*, 1 56–88.

Hart, P. (1996b) 'Understanding Environmental Education: Teacher Thinking and Practice in Canadian Elementary Schools', *South African Journal of Environmental Education*, 16 33–43.

NRTEE (1993) *Annual Review*, Ottawa: National Roundtable on the Economy and the Environment.

OECD (1976) *Reviews of National Policies for Education: Canada*, Paris: OECD.

Paul Hart PhD is Professor in the Faculty of Education and Director of the Saskatchewan Instructional Development and Research Unit, University of Regina, Saskatchewan, Canada S4S 0A2.

THE PEOPLE'S REPUBLIC OF CHINA

BY ZHU HUAIXIN

Environmental education in higher education

In China, environmental education in higher education could be divided into two main categories, one is professional environmental education for those who will go in for environmental work after graduation, and the other is general environmental education for those who will enter various fields of society.

Professional environmental education

Since the 1970s, higher education institutions have been paying much attention to the training of experts or technical personnel of environmental fields, such as biology, ecology, forestry, hydrology, etc., and they have made great progress.

From 1973 to 1978, Beijing University, Beijing Engineering University, Zhongshan University and Tongji University (which are all engineering institutions) took the lead in setting up courses in environmental studies, to train people for careers in environmental fields. Until 1995, there were 79 higher education institutions involved in 15 kinds of environmental programmes for undergraduate students, involving fields of science, engineering, agriculture, medicine and education; 107 centres offering masters' and 38 centres offering doctoral programmes in environmental fields.

Environmental science is a comprehensive field, and the research into and proposed solutions for environmental problems need overlapping and uniting of many disciplines. In China, many institutions have strong research capability, diverse disciplines, advanced equipment and frequent international contacts, thus they have an advantage in developing environmental education as an integrated discipline. At present, the number of institutes for environmental research in higher education institutions accounts for one-third of the total number in the whole country, and they have been training a great number of senior environmental personnel for China.

Since the late 1970s, about 100 engineering institutions have set up a speciality of environmental engineering. Some established a comprehensive department – a Department of Environmental Science. Their duty is to train personnel of the environmental engineering field. Among them, some are under the jurisdiction of the State Education Commission, such as Qinghua University, Tongji University, and so on; some are under specific national ministries, such as Harbin Architectural Engineering Institute, Hunan University and Shandong Engineering University, etc., which are respectively subordinate to the Architectural Ministry, Engineering and Electronics Industrial Ministry and Metallurgical Industry Ministry, etc.; some are under provincial or municipal educational committee, such as Beijing Engineering University, Hebei Chemical Engineering Institute and Zhejiang Engineering University, and so on.

In order to develop students' environmental skills in their future professional fields, those institutions take measures to train their students to apply their professional knowledge to the solution of associated environmental problems. For instance, students from the speciality of chemical engineering should learn to make up programmes of cutting down or removing pollution brought in by the chemical industry with their chemical knowledge; students from the agricultural speciality should learn to solve such problems as soil salinisation and soil erosion with their professional knowledge. In addition, the institutions also adopt field study approaches, by which teachers lead their students to practise observing and solving specific environmental problems with their learned knowledge.

General environmental education

In the late 1980s, most higher education institutions showed concern for the development of environmental awareness in those who will enter such fields as economics, law, science and technology, art, journalism and publishing, and whose work will certainly affect urban and rural environments indirectly.

Many institutions offer elective courses that pass on specific environmental knowledge and concepts in accordance with particular specialities. For example, they offer such courses as environmental chemistry, pollution chemistry, etc., for the students from a chemistry department; pollution and living things, environmental sanitation, etc., for the students from a biology department; natural conservation, protection of resources for the students from a geography department; environmental management, environmental law for the students from a politics department; and environmental literature for the students from a language and literature department. This action can broaden the environmental knowledge of students of various specialities, strengthen their environmental awareness, and develop their appropriate environmental values and attitudes. As many institutions have found, those elective courses cannot provide systematic environmental knowledge, so some departments in many institutions have compiled such relatively comprehensive textbooks as *An Introduction to Environmental Protection* (Liu Peitong and Kong Fande, 1991) in accordance with the needs of different departments.

Other institutions have infused environmental education into basic courses instead of setting up a single course on environmental aspects. These institutions pay much attention to related specific environmental problems in the basic courses. For example, in an analytical chemistry course teachers would explain how to prevent ion from endangering human bodies and the environment; in a physical geography course, teachers would introduce the issue of natural resources and the measures of their conservation. This action has the advantage of relating basic theory with practice.

Moreover, a few institutions offer students regular lectures by specialists from different specialities. These lectures are non-degree courses, but they aim to improve students' understanding of the environment from different perspectives. Take water pollution as an example: a biologist would emphasise the effects of water pollution upon living things, while a chemist would emphasise the relationship between water pollution and chemical reaction. Such lectures will also initiate students' rational considerations. Similarly, some institutions organise environmental seminars, guiding students to engage in theoretical discussion about environmental problems.

One more point should be noted. In recent years, several institutions have begun to set up a course of environmental education for those who are preparing for bachelor or master degrees of education. Such a course does not involve the gaining of specific environmental knowledge and concepts, but involves the pedagogic principles of environmental education, the aim of which is to equip those would-be educationists with some theoretical knowledge of environmental education as a research field. In order to accelerate this work, the Education Department of Hangzhou University took the lead in the research of environmental education theory from 1992, established a 'Centre for Environmental Education Studies' in 1994, which is the first one in China, and has just published a book entitled *Theory and Practice of International Environmental Education* in 1996, which is now used as a textbook for the undergraduate students in some educational departments.

Development of environmental education and its main teaching approaches in basic education in the People's Republic of China

Development and current situation

In 1979, a conference on environmental education in the level of basic education was held by the Environmental Education Committee of the Chinese Association of Environmental Science. The conference recommended that environmental education be undertaken at the primary and secondary stages of education, and chose several schools in different cities and provinces to implement a pilot project. Thus, China started environmental education.

After several years' try-outs, in 1985, the State Environment Bureau and State Education Commission together held a nation-wide meeting in Liaonin Province, and many teachers from various regions attended the meeting to exchange experiences of environmental education activities. As a result of the conference, some documents were published to spread the experience all over the country.

In 1991, the State Education Commission decided that, from that August, environmental education should be arranged as an elective course or extra-curricular activities for the students of grade one in senior secondary school, and from 1993, contents of environmental education should be added in the teaching materials at the stage of compulsory education. Thus, environmental education has become a regular discipline in basic education.

At present, environmental education at the compulsory education stage is infused in different subjects, such as Chinese, mathematics, social studies, geography, science, nature study, art, and so on. Among those, 'nature study' is a core subject for environmental education, including such basic knowledge as air, water, soil, noise, plants and animals, food-chains and ecological balance, etc.

In the senior stage of secondary schools, emphasis is laid on teaching students systematic environmental knowledge, developing their general environmental awareness, establishing their appropriate environmental values and attitudes, and guiding them to participate in investigating environmental problems and attempting to put forward solutions. The teachers in the senior stage of many schools have compiled such printed materials as *Environmental Protection* or *Environmental Knowledge*, which are now used as textbooks for those who take environmental elective courses.

Moreover, the primary and secondary schools also pay attention to developing environmental education through extra-curricular activities. In primary schools, teachers often guide their students to participate in such activities as tree or flower planting, hiking and mountain-climbing, etc., the aim of which is to develop pupils' initial awareness of protecting and improving the environment through observing and experiencing it by themselves. As for secondary schools, teachers usually organise some subject-groups, such as the geography lovers' group, biology lovers' group, etc., in which students could go a step further to study environmental knowledge or do some relevant experiments. Also, many schools make their efforts to disseminate environmental knowledge by holding exhibitions, lectures or forums on the environmental situation.

Main teaching approaches

In addition to the narrative (didactic) approach in the classroom, the main teaching approaches of environmental education are as follows:

Problem-solving approach

Many schools in China instruct students to examine specific environmental problems. The aim of the approach is to help students consolidate learned or study-associated knowledge and concepts. There are two forms of the approach: discovery learning and problem explanation.

In implementing discovery learning, which leads students to explore environmental problems and solutions consciously, on the one hand, teachers usually guide students to find out about and discover hidden environmental problems in the existing situation, which do not show environmental problems directly and obviously, such as we see in the reports in newspapers and magazines. Thus teachers help to develop their students' sensitivity to environmental problems. On the other hand, teachers often ask their students to discuss and make reliable problem-solving decisions by focusing on some existing environmental problems, such as soil erosion, climate deterioration, industrial pollution, etc.

As for the second form of approach, namely problem explanations, teachers usually introduce their students to some general ways of solving certain environmental problems, then guide the students to apply such methods to other problems. This approach helps to develop students' general values in relation to the environment and its problems.

Experimental approach

Most schools enable specific opportunities for their students to operate environmental experiments under controllable conditions, in order that the students can gain direct experience. During experiments, students can observe and understand the origins of some environmental problems, discover some factors influencing them, and can arrive at assumptions of solutions based upon experiments.

The experimental approach includes the conduct of experiments both before and after learning environmental knowledge and concepts. The aim of the former is to help students gain perceptual knowledge and materials by themselves, so that they can understand new environmental knowledge smoothly; the aim of the latter is to help students consolidate and understand the learned knowledge by experimental verification.

Field study approach

Teachers in some schools often lead students to go out to observe such problems as environmental pollution, exhaustion of natural resources and destruction of the ecological environment as part of units within the teaching syllabus.

Most teachers use this approach before teaching theoretical knowledge, the aim of which is to equip students with some related perceptual materials. The advantage of it is that it could enrich the teaching of content, and combine the knowledge provided in the classroom with realistic environmental situations. Therefore the approach can improve students' ability of understanding both knowledge and skills related to the solving of problems.

Simulated approach

In the teaching process of some units, teachers create certain scenes, and ask students to take the roles of the necessary characters in them, i.e. a role play situation. The aim of the approach is to help students learn to think broadly of various factors that influence a certain issue from the environmental perspective, with appropriate environmental values and attitudes.

For example, upon the background that the local government will make a construction decision, the teacher would design a simulated governmental meeting that gains opinions, then assign his students different roles such as economists, environmentalists, engineers, officials and inhabitants, etc. The teacher would first lead them to collect information accordingly, then in the 'meeting' would ask the students to act out their roles, that is, ask them to narrate their opinions respectively. At the end of the simulated meeting, the teacher should make a conclusion on the environmental position. Usually, such play will be acted out for more than once until it reaches the expected or desired results.

References

Liu Peitong and Kong Fande (eds) (1991) *An Introduction to Environmental Protection*, Beijing: Chinese Environmental Science Press.
Xu Huai and Zhu Huaixin (1996) *Theory and Practice of International Environmental Education*, Beijing: People's Education Press.

Zhu Huaixin PhD is Professor in the Department of Education at Hangzhou University in Zhejiang Province, People's Republic of China.

ECUADOR

BY MARCO A. ENCALADA

Background to environmental communication and education in support of sustainable regional development in Ecuador

This account differs slightly from the other contributions to this part in so far as it focuses on a particular case study involving an NGO in the development of an environmental education plan. It is, nevertheless, highly significant and indicative of efforts to promote major environmental and development programmes in southern nations.

In 1995, the Provincial Council of the Pichincha Province of Ecuador (regional government) asked Corporación OIKOS (NGO) to develop the

'Environmental Communication and Education Plan' (ECEP), as part of its 'Western Pichincha Regional Development Program' (WPRDP), aiming to promote sustainable development. The WPRDP has several components, including environmental communication, environmental education, agro-industrial production and municipalities' institutional building.

The central objective of environmental communication and environmental education was to create adequate levels of environmental awareness in the population in order to develop co-responsibility in the characterisation and solution of local environmental problems. It was also hoped to encourage participation in the implementation of parts of the overall programme, which seeks to assure sustainable development within an area of more than 9,000 km², occupied by about 350,000 inhabitants, with a high percentage of rural areas (70 per cent).

The plan put heavy emphasis on systematic planning and programming of educational communication, as well as on intensive training of the work team, whilst retaining a reasonably participatory, overall approach.

It was decided that the project would last a maximum of three years. In the first year, the first three months would be spent developing the ECEP plan, followed by nine months of putting it into action. In the next two years a second stage would allow the continuation of its application and an evaluation of its results. This case study refers only to the first stage, and highlights the methodological approaches and the main communication planning process carried out. Due to time and space limitations, no descriptions are made of the content and instruments used for the communication campaigns.

The planning process

Three major planning steps were established at the outset: firstly, diagnosis of communication and education needs in the region around the WPRDP; secondly, establishment of concrete objectives; and, thirdly, establishment of sets of strategy trees for environmental communication and education.

Diagnosis of environmental communication and education needs

The diagnosis helped to clarify (a) the state of the most important environmental problems and the natural resources of the area; (b) the levels of people's environmental perceptions and consciousness; (c) people's current common practices relating to natural resource management; and (d) current implicit and explicit needs of environmental communication and education.

1 State of environmental problems
   This chapter of the diagnosis comprised a technical characterisation of environmental problems; their causes, effects, and the social factors that have incidence on them.

183

It was found that the most important problems of the region were: water pollution, soil erosion and pollution, deforestation, extinction of wild species of animals and plants, and air pollution.

The main social factors identified were associated with lack of and/or misleading knowledge and practice of: national and regional policies, research, technology transfer, organisational development, municipal institutional building, legal and technical environmental regulations, financing of environmental programmes, and general education.

Findings were later used to inform general orientation for the communication intervention during the implementation of ECEP.

2 Analysis of environmental consciousness

This task was orientated to identify – people's awareness of environmental problems, their effects, causes, the social factors influencing them, and the available feasible solutions; people's attitudes towards confronting solutions and control of social factors that relate to the problems; and the most common behaviours of people in relation to the usage of natural resources and the care of the environment.

An in-depth survey was performed over a sample of 300 households.

3 Environmental practices and habits

A survey of 50 householders selected by occupation was conducted in order to investigate the main environmental practices and habits of the people. A complementary series of in-depth interviews with 10 small entrepreneurs was also undertaken in order to find out about the positive and negative practices that people engage in relating to the processes of production in the region. It was important to determine the conditions under which people would be willing to change their production procedures in order to bring about cleaner production, and pollution prevention.

4 Environmental communication and education needs

Some basic attitudes, behaviours and practices of the population towards environmental communication and education were also explored. Among these were: the level of application of environmental education and communication in schools and communities; types of skills and knowledge that need to be developed to improve the usage of natural resources; the levels of people's sensitisation and motivation towards community participation in environmental programmes, and the most influential groups of local communities.

Establishment of objectives

A special procedure was developed to establish the objectives for the overall communication and education programme: a prognosis mechanism to establish the minimum quantum of knowledge, attitudes and practices people should demonstrate if certain scenarios were to be reached at the end of the programme.

A series of single applications of prospective methods to build up foreseeable futures was applied to characterise which portions of people's knowledge, attitudes, behaviours, practices and habits would need to be reinforced, and which ones reorientated. Based upon the results, sets of strategic objectives were established to be reached within the duration of the project.

Axiologic objectives were clearly a primary need. That meant the need to consolidate certain ecological and environmental principles and concepts, such as: sustainable development; people's participation in pollution prevention and control; the role of environmental communication and education; biodiversity, ecology, environment, and so on. Strategic objectives were established in relation to the action processes that are needed in order to attain certain goals in respect of knowledge, attitudes, practices and habits. Finally, operational objectives were defined for each of the campaigns built around the various specific needs of the programme.

The build-up of strategy trees

The most salient tasks of the planning process were the setting up of a general environmental communication and education model, discussion of this with officials from the WPRDP and the designing of environmental communications and education activities with members of the various audiences: communities of interest, municipalities, workers, householders, politicians, medium and small entrepreneurs, teachers and students of basic education (K-14). Two sets of strategic models were developed: the 'umbrella'-type strategies, and the 'subsidiary' ones.

The first of these was aimed at creating in the audience a minimum common background of understanding of philosophical and axiological ecological principles, as well as of environmental concepts, about which all people should reflect on and be familiar with, at least to some extent. The second set of strategies (subsidiary) was aimed at assembling specific communication and education packages to help the predetermined specific audiences both to raise their knowledge levels about the particular issues they were associated with and also to reinforce and/or reorientate their environmental attitudes, behaviours and day-to-day practices associated with the local problems.

Specific communication and education systems were developed within each of the strategy models to tailor the particular situation of issues, audiences and goals. All of these systems were called 'campaigns' in order to organise the planning process.

The umbrella-type strategies incorporated two directions: the first one to promote some pre-established environmental principles and concepts; and the second one to reinforce basic pre-established environmental attitudes (feelings and emotions).

Six environmental principles and three sets of environmental concepts were chosen, to be delivered through two communication campaigns: one directed

185

towards a group of so-called 'social diffusors' – local people who can pass on information to others (Campaign 1); and another aimed at the general public (Campaign 2). Six sets of attitudes were focused upon to encourage adoption by the communities. These were promoted through a mass communications campaign (Campaign 3). Each communication/education system was organised taking into account the following elements:

- The structure and functions of the system, as well as its technical components, such as: message, media, communication senders and audiences.
- Duration of the campaign.
- Specific goals.
- General activities and operations.

Under the 'subsidiary' strategies two approaches were applied. The first conceives of communication and education as a 'precondition' to attain sufficient changes needed with reference to the social factors that affect the causes of environmental problems. For instance, definition and approval of environmental policies, regulations, and both funding and technology transfer programmes as a way of initiating the process of solving any problem associated with water pollution. The second one conceives of communication and education as a 'tool' to support the pursuing of specific behaviours in people with respect to proposed solutions to concrete problems. For instance, once certain environmental programmes are put into action to prevent environmental damages in any production system, it is necessary to count on the communication's support to adopt either cleaner production technologies or production practices, such as better management of raw materials and wastes.

Under the approach of communication and education as a precondition, two systems were developed: to promote the approval and application of new environmental norms and regulations at the regional level (Campaign 4); and to motivate decision-making to launch complementary local environmental management programmes by the municipalities and local development agencies (Campaign 5).

The strategic approach of communication and education was also developed as an instrument to influence both the informal and formal education sectors.

The informal education systems sought to create opportunities for a wide sector of the population to become well informed and trained to perform and/ or arrive at community dialogues, consensus and negotiations around: the characterisation and interpretation of environmental problems (Campaign 6), and the day-to-day practices people should perform to prevent pollution, to protect the environment, and to conserve the natural resources and wildlife (Campaign 7).

As for environmental problems, it was decided to have two ways of addressing them in practice: an approach to address various problems as a whole, where the role of synergy is important at the moment of characterising them

(Subcampaign 6.1); and a single-problem approach, so that they can individually be addressed with their own characteristics, effects, causalities, social factors and alternatives for solutions (Subcampaign 6.2).

The formal education system addressed the work from two perspectives: one aimed at helping to develop and strengthen the environmental education technical infrastructure in the schooling system of the region, such as: curriculum development, teacher training, educational materials production, and teachers' motivation to perform environmental communication and education in schools; and another aimed at putting the schools in contact with the communities to work out solutions in relation to environmental needs in which both parties can act.

Implementation and results

The management team in charge of the programme was composed of professionals from various sectors: communications (2), informal education (2), formal education (3), engineering of production processes (4) and environmental laws (1). All received intensive training on how to interpret the campaigns' designing process, how to implement them with the people's participation, and how to use feed-back to reorientate activities.

A parallel supervision system was mounted so as to analyse the performance of the planned activities and people's reactions to the programme implementation process.

The plan has been implemented in all its parts. The preliminary results have shown an outstanding participation and good reaction of people to the operational model and the working processes. The various programme's audiences do feel well assisted by the environmental communication and education programme. The production of communication instruments has been achieved, with high levels of people's participation and consultation. Pre-testing of materials and validation of them in practice have been important routine activities applied so far.

Other reports on the performance of the project have shown that people in the communities have been highly motivated to participate in the various actions suggested by the programme, as well as in getting interested in modifying their production processes from the environmental perspective. Some have even already initiated changes in various sectors of production and at home. However, more formal evaluation activity is needed; this is expected to take place next year, the mid-term of the implementation stage.

The main limitation found over the nine months of the implementation process was the lack of institutional support (from the Provincial Council) to encourage the implementation of the communities' initiatives around environmental projects brought out as a consequence of the communication and education programme.

The cost of the overall programme in the first year has been US\$ 270,000, financed by the Interamerican Development Bank (IDB) to the Provincial Council of Pichincha.

Marco A. Encalada PhD is General Manager of Corporación OIKOS, Luxemburgo 172y Holanda, Quito, Ecuador.

GREECE

BY ELISSAVET TSALIKI

The international debate that took place in the 1970s about the need for environmental education had its effect on the education system here in Greece, though this came relatively late in comparison with other European countries. At this early stage, it took the form of some infusion of basic ecological concepts into the prescribed school textbooks for subjects such as science. However, it is arguable that the official introduction of environmental education in Greece happened in 1980, when the Council of Europe organised in Athens a training programme for approximately 30 Greek teachers by European experts. This directly resulted in four schools joining an experimental network of 20 European schools working on a project 'Protection of the Seashores' in 1982. This subsequently led to the Ministry of Education organising a series of training seminars in different parts of Greece, where the experiences of the four schools were presented. Those first seminars were important, as they actually established the way in which environmental education would develop in Greece, by offering comprehensive training that enskilled and motivated teachers sufficiently to go back to their schools and practise environmental education.

Today, 15 years later, I would contend that those seminars determined the kind of methodological approach adopted here. Greek schools have embraced project-based work, a way of working that, when properly applied, is generally accepted as both holistic and successful. What is more, it had the additional benefit of enthusing those teachers who were looking for innovatory approaches in their everyday school life. The teachers felt that, through environmental education that was encouraged by the Ministry of Education, these approaches were legitimised to the mutual benefit of environmental education, the pupils, the teacher and the school.

That said, and despite the ministry's favourable and supportive attitude, probably the worst enemy of environmental education is the Greek education system itself. The extremely centralised and compartmentalised nature of this system which, by tradition, demands that the single textbook and the lone teacher be accepted as the only source of information, mitigates against local issues, for example, being chosen as a topic for study. It is not easy to allow space for inter-disciplinary projects where such a strict timetable exists. This fact has created conflicts and problems from the very beginning that still exist, and will continue to exist until the philosophy for the type of school changes, a real reform of the curricula, happens and a more flexible timetable is introduced. Because of these difficulties, the development of an environmental education programme, which almost exclusively takes place outside the prescribed timetable in what might be termed an 'extra hour option slot', requires lots of effort, energy and often disputes with the school authorities by the teacher. That said, the fact that teachers volunteer to take on the responsibility for environmental education helps it to be taught with enthusiasm.

Despite this, important initiatives have occurred since 1980. A law was passed in 1990 that recognised environmental education as part of the primary and secondary curricula. The law states that environmental education should help students to become aware of the relationship between man and nature, and the social environment in which they live. It should make them aware of environmental problems, and help them, through specific programmes, to play their own part in the solution of them. Another development that helped in the dissemination and decentralisation of environmental education was the secondment of teachers from their schools to local education offices in each county of Greece, where they have the responsibility for helping teachers locally to develop their own projects. This has been the stimulus for more in-service training seminars and increased co-operation with organisations at a local level. A further encouraging initiative was the opening in 1993 of an experimental environmental education centre by the ministry. This was followed in 1996 by the establishment of another six environmental education centres located in different parts of the country.

The initiatives detailed above have all contributed to an increase in the amount of in-service courses held locally, and a subsequent rise in the number of teachers participating in at least some fundamental training. Although there is no one set pattern for this work, a typical example would include lectures dealing with the theory and methodology of environmental education, lectures concerning environmental problems and the presentation of good examples of school projects. Additionally, if the seminar lasts two to three days, the teachers participate in fieldwork exploring the local environment in groups, culminating in the presentation of their experiences to their peers. There are also, although sadly too few, examples of training courses that involve teachers in directly experiencing different active methodologies and which encourage the teachers to use them in their environmental education projects. To assist in-service training in all areas of the curriculum, the state has recently established a network of 'Regional Training Centres', which allows teachers to participate in courses in their free time, in return for some minor remuneration, and includes environmental education in its programme.

During this period, the university sector has also been active in providing some courses for practising teachers in various parts of Greece. Encouragingly, environmental education is now included in the curricula of the university education departments for initial training, although the time specified for this work is woefully brief. This in turn has acted as a stimulus for research which has started to appear in the form of PhDs or research projects at national or international level. Eventually this may lead to the production of resource materials for schools.

The final piece in the jigsaw of teacher training is that provided by the NGOs. Although these tend to be small and underresourced in comparison with some European countries, their contribution is nonetheless significant. Indeed, some very good resource materials have been produced by such organisations. Amongst them is the 'Panhellenic Association of Teachers of Environmental Education', which has helped enormously to create a communications network between teachers all over Greece, to publicise their work, to host in its magazine critical debates and to support the development of new methodologies through the courses it organises.

To conclude, it is arguable that here in Greece there is now a background of accumulated experience. I would contend that this needs to be assessed in the context of the selection of content and the methodological approaches used in the school projects. More in-depth, quality training has to be made available for more teachers, and help should be given to aid research and the development of appropriate resource materials. Above all, courageous steps need to be made by the state towards a real reform of the curricula and the educational system.

Elissavet Tsaliki graduated from the Aristotelian University of Thessaloniki in Greece. She has worked extensively in the field of environmental education (project development, teacher training and research), and is currently based at an urban environmental education centre in Thessaloniki.

HONG KONG

BY ROGER P.K. HO

Origins and development of environmental education in Hong Kong

At the school level, environmental education started as ecological studies in subjects such as biology and geography where scientific knowledge is not presented in a problematic way and reflection was therefore discouraged. Yet elements of environmental education can be found in social science as well as science subjects, and overall development of environmental education remained slow in the early 1980s. At the community level, three pressure groups – Green Power, Conservancy Association and Friends of the Earth – are regarded as the pioneers in environmental education in Hong Kong.

The launch of the White Paper on *Pollution in Hong Kong: A Time to Act* (Hong Kong Government, 1989) had actually served as a bench mark for change: it spelt out clearly government determination in environmental protection through regulatory and educational means. The White Paper noted the low level of environmental awareness in Hong Kong, and the low level of spending by the government (only $0.4 million between 1984 and 1989), aimed at stimulating awareness, explaining government programmes for improving the environment, and encouraging public participation in improvement efforts. Following publication of the White Paper, there has been a substantial increase in funding, from several sources, for programmes to increase public awareness and harness the community's own contributions to reducing pollution. Perhaps the most significant development of environmental education in the 1990s is the publication and distribution of the *Guidelines on Environmental Education in Schools* in 1992. This was the first official document that set out the aims and direction of implementation of environmental education in schools. After the White Paper, a new subject, Environmental Studies, was introduced at senior secondary level.

Environmental education in Hong Kong: definition, teaching styles, learning styles, curriculum pattern

Definition

There is no independent subject for environmental education in Hong Kong schools. Environmental education is understood as a cross-curricular theme: each subject area of the school curriculum focuses on and explores different aspects of human understanding and experience of the environment. Within this interpretation, the way to measure the success of environmental education is not given and the 'learning' produced is therefore not assured, i.e. no one assesses how students come to see, understand, appreciate or feel about the environment. Moreover, as a non-examinable subject, its success is further not assured because environmental education is often marginalised in schools.

Teaching styles

Didactic and teacher-centred approaches still predominate in lessons. Teachers still follow traditional and resource-based strategies in teaching selected topics of environmental education. Lengthy examination syllabuses may encourage teachers to resort to traditional pedagogical approaches such as lecturing or exposition, which are perceived to be safer and more efficient, and do not require the support of resources. There is a general lack of issue-based approach, discussion of value elements and action-learning when teaching environmental topics (Cheng, 1994). Strategies such as role-playing, games and simulation games, which can help pupils examine environmental decision-making and the attitudes and values influencing these decisions, receive less emphasis from teachers. External and internal examinations have not emphasised the assessment of attitudes and values of concern towards the environment. There is a fear by the teachers that the adoption of an integrated approach might lower the pass rate of examinations, as students might not be able to make the necessary intellectual adjustment.

Curriculum pattern

Hong Kong has a centralised education system, but with a *laissez-faire* approach to curriculum implementation (Morris, 1992). Teachers mainly determine the pace of lessons and the contents of teaching (although we have a syllabus for schools that teachers have to cover). Inflexible timetable arrangements are also an important constraint in carrying out fieldwork.

Higher education and community levels

All conventional tertiary institutes in Hong Kong are active in expanding environmental education, with a variety of environmental-related courses delivered by different levels of study programmes. However, related teacher training is confined to catering for the needs of science and social science teachers. As regards initial teacher education in environmental education in Hong Kong, the University of Hong Kong and the Chinese University of Hong Kong prepare graduate teachers through the Post-Graduate Certificate in Education and the Post-Graduate Diploma respectively. These programmes offer elective courses in Environmental Education that adopt a cross-curricular perspective. It exists as a compulsory module in only the Bachelor of Education course for the social science teachers in both universities. Apparently there is the absence of any mandated courses for all teachers. The contribution of the Colleges of Education to developing environmental education (now combined as the Hong Kong Institute of Education), which provide initial training of non-graduate teachers for the primary–lower secondary section through a Teacher's Certificate programme, is relatively small.

Environmental programmes at community level – involving the Environmental Campaign Committee, a growing number of green groups, youth associations, educational institutions, and a new Environment and Conservation Fund together with a parallel private sector fund set up by the Wheelock group – have had some success; but their activities have lacked co-ordination and focus, with no input from communication professionals on ways to stimulate community action to complement the very large sums spent by the government to control pollution and provide an environmental infrastructure. NGOs like the WWF have produced a number of teaching materials to support the implementation of environmental education in schools. Also, a resource centre for environmental education has been established.

The Student Environmental Protection Ambassador Scheme launched by the Environmental Campaign Committee involves 220 schools; and 250 schools take part in a Waste Paper Recycling Scheme (Planning, Environment and Lands Branch, 1996). Other public programmes include the Community Tree Planting Scheme, summer Forestry Work Camps, a Forest Adoption Project, the Clean and Green Scheme, and Greening for the Chest.

Responsibility for Environmental Education

The Hong Kong Government has pledged to pump more funds into environmental education programmes, and business corporations are all too ready to build up a green image for themselves by funding environmental education activities. Schools are considered to be important vehicles for implementing environmental education. Environmental education has become a hot topic in Hong Kong society. Teachers, staff of environmental groups, bureaucrats and others are more open to different and sometimes contradictory philosophical influences from the environmental programmes that they undertake, i.e. they are exposed to different meanings and definitions of environmental education. It should be borne in mind that other professionals such as environmental protection officers, town planners, lawyers and health practitioners etc. could aim at more involvement in the monitoring and control of the quality of environmental education programmes that are taking place in various sectors in the society.

Significant research programmes

Most of the educational research programmes in Hong Kong are quantitative in nature and tend to focus on 'teaching styles' (Yeung, 1995; Wong and Stimpson, 1994). An examination of the journals and publications within the field reveals that the language, methods and approach of studies reflect the role played by, and the value attached to, scientific research within this area of environmental education research. In many cases, researchers are often too self-limiting in the exploratory study they have undertaken, and the potential of these 'exploratory' studies are not always fully explored, using a variety of methodologies.

Prospects

There are two challenges ahead. Firstly, it is for environmental educators to make environmental education happen in schools, and in a more organised and effective way. There are many environment-related activities in schools at present; perhaps it is a transition period for 'environmental education' in Hong Kong from *quantity* to *quality*. We have worked hard in the past years to encourage and facilitate programmes and materials. Now it is time to make a clear movement towards education *for* the environment by having a strategy of support for schools to explore innovative approaches. School support services with a strong academic base for a broad approach to environmental education are essential. Secondly, too few people in the population at large have the chance to receive environmental education. Environmental education at community level has to benefit more from information technology so that the audience base would be enlarged and, furthermore, consumer-orientated education should be an innovative approach of environmental education with emphasis on personal ethics and participation of the public in policy decisions and value choice. Researchers should not get caught in the single approach of 'quantitative research by manipulating variables'. It should be understood and expected that more qualitative research, or a combination of both quantitative and qualitative techniques, will enhance the development of environmental education.

References

Cheng, Wai-mun V. (1994) 'Implementation of Environmental Education through the Teaching of S4–S5 Biology, Geography and History in Hong Kong Secondary Schools', unpublished M.Ed. thesis, Hong Kong: University of Hong Kong, Faculty of Education.
Hong Kong Government (1989) White Paper: *Pollution in Hong Kong: A Time to Act*, Hong Kong: Government Printer.
Morris, P. (1992) *Curriculum Development in Hong Kong, Education Papers 7*, Hong Kong: University of Hong Kong, Faculty of Education.
Planning, Environment and Lands Branch (1996) *Heading Towards Sustainability: The Third Review of Progress on the 1989 White Paper: Pollution in Hong Kong: A Time to Act*, Hong Kong: Government Printer.
Wong, E.M.O. and Stimpson, P. (1994) 'Teaching Styles of Hong Kong's Environmental Educators in Secondary Schools', *Research in Education*, 52 1–12.
Yeung, S.P.M. (1995) 'Environmental Consciousness and Geography Teaching in Hong Kong: An Empirical Study', *Environmental Education and Information*, 14 (2) 171–194.

Roger P.K. Ho has worked in the field of curriculum development for environmental education in Hong Kong and other developing countries. He is currently a PhD student in Environmental Education at the University of Cambridge Department of Education, 17 Trumpington Street, Cambridge CB2 1QA, UK.

LATVIA

BY DIANA SHULGA

The present-day educational system in the Republic of Latvia is based on the Education Act of 1991 (though amendments to this are on-going).

The Ministry of Education is responsible for the governmental school system and it also co-ordinates newly established private schools, whilst local school boards have independence in decision-making on practical (including administrative and economic) matters (Meza, 1996).

Until very recently, environmental education has had no official status or documentation. Traditionally, elementary school pupils (Grades 1–4) have undertaken 'nature studies', whilst any inclusion of environmental education activities beyond this stage has tended to derive from individual teachers' enthusiasms – notably teachers of biology, chemistry and physics. Meza (1996) reports as a result of an investigation of primary schools in Latvia that 90 per cent of teachers identified a need to incorporate environmental education into the curriculum far more extensively, and to develop it as an inter-disciplinary field – augmenting existing out-of-school activities such as hikes, camps, excursions and so on.

Now we are in an important period of transition, and a great deal of activity and development is taking place at a variety of levels: internationally, nationally and locally. In the autumn of 1996, draft guidelines for environmental education in primary education (Grades 5–9) were published and introduced into schools by the Republic of Latvia Ministry of Education and the Science Centre for Education Content and Examination. Thus the school year 1996/97 (as this book goes to press) is the first test year when schools are asked to send in their opinions and remarks on the proposal. This initiative builds upon previous action in 1994 when a Draft Concept of Environmental Education was offered to the Ministry of Education by three active environmental education NGOs – namely the University of Latvia Ecological Centre, the Children's Environmental School and the Society for Nature Conservation. This Concept was utilised in the development of the national guidelines, illustrating how NGOs in Latvia have been a driving force behind the planning for implementation of environmental education into the formal education system

Within the guidelines document, environmental education is defined as a cross-curricular education theme, i.e. as an approach to education rather than a discrete subject with clearly specified content. It is made clear that environmental education should incorporate aspects of education 'about' the environment, 'in' the environment and 'for' the environment. (Other related cross-curricular themes taught in schools in Latvia include health education and global education.)

So we eagerly await the responses to the guidelines introduction; though it must be emphasised that whilst teachers may be enthusiastic and the documentation is in place, schools still face and will no doubt be facing for a long time the problem of a lack of appropriate resource materials.

Alongside this important effort by the ministry and NGOs to establish and promote environmental education in the formal education system, other important initiatives are also taking place:

- An Association of Environmental Educators in Latvia was founded two years ago in order to bring together educators committed to working in this field. As the Association is still young, its membership numbers are small so it cannot be considered as a significant influence yet; but nevertheless its establishment represents a very important development.
- Schools in Latvia are involved in several national and international environmental education projects. Some widely known international ones of which Latvian schools are a part include 'The Baltic Sea Project', 'Air Pollution Project Europe' and 'School Project on Saving Energy and Resources'.*
- The University of Latvia Centre for Environmental Science and Management

Studies (UL CESAMS) provides MSc degree programmes in environmental pedagogics for teachers in general and vocational schools who are working or interested in this field.

- The vocational school system has been working on the introduction of environmental education into their curriculum since early 1996.
- A National School student Olympiad of Environmental Projects is organised annually by the Ministry of Education, involving other institutions in the field.
- Environmental education at the community level has developed extensively over the past 10 years. The importance of the role of the local community and of the use of community resources in environmental education has been identified and emphasised as an ongoing topic for discussion and action among educators, local authorities, regional planners and other community-based organisations and individuals. Indeed it has been recognised that it is members of a community who manage interactions between different components of the environment – natural, social, economic, cultural and historic – at a local level, and therefore involvement and awareness of each individual community member is essential in terms of sustainable development of the community. Only a minority of communities in Latvia have so far developed their 'Local Agenda 21s', but significant initiatives are being undertaken with schools. In order to encourage community-orientated Environmental Education in Latvian schools, the University of Latvia Ecological Centre has undertaken several environmental education projects with a community focus. One project, for example, aims to use community-based environmental education as a tool for raising student awareness of local issues and for raising self-esteem relating to personal involvement and action. This project involves Dagda Secondary School and is a part of an international project on Environmental Education initiated by the European Commission and the European Secondary Heads Association. Its aims are:

1 To encourage school students to explore their natural environment;
2 To encourage students to learn about the cultural and historic environment and to appreciate their heritage;
3 To evaluate advantages and disadvantages of their particular community and find reasons for both;
4 To find their future role and place to play in the development of their community;
5 To generate ideas on different environmental, social and economic problem-solving to share with the local municipality;
6 To find the motivation for further education to be able to contribute to the further development of the community.

This provides a brief insight into one test project currently run in co-operation between two educational establishments, i.e. university and school, and very positive results are expected * (for further details see also Shulga, 1996).

- UL CESAMS is engaged in a major project that links the Ministries of Education in Latvia and Norway in the development of the integration of environmental education into school subjects and the development of a multidisciplinary team project method as an approach to environmental education in Latvian schools. This substantial project aims to promote the development of environmental education in Latvia, focusing on pedagogical methods involved in school and class projects that successfully implement an integrated cross-curricular approach. It is featured as a case study within Part IV of this text.

In conclusion, Latvia is at an exciting stage in the development of its provision of environmental education at all levels. Most importantly, the need for it is recognised at national (government and NGO) levels, teachers are supportive and enthusiastic, and a number of influential initiatives are in progress, including those that involve local community involvement and action.

References

Meza, L. (1996) 'Environmental Education in Primary Schools of Latvia', in R. Wikstrom (ed.) *Implementation of Environmental Education in the Community*. Proceedings of the 5th European Conference on Environmental Education in Europe, 22–27 October 1996, Mid Sweden University, Sweden.

Shulga, D. (1996) 'Community Based Environmental Education School Projects and European Dimension: Possibilities and Practice in Latvia', in R. Wikstrom (ed.) *Implementation of Environmental Education in the Community*. Proceedings of the 5th European Conference on Environmental Education in Europe, 22–27 October 1996, Mid Sweden University, Sweden.

* Further details of these projects and initiatives are available from the author, as detailed below

Diana Shulga MSc is Head of the Environmental Education Department at the University of Latvia Ecological Centre, Raina Blvd. 19, Riga, LV-1586, Latvia.

ROMANIA

BY IULIAN MIHNEA

Introduction

We Romanians are privileged to be located on the 45th parallel, meaning in the middle of Europe.

The pollution of the environment is multilateral. We have the pollution of the land, of the waters (surface and sub-surface) and pollution of the air. All this is a man-made pollution, that is, through man's activity. We have the hope that with a proper knowledge and attitude towards the environment, man can decrease the damage now and prevent it for the future. That means that education has a big part to play in improving the environment.

Background facts

Area:	238.291 km²
Population:	22,854,622 at the last census (1992) and decreasing
The country is divided into:	41 (*Judete*) counties
Number of towns:	260
Number of communes:	2,688
The agricultural area is:	14,793,062 hectares, 62 per cent of the total
Forestry takes from the area:	6,681,057 hectares, about 28 per cent of the total

The other 10 per cent consists of waters, cities, villages, roads.

Let us now return to pollution. This is the result of floods, waters released by industry, cities' sewerage, and agricultural complexes that specialise in animal farming. All this is seriously damaging the environment. We can add: the inadequate storage of the industrial residues; inadequate city sewerage evacuation; rural farm complexes; and, even worse: places that deal with pollutants and do not have sewerage at all, as in many places in the rural area. On top of all this we have pollution from the petrol extraction from the soil. This pollution includes petrol itself and salty water. We have mines of all kinds and resultant damage to the environment. We find erosion of the soil, flooding and creation of swamps, quagmires and areas of marshy ground. The soil in these places becomes acidified and saltified, and then the deficit of humidity becomes apparent.

The formal educational process

The schooling system of Romania, organised on a modern basis, has evolved ever since the government of Alexander Ioan Cuza, the first power holder of the united Romania. The schooling system has gone through three stages:

- The first stage: from the creation of the modern Romania, after the War of Crimea (1856–1859) and the peace treaty that followed, until the end of the Second World War (1945).
- The second stage: from the end of the first stage until the Romanian Revolution on 21 December 1989.
- The third stage: beginning December 1989 until now.

The schooling system has included, with small differences, in all its stages: a kindergarten stage; the primary school (grades 1–4); middle stage named 'Gymnasia' (grades 5–8); and secondary school or 'lyceum' (grades 9–12). Beyond this it is possible to undertake professional studies (for apprenticeship in a profession) or to follow superior studies such as medicine and agronomy in universities.

The educational process has included, along with basic matters, aspects of environmental protection, especially relating to agriculture. During the first stage of development of schooling, a key contribution in the educational process came from the villages, agricultural schools and pedagogical schools which prepared teachers for working with grades 1–4. In the villages, priests worked together with teachers, following the same goal.

They organised, especially in the winter, conferences and lessons, and discussed with the people practical problems of their lives, including farming issues.

The second stage of organised schooling system was influenced by the philosophy of the Soviet schooling system. Close to the year 1980 one could see a remarkable difference from the first stage: the technical secondary schools were greatly developed but care for the environment was forgotten. We left the West to deal with such 'small matters'. Only after 1975–1980, under the influence of actions on a global scale, were courses introduced for the preparation of the staff to deal with pollution problems and the economical implications of their damages.

After this time the schools' curriculum changed to include details of preventing ecological calamities (disasters) and the protection of the environment (e.g. how to avoid drought, flood, erosion of soil and other damages).

In the third stage (after the revolution) the educational process has developed considerably. Alongside the state system of education, private institutions have appeared which have involved themselves in an education of the population that does not neglect their everyday lives and practical activities.

So, in the kindergarten stage of schooling a weekly hour has been introduced with lessons and explanations about how the environment must be protected. In the curriculum for the primary school, an hour is also provided for general knowledge of ecology and environmental protection. Biology in the secondary school includes concepts of ecology (definition, ecosystems, types of ecosystems, biosphere). In the eleventh grade pupils study 'geography of the surroundings'. Courses teach the pupils notions about the environment around us, what it is made of, the relation between the component elements, the influence of human activity on the environment around us and priority areas for the protection and conservation of the environment.

The 'superior learning' curriculum includes environmental engineering, disciplines that deal with the protection of the environment, civilian constructions, industrial and hydrotechnics, machinery, mines, etc.

The role of the public services, companies and NGOs

The protection of the environment in Romania is a state problem under the supervision of the Ministry of Water, Forests and Environment Protection and the Commission for the Protection of Natural Monuments from the Romanian Academy. 'Agencies of supervising and protection of the environment' are established and working at the *Judet* level (the administrative form of the land division). At present 41 agencies that deal with the protection of the soil, sub-soil and terrestrial ecosystems have imposed adequate measures of territorial management, conservation and planning that shall be compulsory for all landholders according to the law for environmental protection. To make sure that the process of education is thoroughly observed and the protection of agricultural land is implemented, a great number of state institutes or public institutions (for research, planning, development) are involved together with non-governmental and private organisations and research institutes. A number of consulting institutes such as ISPIF (see below) organise courses relating to agricultural science and conservation. These are for people coming from nearby villages or groups of villages named *Comuna*. This form of teaching is approved and sustained by the Ministry of Waters, Forests and Environment Protection and help is provided through the local agency for Environment Protection and Supervising at the *Judet* level. Other essential work is done by NGOs, Ecological Foundations and the Professional Ecological Associations. At present the number of NGOs that engage in key activities in the field of environment protection is four to six associations per administrative division of land (*Judet*). The aims of the NGOs are:

- to put into practice the ecological achievements;
- to protect natural resources;
- to sound the alarm against pollutions;
- to protect the zones already polluted;
- to clean the areas affected by pollution;
- to clean areas with polluted water;

The Ecological Foundations (10–15 of them) have a wider scope for environment protection. One of them, the Ecological National Foundation for Environment Protection, has as its primary aim the promotion of new technologies for Environmental Protection in Romania.

The Professional Ecological Associations, staffed with specialists in environmental engineering and young students, are focusing on environmental improvement in rural areas.

All that has been said up to now is still far from what is needed at a practical level, so let us turn to an example of a planned project.

Proposal for the organisation of a schooling system in the Vrancea administrative land (*Judet*)

The villages of this district maintain the traditions of thousands of years of the Romanian people. The land has been seriously exploited and degraded. A consulting institute (ISPIF) is trying to help the people of this land and has applied to the Vrancea Agency for the Supervising and Protecting of the Environment together with the town of Focsani to enable the mayors (heads of local administration) and researchers from three villages to establish three educational centres for putting into practice agricultural knowledge, its ecological content, and measures for environmental protection for the three characteristic forms of landscape (mountain, hills and plains). The teaching will be attended also by specialists who hold positions in the villages and by children (kindergarten and primary school children). Youngsters and old people from these settlements are also invited to attend these courses. Alongside the educational programmes it is intended to achieve the following practical goals:

- the preparation of the platforms for compost-making;
- sanitation;
- the construction of platforms for the growth of worms;
- the provision of drinking water in a centralised form;
- the execution of the installation of a familial type: Biogas;
- the working of a plot of land in an ecological manner.

Together with all this in the communes (the smallest land administration), an educational programme to improve the sanitation level of the people living there will be created in Focsani town. It is the hope that this project will successfully link theory with practice in environmental education in Romania.

Iulian Mihnea PhD is an Adviser Engineer with ISPIF Engineering and Consulting Company and Associate Professor, Bucharest.

SLOVENIA

BY BARBARA BAJD

The present situation

Slovenia is a young country: originally the most northerly republic of the former Yugoslavia. It declared independence in June 1991. However, its distinctive education system and curricula pre-date independence. In 1983 environmental education was purposely included within the country's programme of elementary and secondary education. The basic document governing the curriculum is *The Programme of Life and Work for Elementary School*, devised on the recommendations of the Ministry of Education and Sport. The document sets out the general aims and content of the elementary schools syllabus, as well as the organisational forms and approaches by which these can be implemented.

Elementary school in Slovenia (or primary school) includes classes (year groups) 1–4, and lower secondary school classes 5–8. Environmental education is not organised as a separate subject in primary schools, but some of its elements are integrated in different broad subject areas such as science and social studies. Teaching in lower secondary schools is on a subject basis.

Educational reforms of upper secondary schools (gymnasia) in 1980 and vocational secondary schools in 1981 legislated for the introduction of ecological topics within different areas of the curriculum. Biology as a core subject was included, with some basic areas (cytology, life processes and general ecology) taught within the curriculum of vocational secondary schools.

In general, besides core subjects, upper secondary students select options in, for example, animal and plant systems, genetics or ecology, together with associated fieldwork. Every pupil therefore has the opportunity to acquire at least basic ecological knowledge. School legislation in Slovenia and the curriculum require all schools and their teachers to plan and work on a range of projects – in part fieldwork based – with an ecological content, and emphasising environmental conservancy and nature protection. Such projects extend the range of ecological topics covered, and are of greater variety than the specific attainment targets within the curriculum.

Since 1993 Field Centres have been established in Slovenia; they are currently organised as semi-independent institutions, directly financed by the Ministry of Education and Sport. Field Centres cover a range of activities – sport, climbing, cycling, survival skills, social activities, skiing, etc. There are currently 10 Field Centres, with an eventual 20 planned. They are located in different places around Slovenia (in the mountains, near lakes, at the sea coast, etc.), both to allow proximity for all school children, and to reflect the varied land forms in the country.

All the Centres are residential, very well equipped, and can accommodate 40–50 pupils at any one time. The new (1996) educational legislation intends that each child from primary and secondary school spends one week on fieldwork, with the opportunity to participate in a variety of ecological and conservation projects.

There are also a number of Day Centres – at the zoo, the technical museum in Bistra, at the arboretum – that provide shorter courses on specific ecological topics.

New educational legislation, introduced in 1996 (see below), incorporates specific reference to nature education and environmental protection, so it can be expected that those involved in preparing new teaching programmes will necessarily define basic targets for nature education and protection within those programmes.

Within higher education the different faculties (e.g. the Biotechnical Faculty, Philosophical Faculty, Faculty of Natural Sciences and Engineering, etc.) provide first degree programmes which may include many aspects of ecology and associated areas of environmental and conservation science. Examples of subjects available for undergraduate study include: marine ecology; animal ecology; plant ecology; environmental science; protected area management; landscape ecology, etc. Most postgraduate studies in the field, including National Heritage

Protection and Environmental Protection, are inter-disciplinary and organised between faculties.

The School of Environmental Sciences in Nova Gorica, which opened in the academic year 1995/96, is the first such international postgraduate school in Slovenia. The school has the status of an independent faculty, and is a joint venture between the Nova Gorica municipality, and the Jozef Stefan Institute, Ljubljana. Last year there were 14 students, and this year about the same number. Maximum enrolment in any one year is deliberately limited to 20.

Prior to the 1996 educational reforms, the Board of Education was responsible for attainment targets in schools in Slovenia. The recent legislation has introduced new arrangements: The National Curricular Council is now responsible for oversight of curricula at all levels of education. Under the Council's auspices, separate Curricular Commissions, responsible for particular levels of school education (Curricular Commission for Nursery Schools; Curricular Commission for Elementary and for Secondary Schools, as well as for General and Vocational Secondary Schools, etc.), will prepare the guidelines for subject curricular commissions (mathematics; chemistry; biology, etc.) which in turn will plan and co-ordinate the content and levels of achievement in their individual subjects.

The main influence on the design of educational programmes and the responsible bodies for their implementation are the several educational commissions, which include experts from the different faculties and research institutes, as well as representatives of the schools, and the Board of Education. The Commission for Environmental Protection has overall responsibility for environmental education in Slovenia. Commission members include relevant specialists (biologists, chemists, psychologists, technical experts, etc.). Delivery of the programme in environmental education is also evaluated by the Ministry of Environment and Physical Planning, but this is not involved in curriculum planning or in achieving the attainment targets in schools.

In Slovenia there are over 100 NGOs with extensive and varied involvement in environmental activities. Most are primarily involved in environmental and nature-protection issues, and promoting sustainable development projects within Slovenia, while the remainder have been founded very recently. While some NGOs organise courses for teachers and fieldwork for pupils, these organisations have no direct or formal influence in the planning of environmental education.

The Regional Environmental Centre for Central and Eastern Europe (REC) is situated in Ljubljana. This commenced activity in 1993 and was officially opened in 1996. REC supports and facilitates NGOs for nature protection, provides some financial support, and serves as a link between Slovene organisations and international ones.

Within Slovenia there are numerous projects that influence the teaching of environmental education, especially in elementary schools. These include:

1 Environmental and School Initiatives Project (OECD/CERI) (see p. 116). In the second phase of this international programme, which ran from 1990 to 1994, Slovenia was one of 21 participating countries. In the project, participants from the Philosophical Faculty, Faculty of Education and Board of Education, and teachers and students from eight Slovenian elementary schools worked together. The pupils had an important role in selecting their environmental projects, as one of the central objectives was to develop their personal qualities, such as responsibility, independence and self-confidence. The third phase of this project is currently in preparation.

2 The Board of Education is working on a project 'From the Environment to the Environment', the results of which will help to plan a new curriculum for the first six years of education.

3 'Education for Environmental Protection.' This is a joint project between the Faculty of Education, University of Ljubljana, and the School of Education, University of Durham, England. The collaboration is part of an international network of related projects involving participating institutions from many different countries, directed by Dr Joy Palmer at Durham.

Prospects

Public awareness of environmental education, nature conservancy, environmental protection and sustainable development has increased considerably in recent years. Within the formal structures of Slovenian education the prospects for the immediate future are :

- That environmental education will form part of the national curricula for all schools in Slovenia.
- That the national curriculum will promote fieldwork studies and that as much environmental education as possible will be through 'hands on' projects.
- That all pupils will have a sound base of knowledge of the environment and nature protection, and ecological issues generally, so as to secure Slovenia's future development in environmentally safe and responsible directions.
- That researchers will continue to engage in collaborative national and international projects.

Acknowledgements

I thank Irena Perenič and Sonja Artač from the Board of Education of Slovenia for providing data for this report.

Barbara Bajd PhD is an Assistant Professor at the Faculty of Education, University of Ljubljana, Kardeljeva ploscad 16, 61000 Ljubljana, Slovenia.

SOUTH AFRICA

BY CALLIE P. LOUBSER

Development of the concept in South Africa

Environmental conservation has probably been practised since earliest times in South Africa. Hugo (1993, pp. 43–45), for instance, argues that the indigenous people of Africa have been utilising the environment wisely through the ages. This statement is not agreed upon by everybody, because of the fact that some people also see the actions of hunter-gatherers as environmentally harmful. We do not know, therefore, whether any active environmental education was provided in those days. It seems likely that the study, practice and definition of environmental education in South Africa began to take shape only fairly recently. Irwin (1990, p. 6) maintains that environmental education in South Africa has gained momentum over the past 15 (by now 20) years and has reached a level where individuals and organisations can play a significant role in the solution of environment crises.

From its small beginnings, environmental education has grown into a movement that is attracting the attention not just of the general public but increasingly of formal educationists as well. Many agencies are involved in environmental education today and one can draw up a long list of environmental education projects. The first international congress on environmental education in South Africa was held at Mooi River in 1982, and by now several environmental education congresses are held annually. One of the first organisations to become active in environmental education was the Wildlife Society of Southern Africa, which launched the Umgeni Valley Project in Natal in 1973. This project designed the first teaching materials for environmental education in South Africa and also promoted co-operation between organisations in the non-formal education sector (the former Natal Parks Board) and the formal education sector (the former Natal Education Department). Nowadays there are many other organisations that undertake environmental education projects. In Soweto thousands of teachers, children and youths participate in environmental education programmes arranged by the National Environmental Awareness Council (NEAC). In Mpumalanga Province, Ecolink is running important holistic environmental education programmes for the local population. Many other community projects have also started.

Before the Wildlife Society started with environmental education, educational actions were limited to conservation education, and conservation was seen simply as the wise management of natural resources and basic ecology (Irwin, 1990, p. 4). People moreover considered environmental education as a synonym for various other concepts such as *ecology, outdoor education, biology and nature conservation*. Although it includes all these aspects, the concept *environmental education* today is seen as a much broader concept.

As far as formal training is concerned, environmental education courses were first offered at the former University of Bophuthatswana. The Universities of Rhodes and Stellenbosch followed suit, and nowadays several other universities, such as the University of South Africa, offer environmental education in their teacher training courses. Certain teacher training colleges are also taking note of this important field of teaching. Consequently, the list of universities and colleges that teach environmental education is growing steadily. In the non-formal education sector several environmental education centres offer facilities to schools that want to take part in their programmes. From the aforementioned it is clear that there is growing interest in environmental education in South Africa and that teachers, as well as people in the private sector who are involved in education, formal or non-formal, cannot delay its inclusion in their teaching programmes any longer.

Inclusion of environmental education in formal education in South Africa

People involved in environmental education in South Africa decided that, apart from the significant work done in this field by government agencies, environmental education should take its place in formal education too. The Department of Environment Affairs and Tourism and the Environmental Education Association of Southern Africa (EEASA) decided to start a process to establish environmental education in the formal education set-up. As a result, a number of formal educationists gathered in 1993 to launch the process, which soon became known as the Environmental Education Policy Initiative. Since the process was to be a democratic one, as many stakeholders as possible were involved and regional workshops were run to introduce the project to people at grassroots level. This process also has implications for the non-formal sector. More communication between formal and non-formal education should take place.

Eventually, at a workshop held at Dikhololo near Brits in August 1993, the idea of including environmental education in formal education was discussed by leaders of all the major agencies involved. These agencies included all the education departments of the education system at the time (17 in total), members of the education desks of political parties, educational associations, members of progressive education movements like the National Education Co-ordinating Committee (NECC), student associations such as COSAS (Council of South African Students), university representatives and some individual stakeholders. The decision of the meeting was unanimous: the process had to continue and the existing working committee should run it.

The working committee had talks with the former Department of National Education and political parties such as the ANC. Members of the working committee ensured that environmental education was mentioned in the document on the Reconstruction and Development Programme (RDP) (ANC, 1993, p. 40), as well as the ANC discussion document on education (1994), and finally in the White Paper on Education (South Africa, 1995a, p. 18). The following statement in the White Paper is noteworthy:

> 20. Environmental education, involving an inter-disciplinary, integrated and active approach to learning, must be a vital element of all levels and programmes of the education training system, in order to create environmentally literate and active citizens and ensure that all South Africans, present and future, enjoy a decent quality of life through the sustainable use of resources.
>
> (South Africa, 1995a, p. 18)

Prior to these references, environmental education had merely been mentioned in passing as a possible cross-curricular theme in the Curriculum Model for South Africa (CUMSA) document (Department of National Education, 1991, p. 32). However, the document *Norms and Standards and Governance Structures for Teacher Education* (Committee on Teacher Education Policy [COTEP] 1995) contained a list of environmentally related requirements. Examples of such requirements are the following:

- Teacher education should enable the prospective teacher to develop skills such as the ability to develop a sense of environmental responsibility in students (p 9).
- Teacher education programmes should ensure that the teacher is able to:
  identify areas of knowledge, for example language and environmental education, which can contribute to a cross-curricular, integrated approach to learning (p. 18).
- Teacher education programmes for the secondary phase should ensure that the teacher will be able to:
  teach about environmental issues within the framework of their subjects and/or as a cross-curricular study (p. 29).

> (South Africa, 1995b)

These quotations indicate the importance of environmental education in teacher training.

At present, negotiations are on to determine the exact role and place of environmental education in the formal curriculum. A cross-curricular approach seems to be favoured, but the full implications of this should be researched. Some research projects to address this have started, but the need for further projects is evident.

References

ANC (1993) *The Reconstruction and Development Programme* (RDP), Johannesburg: Umanyano Publications.

ANC (1994) *Discussion Document on Education*, Pretoria: Government Printer.

Department of National Education (1991) *A Curriculum Model for South Africa*, Pretoria: Government Printer.

Hugo, A.J.W. (1993) 'African Traditions and Environmental Education', *South African Journal of Cultural History*, 7 (3) 43–45.

Irwin, P. (1984) 'The Origin and Development of Environmental Education: A World Perspective', *Southern African Journal of Environmental Education*, 1 7–9.

Irwin, P. (1990) 'The Concept of Environmental Education and the Development of Environmental Education in Southern Africa', *Southern African Journal of Environmental Education*, 11 3–7.

South Africa (Republic) (1995a) *White Paper on Education and Training*, Cape Town: Government Printer.

South Africa (Republic) (1995b) *Norms and Standards and Governance Structures for Teacher Education*, Committee on Teacher Education Policy (COTEP), Pretoria: Government Printer.

Callie P. Loubser PhD is a lecturer at the largest distance education university of South Africa – the University of South Africa, 392 Pretoria, 0001, Republic of South Africa.

SPAIN

BY SUSANA CALVO, JOSÉ GUTIERREZ AND JAVIER BENAYAS

Social and political context of the Spanish educational system

After 40 years of Franco's dictatorship (1936–1975), Spanish society set about building the transition to a modern society and a European democracy. Between 1978 and 1983, a total of 17 regions were established that have an autonomous status in the government and administration of the country. Each one of these *autonomous communities* has its own responsibilities and power to make decisions relating to management of the economy, health, social services, employment and education; yet each should follow some general framework established by the central government. In educational matters, the autonomous communities have powers relating to development and implementation of the curriculum, including full responsibilities for programmes, teaching content, appointment of teachers, provision and maintenance of school buildings, staff competencies, research, examinations and pre-service and in-service training of teachers. In 1990, an innovative law reformed the Spanish educational system (LOGSE). This law emphasises processes and attitudes rather than knowledge; it incorporates a constructivist view of the teaching and learning process, wherein the students have more autonomy and responsibility within their educational activities; and it gives parents greater capacity for decision-making relating to pupils' education. This law extends the period of compulsory schooling to the age of 16. It is being introduced at all levels of education in systematic stages.

One of the more innovative pedagogical ideas of the present curriculum is the introduction of cross-curricular subjects in order to connect school-based work with events and issues of the natural and social environments. Environmental education, health education, democracy education and equal opportunities are cross-curricular themes. *Environmental education* as a cross-curricular subject offers the possibility to work in an inter-disciplinary way and it provides a new opportunity to transform the traditional methodology of 'classic' subjects.

Environmental education in the formal education system

At the pre-primary (0–6 years) and primary school (6–12 years) stage, environmental education is not considered as a separate curriculum subject like mathematics, language or the natural sciences. Environmental education is an area of study whose contents are more related to life and social problems. The new education law incorporates environmental education as a cross-curricular subject, but it is not compulsory in schools at this level. Nevertheless, schools that choose to incorporate it into their curriculum planning receive more support (financial) and resources to develop specific projects on the environment. Each year the different regions organise a range of environmental activities including conferences, seminars, research projects, campaigns and celebrations in order to stimulate teachers', students' and parents' participation. The ALDEA programme in Andalusia is an example that has become a point of reference of this sort of initiative. (This includes activities such as 'put green in your class', 'green schools', 'grow with your tree'.) The role of environmental education in such projects is to suggest ways to reform and improve the curriculum in general and to make connections between school and life, classroom and community. Unfortunately, too few teachers have so far taken part in elaboration of the curriculum to include environmental activities – they are overburdened with the many other responsibilities required of them by the law.

In the secondary school (12–16 years), students follow five core 'speciality' subjects – science, humanities, art, new technologies and modern languages. At this stage, environmental education may be incorporated in one of three ways: as an optional subject for all students of the five core subjects; as a compulsory subject for all students whose speciality is science; or as a cross-curricular theme incorporated into the compulsory subjects with an inter-disciplinary methodology.

At the level of professional training, for students who will not be following a university course (post-16 years), two options are available: the 'professional modules' and the 'social guarantee programme'. In the first of these we find some technical programmes relating to the environment (e.g. expertise on environment for natural parks and forest, environmental health, agent for the community, tourist agent); and in the second is included training for such activities as gardening, farming and bricklaying, which obviously have environmental impact.

In post-secondary education, for two years after compulsory schooling (16–18 years), students may study optional subjects such as ecology and environmental issues, or may take a specific course on 'Sciences of the Earth and the Environment'.

During the past two decades, environmental education in the university sector has increased greatly. There has been a massive increase in masters' and doctoral courses, in seminars, conferences, research and optional subjects (see table below). There has been much strengthening in the place of environmental education in teacher education courses. For example, in each autonomous community, in-service training of teachers (through teacher centres) includes courses focused on environmental education methodology, constructivism as an approach to learning, environmental issues (pollution, problems of rivers, cities and industries, recycling techniques) and on skills to evaluate attitudes and cross-curricular subjects.

Educational level	Role of environmental education
Pre-primary (0–6) and Primary school (6–12)	Cross-curricular subject Multidisciplinary view Workshop activities Field trip and visits to natural centres
Secondary school (12–16)	Optional subject with inter-disciplinary view Compulsory subject for sciences specialty Cross-curricular enclosed into the classical compulsory subject Visits to natural parks and interpretation centres
Professional training (after 16)	Professional modules: expertise on environment for natural parks and forest, environmental health, tourist agent and agent of the community Social guarantee programmes: classical profession as gardener, farmer or bricklayer for old buildings
Post-secondary school (16–18)	Specific subject: Sciences of the Earth and the Environment Optional subject: ecology, EE, environment problems
University (after 18)	Optional subject in courses in sociology, political and juridical studies, psychology, economy, environment and health sciences, pedagogy, psychopedagogy and education degree Doctorate course, master, seminar, congress

Out of school environmental education

In Spain there are many possibilities for developing out of school studies, perhaps involving NGOs, ecologists' groups and Field Centres. The involvement of NGOs has increased in the past 10 years, coinciding with rising public awareness about environmental issues. There are currently some 150,000 people associated with some groups of national or international ecology associations (e.g. Greenpeace, WWF, Friends of the Earth, CODA). Such groups organise participatory activities, field trips, campaigns, publicity, and they collaborate with schools.

The opening of Field Centres in Spain is closely tied to the reconstruction and rehabilitation processes relating to farmhouses and ancient lordly mansions after the totalitarian regime. At the beginning of the democracy, some groups with reformist ideas in the political, social, economic and educational areas began to develop ambitious educational projects. A great variety of Field Centres proliferated (now around 500), including ecology centres, nature classrooms, interpretation centres and farm-schools. Between them they offer a collection of dynamic, active and participant possibilities to enjoy the environment and to generate conservationist attitudes towards it. During the 1980s, farm-schools became a prevailing model; the aim of these establishments is to introduce children and young adults to the traditions, forms of life and models of economic organisation of the rural environment. In the 1990s, the prevailing model is that of Environmental Interpretation Centres: structures destined basically to manage the public use of the protected natural spaces, to receive visitors and to provide environmental information.

The co-ordination of a national strategy on environmental education

Spain is making the institutional arrangements for a national environmental education strategy as proposed in *Agenda 21*. The main aim of this strategy is the co-ordination of the formal and non-formal programmes. This fact prompts an approach from different angles, with each environmental agency of the administration becoming responsible for defining its objectives and work programme. The agencies should think of environmental education as a tool for implementing their policies and not direct their efforts exclusively towards school programmes. A technical working group, with representation of the different autonomous communities, has the competencies to make a repertory of action being carried out in the field of environmental education nation-wide, analyse the data collected and prepare a plan for the implementation of an environmental education strategy for Spain that takes into account the limits of sustainable development. Another working group is trying to lay the foundations for environmental education within regional environmental administration agencies. This working group is also preparing guidelines for co-operation with working groups dealing with environmental education in the formal education system, and in the fields of health and consumer education. Work that is being done – or that could be done – in the field of environmental education by NGOs is being analysed by a third working group. The volunteer programmes and activities are an important part of this group. The forum constituted by the Spanish Commission on Environmental Education of IUCN–The World Conservation Union, in which government and NGO members participate on an equal footing, is also making an input to the creation of an environmental education strategy for Spain.

Popular participation in the solving of environmental problems in order to achieve sustainable development is the main objective of this general plan. This calls for a process of reflection with the widest possible public participation, in a way of participant-action-research with the collaboration of the various social sectors. For this process, the status of a horizontal communication and an active dialogue is the base of our skill. A government's key role is to facilitate the involvement of community groups with government and non-government organisations. The process of convergence in the working parties to arrive at a national strategy is important because it is in itself educative, and commits the participants to the future evolution of the programme. The objectives of the preparatory work are:

• To achieve by consensus a flexible statement, containing guidelines for environmental education within the limits of a project for sustainable development.
• To encourage all social sectors to take part in a common effort to improve relationships with the environment.
• To outline a plan that organises and arranges priorities in environmental education activities, now carried out in a sporadic and disorganised manner.
• To promote research into social behaviour and its effects on the environment.
• To rationalise the funding of projects and make the evaluations necessary to ensure that the objectives laid down are achieved.
• To define the social groups for preferred attention.
• To design and co-ordinate planning in the national and autonomic levels.

But a number of problems arise in trying to implement a national strategy on environmental education in a systematic and dynamic way. In particular is the change to the decentralisation model of autonomous regions, and the differences between the environmental and cultural situation in the 17 autonomic regions, which leads to different ways of looking at the role of environmental education. Also there is a variety of competencies in the administration, which sometimes gives rise to a fragmented view of the environment. It is also necessary to develop research about the evaluation of activities or programmes to see how the objectives are attained. Evaluation is the key to improved programming. The power and efficacy of education will be realised as programmes are evaluated, the results reported to all concerned, and the information used to make future educational decisions even better. To define some empirical indicators and standards of quality in environmental education, we need the research in a qualitative or quantitative view to measure or identify tangible or intangible results of the environmental projects.

Conclusion

What has been achieved during the past two decades in the field of environmental education has clearly been limited because of both space and time. Yet the future looks optimistic: new initiatives will learn from past mistakes. And indeed, past achievements are numerous: more than 200 books focused on environmental education, four specific autonomous associations, more than 15,000 educators with direct or indirect competencies in the field, more than 20 doctoral theses, 15 universities with specific environmental degree subjects, five masters' programmes, three international congresses, 10 international conferences, more than 20 autonomic meetings and around a dozen research groups that focus on environmental education together add up to a solid platform for further developments. The prospects are good for collective effort and achievements.

Susana Calvo is at the Evaluation and Information Department of the Environmental Ministry, Plaza San Juan de la Cruz 28071, Madrid. She was a member of the working group to prepare the Spanish national strategy in environmental education.

José Gutierrez PhD is Associate Professor in the Educational Research Methodology Department of Granada University, Faculty of Education, Campus de Cartuja s/n, 18071 Granada, Spain.

Javier Benayas is Associate Professor in the Dept de Ecologiá, Módulo C-XV Facultad de Ciencias, Universidad Autónoma de Madrid, 28049 Madrid.

SRI LANKA

BY MARJORIE PERIES

Sri Lanka has a long and varied history of cultural development dating back 2,500 years. It is a history also of the development of kingship and a history of wars and social upheavals. The north central plain was the first centre of government when large cities such as Polonnaruwa and Anuradhapura developed. A visitor even today can visualise the 'greatness' of the past when viewing the ruins there. As the centuries progressed, constant invasions from India led to a drift to the south-west of the country where new cities were established. The rulers even in those early times were aware of the need to preserve the environment. Vast tracts of jungle land were kept intact. The central hill country, which is thickly forested, was kept untouched. This was the source of many of the country's important rivers. The beautiful waterfalls and streams helped to feed the great tanks or lakes constructed by the kings in the old capitals. There are specially marked forest reserves in Sigirya, Mihintala, Kataragama and Maligawila, and today the most well known are the Udawatta Kele in Kandy and the Sinha Raja Forest. In many of the old books and stone inscriptions attention is paid to the need to maintain forests. This clearly shows that environmental education of a kind was carried out even then.

Colonial policy

The colonial rulers of Sri Lanka from 1789 to 1948 did not pay much attention to forest protection. The central virgin forests of the hill country preserved by the kings were cleared to make way for coffee and later for tea plantations. Serious soil erosion was a result of this. However, it must be noted that large jungle areas were preserved in between groups of tea plantations so that they could provide sanctuary for the beautiful flora and rare fauna.

Problems due to ancient agricultural methods

A system called 'chena' cultivation, where valuable forest land is indiscriminately cleared for about an acre or so, then cultivated for a few years and then abandoned, led to the denudation of forests. Further, illicit logging and cutting of valuable timber was also practised. In fact even in the Sinha Raja rainforest valuable trees and fauna have suffered. Environmental problems have therefore been serious since the nineteenth century, resulting from forms of agricultural practice.

Global problems in environmental protection

The whole world has an enormous problem to tackle. Population growth is out of balance with resources that are required to sustain it. In both Asian and African continents the pressure on land due to population growth is very great. In addition to this it has been found that water-borne diseases kill an average of 2,500 people annually, and this has been brought about due to water pollution, attributed mostly to deforestation. Sri Lanka shares these global problems.

Developments in creating awareness through education

The government of Sri Lanka is acutely aware of the urgency of the environmental situation. Both teachers and students are encouraged to become environmentally aware. The children, the future 'citizens' of the world, should have at least a basic functional environmental education – only then can an environmentally literate society be created. The emphasis must be on *sustainable development*. There has then to be an understanding of the interconnection of goals – namely economic, environmental and social. The main approaches to teaching and learning in schools and communities is to develop an environmental ethic that will foster environmental literacy. Students are encouraged to 'experience' the environment, and, in the words of René Dubos, children are helped to 'think globally and act locally'. The concept of sustainable development is conveyed through practical implementation of its principles. In order to achieve this, the state has encouraged the schools to observe 'Environment Day' in a positive manner. This is an important date in the school calendar. The private sector and also NGOs draw up special programmes. These include tree planting campaigns, drama 'skits', speeches, and public marches through cities with banners and slogans. The schools draw up rosters of children to look after the newly planted seedlings and plants.

Environmental education in the classroom

Environmentally related topics are included in Sri Lankan schools as part of the school curriculum. These are included in agriculture, science, social studies and English language subjects. Special studies are made of the problems of local air and environmental pollution. The need to protect both plants and wild life are emphasised. An emphasis is also placed on the relationship between various species: human, animal and other forms of life. There are lesson units in the English language texts where topics of trees, forests, and animal and bird life are included. The English literature syllabuses include, among many others, Chief Seattle's speech 'Our Sacred Land' which highlights how precious the environment is to man's well-being. Poems such as 'Binsey Poplars' by Hopkins is included in the A Level Literature syllabus. Children visit the Sinha Raja forest and get first hand information on the dangers of pollution and also how wonderful nature is as it sustains itself. They are made aware of the need to see that industrial factories are sited away from towns or any habitation. The government's policy of reforestation is highlighted always.

Higher education and environmental education at teacher colleges

Environmental topics are included in the curriculum in 'Principles of Education', 'Population Education' and studies on the 'Family in Environmental Development', to mention a few. At these colleges there are special societies that relate to the environment; students are trained to organise trips and to give speeches on the subject to colleagues. 'Environment Day' is also filled with related activities. Their training here helps teachers to encourage children to 'experience' the environment.

At the community level

Parliamentarians and local government authorities give the lead in public demonstrations and activities related to the environment. The media – television, radio and newspapers – publicise these activities.

Women's role in environmental education

Research studies have shown that women are good advocates for the environment. It is an accepted fact now that women play a leading role in economic and social development, and in the well-being of society. Sri Lankan women

215

help in agricultural activities such as transplanting paddy, and in maintaining market gardens where vegetables are cultivated. Agricultural officers advise these workers to protect the environment by instructing them on correct methods of terracing land and cutting trees in a sustainable manner.

Poverty alleviation is an important component of the programme called 'Jansaviya' and 'Samurdhi', where youths are trained in self-employment projects so that their economic status improves. Women who work in craft-based activities such as rope and cane and basket weaving, requiring plants and trees, are very much aware of the need to protect the environment.

Those responsible

In the government there is a ministry that sees to women's affairs as well as the environment. Private firms and NGOs all co-operate in the projects undertaken. They help to maintain sanctuaries for bird and animal life and in school projects. The leadership is from the top and that is encouraging.

Research programmes

These are constantly on-going especially at the Sinha Raja forest where a constant survey of fauna and flora is carried out. The plant genetic laboratory set up with Japanese aid helps in protecting and collecting rare herbal plants and other indigenous plants for posterity and research. A special project called the 'greening of Sri Lanka' took place in the 1980s. About 578 acres of land were reforested and three-quarters of a million seedlings were raised in government nurseries. Later these were handed over to farmers and cultivators who were responsible for overseeing the protection of these areas. Today these maturing forests are looked after by the farmers, thereby easing the financial burden of the government.

The prospects

There are many problems where illicit activities take place, but the prospects are hopeful because Sri Lankans in general are environmentally alert and are trying to keep the environment green and beautiful – as it was so many years ago.

Marjorie Peries MA is a former principal of an English Specialist Teachers' College in Sri Lanka and is presently a part-time lecturer for the Bachelor of Education Course at the National Institute of Education, Maharagama and at the Open University, Polgalla, Kandy, Sri Lanka.

TAIWAN

BY PEI-JEN CHEN

The official launching of environmental education in Taiwan can be traced back to 1987, when the Environmental Protection Administration (EPA) was established. Recycling was, and still is, the major environmental education activity led by EPA. Since then, the Ministry of Education, the Ministry of Interior, the National Science Council, the Agriculture Council and the Energy Council have been sharing the responsibility of doing environmental education. While the National Science Council has been responsible for the 'fundamental' research, the rest are responsible for the practices of environmental education either in the formal education sector or the non-formal one.

As in most other countries, environmental education cannot be found as a separate subject in the formal education sector, and there is no mandate to teach it in the schools. Analysis of the current k-12 schools' textbooks (curriculum) indicates that a few environmental education concepts are scattered in the textbooks, in various grades/subjects. Infusion model is, hence, advocated to integrate environmental education concepts in the schools' curriculum. Supplementary instructional materials have been designed mainly by the individual teachers' colleges and universities to help school teachers to do so. However, environmental education is often regarded as an alternative term to solid waste recycling. More in-depth coverage of environmental education, ranging from environmental knowledge and sensitivity to strategies of resolving environmental issues, is not included in the supplementary materials. It is also found that environmental education is implemented most effectively in the elementary schools, and gradually declines as students grow older.

Twelve environmental education centres, located in the normal universities and/or teachers' colleges, are responsible for pre-service teacher training and the provision of in-service teacher workshops on a regular basis through contracts with the Ministry of Education. Environmentally related courses, especially environmental sciences, are offered to help pre-service teachers to become competent in teaching environmental education. In most cases, only students from the departments of mathematics and science education are required to take such courses. Meanwhile, most school teachers have not been trained environmentally during their formal training. Many week-long workshops are offered to in-service teachers to help them to be environmentally trained. A few in-service (two to three hours long) workshops are held on Wednesday afternoons by concerned schools.

On the other hand, five national parks (another one being planned), several nature centres and science museums are responsible for the non-formal education sector. Interpretation services and nature tracks are provided to help citizens to get to know more about wilderness in the national parks and the nature centres. Environmental education at the community level is interpreted as being equivalent to recycling, or cleaning up the mess, or saving the old trees at most.

The Chinese Society for Environmental Education, established in 1993, has more than 1,000 members. This society has been the major focus for many professionals from the academic field. Little has been done to raise environmental literacy among the general public by this organisation compared with the effort done by the various NGOs.

Over 100 NGOs have contributed significantly to the increase of environmental literacy among the general citizenship. The Union of Housewives, for example, has done so through nature walks. The Chinese Wildbird Society has constantly offered summer camps and various informal courses for citizens. In fact, it might be fair to say that NGOs have contributed more than government offices as far as environmental literacy is concerned.

In order to identify effective strategies to promote environmental education, and to solicit appropriate channels to implement environmental education in the schools, research projects have been supported mainly by the National Science Council during the past few years. Major research projects, in the past few years and possibly in the future, can be roughly divided into the formal education sector and the non-formal education sector as listed below:

Formal education sector:

1 environmental education concept study
2 environmental value teaching strategies
3 environmental behaviour
4 environmental literacy
5 pre-service teacher preparation model
6 in-service teacher preparation model
7 outdoor education, and
8 teacher educator's training

Non-formal education sector:

1 effective environmental education models that can be applied to communities, NGOs and government offices
2 effective environmental education training programmes that can be applied to business and industry, and
3 effective environmental education media coverage

It is expected that fundamental research projects can further the effectiveness of contemporary environmental education programmes. However, it is agreed by most environmental educators that environmental education is a field that crosses many subjects, and that more effective teaching strategies should be developed to achieve the ultimate goal of environmental education. The current understanding of a cross-curricular approach is used in developing a new form 'green curriculum', instead of altering the out-dated curriculum. Some educators call it the transdisciplinary approach; others call it the sansdisciplinary approach; still others call it the coherent approach.

A major educational reform is taking place in 1996, and is expected to continue for the next few years. Open education and curriculum integration are two ideas that have been raised to improve schools' learning. Some elementary schools are assigned to try out these ideas, with little governmental help. Networking with these educational reforms, we can witness the success of environmental education. If reform does not take place, environmental education will fail because of the overloaded curriculum placed upon teachers' shoulders.

Pei-Jen Chen PhD is director of the Environmental Education Centre at the National Taipei Teachers' College, 134 Ho-Ping East Road, Section 2, Taipei 10659, Taiwan.

UGANDA

BY J.K.W. OFWONO-ORECHO

Historical background

While the concept of environmental education and creating public awareness is relatively new in Uganda (Ministry of Natural Resources, 1995, p. 45), in the formal school curriculum, its concept is not a new thing. Before the 1970s environmental education was taught in schools as nature study. In the mid-1980s, mainly due to a new and enlightened political and social situation that prevailed in the country, environmental problems such as soil erosion and land degradation, pollution, devegetation, drainage of wetlands, noxious water weed/hyacinth, loss of biological diversity and environmentally related diseases began to receive more public attention and be addressed more vigorously by both the Government of Uganda and NGOs. The Ministry of Environment Protection (now the Ministry of Natural Resources) was set up in 1986.

In 1987 there was a major curriculum reform in the primary science syllabus. In this particular review, some aspects of environmental topics were incorporated into the curriculum and are being taught to about 3–6 million children. Similarly, more and more environmental topics are being integrated in the traditional history and geography to give a new blend to a discipline commonly known as social studies.

A continuation of these low-key efforts exerted at the primary level of education is systematically being emulated at the secondary and tertiary institutions. For example, at Makerere University and the Institute of Teacher Education, Kyambogo, environmental course units have been developed and are being taught in some undergraduate courses as a basic ingredient and requirement of higher education. A similar approach has also been adopted at teachers' colleges.

Since 1991, because of the ever-increasing environmental problems enumerated above and the urgent need to address them, the Government of Uganda has been developing a National Environment Action Plan (NEAP) with the aim of providing a framework for integrating environmental considerations into the country's overall economic and social development (Ministry of Natural Resources, 1995, p. xii). It should be noted that prior to the publication of the Government White Paper on Education in 1992, there was no public policy to guide or facilitate environmental education at any level of formal education. At the non-formal level, environmental education and public awareness has been the preoccupation of NGOs such as Wildlife Clubs of Uganda and Harmony.

In 1995, a national workshop on integrating environmental education into the formal education system in Uganda was held at the Institute of Teacher Education, Kyambogo. It was organised by Harmony and Kyambogo Environmental Education and Management Association. One of the landmarks of the workshop was the founding of the Uganda National Environmental Education Association (UNEEA).

The objectives of UNEEA are to:

* influence the incorporation of environmental education into the formal education system in Uganda;
* promote professional needs and activities of environmental educators;
* review, formulate and disseminate environmental education curricula; and
* co-ordinate environmental education research activities in Uganda.

Who is responsible for environmental education in Uganda?

There is a government institutional arrangement responsible for environmental education in Uganda. The National Environment Statute, 1995, which established the National Environment Management Authority (NEMA) under section 5 (1), provides that 'The Authority (NEMA) shall, in collaboration with the Minister responsible for education, take measures necessary for the integration in the school curriculum of education on environment' (Section 88, p. 66). NEMA is empowered under the statute 'to promote public awareness through formal, non-formal and informal education about environmental issues' (Section 7 (1) (g), p. 18). Therefore, NEMA, a government organ, is authorised by law to co-ordinate, monitor and supervise all matters incidental to or connected with sustainable management of the environment, including environmental education. Environmental education is also firmly enshrined in the Constitution of the Republic of Uganda, 1995. For example, Article 245 states that 'Parliament shall, by law, provide for measures intended – (c) to promote environmental awareness' (p. 150).

In 1996, NEMA and the Uganda Ministry of Education developed a National Environmental Education Strategy for the Formal Education Sector. The strategy is intended to guide the implementation of environmental education by giving direction and vision, as well as clarifying its goals, objectives and principles (Ministry of Education and NEMA, 1996, p. 6).

The National Environmental Education Strategy emphasises that

> every subject has the capacity to teach environmental education, which entails using the entire curriculum process to convey environmental messages and contribute to awareness creation, and the transmission of knowledge, skills and values that will motivate the desire in the individual to take action. Environmental education concepts, values, and skills will be infused into all disciplines.
>
> (Ministry of Education and NEMA, 1996)

The Strategy further clarifies 'the pedagogic methods advocated both in and out of the classroom consist of three main elements: *dialogue, encounter* and *reflection*'.

Environmental education in formal education

At the formal level of education, the responsibility for environmental education mainly rests with schools, colleges and universities and other tertiary institutions in the country. At the school level, in spite of all that has been said and done so far, environmental education is still in its infancy and is yet to set a pace that is considered adequate. Its concepts and approach are yet to be articulated. It has, however, been accepted as a useful approach to halt degradation of the environment and restore the degraded ecosystems. Unfortunately, no discernible attention has yet been given to train and motivate teachers who would integrate environmental education into the school curricula. At the same time, no attempt is being made by teachers to use the environment itself as a natural laboratory for environmental education. The teachers appear to teach *about* and *from* the environment rather than *for* the environment.

The National Environment Management Policy for Uganda (1994) states that environmental education be made mandatory in all formal education institutions in Uganda. It should be taught on a multi-disciplinary basis and be integrated into on-going curricula, and not as a separate or additional subject.

A brief look at the status of environmental education in Uganda as outlined in the National Environmental Education Strategy for the Formal Education Sector (Ministry of Education and NEMA, 1996, pp. 5–6) indicates the following:

- *Pre-primary level*
  A standardised curriculum has been prepared and it provides room for environmental education. One of the objectives of education at this level is

to help 'the child to develop right attitudes towards the environment'. There is no known teacher capacity, support materials or even clear perception of what environmental education is at this level.

- *Primary level*
  There is a general focus on learning *about* the environment and some aspects of its conservation, particularly in science and social studies. Approaches used to strengthen this integration include: development of support materials, orientation of some of the teachers, and changes in the techniques of setting questions. Improvement in teacher competence to handle environmental education and additional educational materials are urgently required.

- *Secondary level*
  Although aspects of environmental knowledge and conservation are covered in the specialised subjects such as geography, agriculture, chemistry, physics and biology, their overall inclination to environmental education is rather minimal. The testing techniques do not emphasise exposure to the environment even where practical experience is expected in their teaching. Development of environmental education responsive to curriculum content and teachers' competence are key requirements at this level.

- *Tertiary level (universities, teachers' colleges and vocational institutions)*
  As in the primary and secondary schools, some environmental aspects are covered in the various academic subjects. The curricula, however, reveal compartmentalisation rather than holistic approaches and strategies as well as inadequate co-ordination. Again, there is concentration on education *about* rather than *for* the environment. The *education* component is neither *emphasised* nor *mentioned*.

In promoting environmental education in the formal education system, Uganda faces three problems: lack of clear policy, lack of funds, and lack of trained human resources (Ministry of Natural Resources, 1994b, p. 221).

Definition of environmental education

In Uganda, environmental education has been defined as the process of recognising values and clarifying concepts in order to develop the skills and attitudes necessary to understand and appreciate the inter-relatedness among man, his culture and his biophysical surroundings (Ministry of Education and NEMA, 1996, pp. 2–3; National Environment Statute, 1995, p. 9; Makerere University Institute of Environment and Natural Resources, 1994, p. 6; Ministry of Natural Resources, 1993, p. 1). This definition is based on the first international definition given by the World Conservation Union (IUCN), Commission of Education in 1970.

The role of NGOs in non-formal environmental education

Some of the most outstanding efforts in non-formal environmental education and conservation action are being done by the indigenous and international NGOs in Uganda. NGOs all over the country are becoming increasingly involved in environmental education. The indigenous NGOs such as Wildlife Clubs of Uganda and Harmony in particular should spread environmental education throughout the country by embracing Ugandan children and youth. All the NGOs need to be co-ordinated and should 'realign their campaign towards agreed objectives' in public education and awareness. The NGOs, however, are severely handicapped by low capacity (management skills).

The main constraints facing the effective delivery of environmental education by local NGOs include lack of supplementary environmental materials and equipment, and lack of sufficiently trained personnel (Ponniah and Lazarus, 1990, p. 20).

The Government of Uganda has decentralised environmental management, realising that the immense environmental problems can only be well tackled using grassroots and local government approach. Government takes the role of NGOs to be very crucial and works in partnership with them in the field of environmental management in the country.

Environmental research

Environmental education must be based on sound principles of learning and appropriate methodological approach supported by research. Research in environmental education is yet to make a breakthrough in the traditional research agenda in Uganda. For example, up to 1992, cultural research accounted for zero per cent of projects having in-built environmental consciousness in the Uganda National Council for Science and Technology (Ministry of Natural Resources, 1994b, p. 229).

This is a very serious issue, bearing in mind that Uganda is rich in indigenous knowledge on environment and its conservation, which if incorporated in current efforts could go a long way in resolving environmental problems in the country. Environmental educators should recapture the ordinary Ugandan indigenous knowledge of specific natural resources, and cultural values relating to worship and love of nature. Indigenous knowledge played a key role in sustainable environmental management during the pre-colonial era.

Environmental research faces many daunting problems: its system is not responsive and productive; the dissemination of research results is poor with no central place where results are stored and catalogued for easy accessibility; and research networks virtually do not exist. It also suffers from lack of research facilities, insufficient human resources and lack of support services (Ministry of Natural Resource, 1994b, p. 227).

But this gloomy situation is likely to be reversed for two reasons. Firstly, Uganda has now become the twelfth country to join an 'International Research Project: Emergent Environmentalism' based at the University of Durham, England. The database has been collected from over 120 Ugandan adults. It will add to the rapidly expanding international data, which will reveal important insights into the impact of different cultural and geographical backgrounds on the environmental educators and policy makers alike. Secondly, the National Environmental Education Strategy for the Formal Education Sector (Ministry of Education and NEMA, 1996) has included research in environmental education as one of its fifth programme areas, especially research in environmental education curricula formulation, pedagogy, materials development, attitudes, beliefs, values, skills and assessment and evaluation.

Conclusion

With the development of the National Environmental Education Strategy for the Formal Education Sector by the Uganda Ministry of Education and NEMA, the future of environmental education in Uganda looks bright. However, an area that deserves the government's immediate attention in environmental education is the teacher training courses. Environmental education should be made an integral part of every teacher training programme so that a cadre of trained and committed teachers capable of creating the right kind of attitudes and ethics related to environment among Ugandan children and youth is built up. Environmental education should lead to behavioural transformation in the society, creating a sense of stewardship towards the environment and effective management of the natural resources to enhance the quality of life of the present and future generations.

References

Makerere University Institute of Environment and Natural Resources (MUIENR) (1994) *Environmental Education: A Source Book for Teacher Educators in Uganda*, Kampla: Environmental Education Unit.

Ministry of Education and NEMA (1996) *National Environmental Education Strategy for the Formal Education Sector*, Kampala.

Ministry of Natural Resources (1993) *Final Topic Paper on Education, Research, Human Resource Development and Information Systems, Vol. II B*, National Environment Action Plan Secretariat, Kampala, September.

Ministry of Natural Resources (1994a) *The National Environment Management Policy for Uganda*, National Environment Action Plan Secretariat, Kampala, January.

Ministry of Natural Resources (1994b) *State of the Environment for Uganda*, Kampala: National Environment Information Centre (NEIC).

Ministry of Natural Resources (1995) *The National Environment Action Plan for Uganda*, National Environment Action Plan Secretariat, Kampala, June.

Ofwono-Orecho, J.K.W. and Bagoora, F.D.K. (1996) *Promoting Public Environmental Awareness in Uganda*, unpublished mimeo.

Ponniah, W. and Lazarus, D. (1990) 'Public Education and Awareness in Uganda',
   Mission Report, United Nations Environment Programme, Nairobi, November.
Uganda Government (1995) *Constitution of the Republic of Uganda.*
Uganda Government (1995) *The National Environment Statute*, Statutes Supplement
   No. 3, UPPC, Entebbe, May.
UNESCO (1985) *A Comparative Survey of Environmental Education into School
   Curricula*, UNESCO–UNEP International Environmental Education Programme,
   Environmental Education Series 17, Hamburg: UNESCO.
UNEP (1988) *Strategic Resources Planning in Uganda, Vol. VIII: Environmental
   Education*, Nairobi.

J.K.W. Ofwono-Orecho is a lecturer in business studies at the Institute of
Teacher Education, Kyambogo, Kampala, Uganda, and visiting lecturer at the
National University of Rwanda, Butare. Address for correspondence: PO Box
574, Kampala, Uganda.

THE UNITED STATES OF AMERICA

BY JOHN F. DISINGER

Some say that environmental education in the United States took initial
root during the early days of the nature study movement in the 1890s – *Study
nature, not books*. Others identify as environmental education's touchstone the
emergence of the outdoor education movement during the 1920s – *Teach
outdoors what is best taught outdoors, and indoors what is most appropriate there*.
Still others name the conservation education movement of the 1930s as the
legitimate forebear – *Americans must learn to manage natural resources scientifically, for utilitarian purposes*. As each of these movements evolved, it co-opted
elements of the others. What resulted were uneven mixtures, in many instances
excellent, of intellectual content and educational process, of science, social
studies and humanities, of education *in* the environment and education *about*
the environment. What did *not* result were commonality of focus or broad
acceptance within the educational community.

   Primarily as a result of an irruption of public concern about environmental
quality, a substantially different focus, environmental education, emerged in the
1960s – different because it involved values focusing on the quality of the
human experience and hence of the human environment. The movement
spawned an interest in education *for* the environment – education fostering
responsible environmental citizenship. The US federal government's initial
education-related response was the National Environmental Education Act of
1970, which quickly became a rallying point for those interested in education
dealing with the environment from all perspectives. Although limited in scope
and funded at much lower levels than authorised by the legislation, the 1970
Act resulted in the creation of an Office of Environmental Education in the
US Department of Health, Education and Welfare and the funding of a

modest grants programme. The Act was funded from 1971 to 1975 and was not reauthorised in 1981. Also during the 1970s, state, local and commercially focused environmental education efforts proliferated – master plans, curriculum guides, teacher guides, sections of science texts, ancillary materials – sponsored and produced by varying combinations of educators, textbook publishers, resource managers, environmentalists, and business and industry. Many were (and still are) accused of attempting to advance their own agendas in this manner, and many were (and still are) doing so. In terms of quality, these materials ranged, and still range, from excellent to abysmal, from pedagogically sound to very weak, from scientifically and educationally responsible presentation to blatant propaganda.

Shifting political and economic priorities during the 1980s led to the demise of the 1970 Environmental Education Act, so for a time environmental education evolved with minimal support from the federal government. But lack of federal funds and leadership forced environmental education programmes to become more self-reliant, focused on community needs and based on vigorous grass roots support. That self-reliance typically came at the expense of broad perspectives and of general acceptance into the educational mainstream. It also opened more widely the door for those with other agendas to develop and promote one-sided teaching/learning materials because they were willing to make the investment of time, energy and money.

A national renewal of concern for environmental quality led to legislation directing the US Environmental Protection Agency to spearhead the implementation of a new National Environmental Education Act in 1990. The establishment of an Office of Environmental Education in that agency today provides a federal focal point for the furtherance of environmental education. A modest grants programme supports innovative state-wide and local activities targeted at improvement of the state of the art in environmental education. But the federal government's role is neither to lead nor to co-ordinate; those tasks are reserved for the 50 states, each of which makes its own decisions in these areas. No state requires comprehensive environmental education programming, though many specify minimal requirements for specific components (for example 'Plant a tree because it's Arbor Day!') and a few require minimal preparation in environmental education as parts of teacher certification programmes.

Over the years, much of the national leadership in environmental education has come from professional associations – the American Nature Study Society, the Outdoor Education Association, the National Association for Interpretation, the Conservation Education Association and the North American Association for Environmental Education. The latter organisation, formed in 1971 as the National Association for Environmental Education, officially broadened in the 1980s to include representation from the entire North American continent. It provides a professional home for academics and practitioners of all varieties of environmental education, and is currently engaged in the development of rigorous professional standards for the field.

In some ways present-day environmental education in the United States is a logical 'next step' beyond its predecessors, but in others it is fundamentally different. Environmental education in the US is now characterised by focus on the explicit and implicit interconnections among human health, science and technology, society's environmental, economic and social problems and issues, and other quality of life concerns – fear of severe deterioration of human health and quality of human life caused by dramatic declines in environmental quality. A current criticism of environmental education is that, though its intent may be admirable, it is in fact 'soft' – its science base is weak, it ignores economic realities, it preaches unthinking environmentalism. It is possible that these criticisms will foster rigorous self-examination, leading to substantial improvements in materials and practice.

At its heart, today's environmental education places special emphasis on the social dimensions of environmental problems locally, nationally and globally – education *for* the benefit of people affected by environmental problems, education keyed to the solution of environmental problems, perhaps education *for* the intrinsic benefit of the environment itself. Nonetheless, environmental education continues to include widely varying mixtures of nature study, outdoor education and conservation education, of science and aesthetics, of objectivity and subjectivity, of environmentalism and anti-environmentalism, in different mixes, in different places, at different times. Thus, environmental education is defined differently by different groups, all of them certain that their formulation is the proper one. They are generally amicable, that is, they frequently talk *to* each other, though not necessarily *with* each other. Nonetheless, all are committed to 'environment' as an appropriate, indeed essential, focus for formal and non-formal education in the United States. The debate appears to be healthy.

John F. Disinger PhD is Professor Emeritus at the School of Natural Resources, The Ohio State University, USA. He was also Associate Director of the ERIC Clearinghouse for Science, Mathematics and Environmental Education, 1971–1991, and President of the North American Association for Environmental Education, 1985–1986.

Footnote

As stated at the outset of this part, the above descriptions provide numerous avenues for debate that readers are invited to pursue. It is not appropriate here to summarise, to compare or contrast the various statements in any rigorous sense, since they vary so widely in their breadth of content and depth of analysis. They give a 'flavour' of what is happening around the world; by design, they were not written to a single prescribed format and they do not all answer the same questions.

Yet before bringing the part to a close, it is nevertheless appropriate to highlight a number of features that the majority of the accounts draw to our attention.

In the first instance, they speak very positively and optimistically about the general state of environmental education. For example, from Australia we hear that 'the prospects remain bright . . . teachers find a way of engaging in environmental education even in circumstances where this is against the grain'; in Canada 'there is evidence to support the notion that environmental education-related activity is thriving within elementary schools'; in Slovenia it is envisaged that environmental education will form part of the national curricula for all schools; in Spain 'the prospects are good for collective effort and achievements'; in Uganda there is the new National Environmental Education Strategy for the Formal Education Sector, and from the United States of America we are told that 'environmental education is defined differently by different groups . . . all are committed to "environment" as an appropriate, indeed essential, focus for formal and non-formal education. . . . The debate appears to be healthy.'

At a global level, debate *is* healthy, but there are numerous ongoing issues to resolve and serious challenges ahead. A number of the more commonly recognised challenges are highlighted within the national statements. These include the need to:

- work out the implications of centralised curriculum control and reduce marginalisation of environmental education (Australia, Greece, Hong Kong);
- continue the shift of emphasis from environmental education as 'science' to that which has an explicit social agenda (Australia, USA, Spain, Latvia);
- relate the implications of such trends to the theory and practice of curriculum development, professional development and educational research in the field of environmental education (Australia);
- increase levels and quality of teacher training in environmental education (Greece, Hong Kong, South Africa, Taiwan, Uganda);
- increase the environmental education research base and broaden approaches to research (Greece, Hong Kong, Slovenia, Taiwan, Uganda);
- develop resource materials and support for schools (Greece, Hong Kong, Taiwan, Latvia);
- develop programmes at community level (Hong Kong, Romania, Ecuador, Taiwan, Uganda);
- promote fieldwork studies, and 'in' and 'for' the environment experiences (Hong Kong, Slovenia, Spain, Uganda);
- co-ordinate formal and non-formal programmes through sound national strategies (Spain, Uganda);
- evaluate programmes and strategies (Spain, Ecuador).

How encouraging it is to reread and cross-reference the accounts and to ascertain that each of these needs is being addressed to some extent at least, within one or more of the countries included in the part. Many of the challenges articulated have also been identified and discussed either from theoretical or practical perspectives in this book's earlier sections. Thus we now return to the general scene in environmental education, and to further consideration of its progress and potential in the next few decades.

Part VI

TOWARDS PROGRESS AND PROMISE IN THE TWENTY-FIRST CENTURY

What can be done towards making progress in terms of helping environmental education realise its maximum potential? What can be done to help the formal educational process achieve its various purposes – of helping citizens be informed about their roles as producers and consumers; encouraging appropriate behaviour in relation to the environment; enabling the decision makers of the future to adopt environmentally responsible approaches; helping young learners to appreciate and enjoy the world around them; and generally encouraging 'ecological thought' and a realisation of the key role of environmental thinking and action in promoting international understanding and sustainable development?

Answers to these questions clearly lie at two levels: firstly at the macro or radical level, which calls for a substantial rethinking of paradigms and approaches to environmental education – or even education itself; and secondly at the more conservative level, at which small yet significant steps can be taken to change or modify existing educational policy and practice.

RADICAL RETHINKING

As pp. 99–102 have already indicated, for some, the answers to minimising the conflicts, inconsistencies and limitations of the rhetoric–reality gap in environmental education lie in substantial changes or paradigm shifts relating to the environmental field, or even to education itself. We have seen, for example, that Gough (1987) argues the need to shift from a materialistic and atomistic world view and epistemological paradigm towards an ecological paradigm for education. Other writers similarly challenge the dominance of a scientific, epistemological paradigm – for example Fien (1992), Elliot (1991), Robottom and Hart (1993). As this macro level of change has already been addressed in its appropriate place in this text, i.e. in conjunction with an overview of theoretical perspectives, only two aspects will be elaborated upon here, both relating specifically to environmental education. These are a focus on the goals and then on the terminology of the field.

For Robottom and Hart (1993), one of several fundamental issues that needs addressing by way of substantial challenge is the 'taking for granted' of goals

233

relating to environmental education. It is argued (p. 39) that there exists a public statement of goals for curriculum development in environmental education that is strongly reinforced by a number of influential educators and researchers in the field whose approach to environmental education is grounded in the positivist paradigm. For example, Hungerford *et al.* (1983) indicate that their own work on developing an accepted statement of goals (validated against the Tbilisi objectives) in order to 'bring increased order to the field and to operationalise the structure of environmental education' is beyond critique:

> We submit that EE does have a substantive structure that has evolved through the considerable efforts of many and that the framework has been documented formally in the literature. . . . One would dare hope that this question (about definitions of environmental education) could, at long last, be laid to rest. No doubt, it would behove the EE community to keep a critical eye on its goals and to reassess them as necessary, but the field is quite definitely beyond the goal setting stage and into the business of goal implementation.
>
> (Hungerford *et al.*, 1983, pp. 1–2)

Robottom and Hart (1993) consider that many of the accepted goals at that time were outdated and that dominant research trends merely served to reinforce them, 'thereby making it increasingly difficult for environmental educators to determine their own, more locally appropriate, just and equitable goals' (p. 38). Certainly this argument continues to hold true at the present time, as it would appear that in many educational situations, the appropriateness of a particular set of goals (set by others), and their value in every sense, is taken for granted. Hence research aimed at evaluating environmental education programmes is rendered ineffective, since the goals themselves are not being appraised. What is required is a substantial shift in thinking, away from the belief that a single set of internationally agreed goals for teaching and curriculum development can have lasting relevance for all educational situations, and towards the view that goals should be subject to ongoing appraisal and reappraisal by educators themselves. Such appraisal would consider the appropriateness of a set of goals in a given and particular context, taking account of social, political, ecological, cultural and historical circumstances.

For other environmental educators, radical rethinking should occur, not just in relation to a definition of goals in the field, but also to the terminology used to describe aspects of the educational process. Gough's (1987) argument for a major paradigm shift in the direction of an ecological world view has been referred to. He calls for a future wherein individuals do not learn about, from or for environments; rather they live 'with' them. 'As a foundation for educational inquiry, an ecological paradigm should give us cause for optimism that we might someday learn to live, and live to learn, *with* environments' (p. 50). This idea is grounded in a deep ecology world view that cultivates a 'state of being . . . that sustains the widest (and deepest) possible identification' of oneself with one's environments (Fox, 1987, p. 7). This sense of identification, or, as Devall and Sessions (1985) call it, 'ecological consciousness', is so profound that its proponents have no word for nature but see themselves and nature as part of 'being'. For Gough, the slogan of education 'for' the environment is not much of an improvement on what for him and others are the inadequacies of education 'about' and 'in/from' the environment.

> Apart from being somewhat patronising and anthropocentric (who are we to say what is 'good for' the environment, and which environment is '*the* environment', anyway?), this slogan maintains the sorts of distinctions that tend to work against a deeply ecological world view – distinctions between subject and object, education and environment, learner and teacher.
>
> (Gough, 1987, p. 50)

It is suggested that if we are to have a profoundly ecological understanding of education, attention must be shifted away from the *objects* of environmental education (e.g. desired states of the environment or changed human attitudes) and towards the interactions or *inter-relationships* that exist among people and environments.

> We can try to trust our personal subjective experiences rather than defer habitually to the entrenched status of accumulated propositional know-ledge . . . we can try to educate our own senses so that we become better at searching out the characteristics of the personal, social and physical environments in which we conduct our educational practices. Above all, we can try to see such searching – like all learning – as a relationship . . . we should perhaps put less faith in what is possible to learn *from* lecturers or textbooks *about* children or schools. Rather . . . we should have more faith in what we can learn *with* our peers, *with* those we now call our learners, and *with* environments.
>
> (Gough, 1987, p. 64)

Jickling and Spork (1996) also engage in a critique of the nature of environ-mental education and outline particular concern for the use of the slogan 'education for the environment'. They rightly point out that there has been very little questioning of the categorisation of environmental education as education about, in and/or for the environment, and that these categorisations have become commonly accepted slogans. Also correctly, they indicate that 'educa-tion for the environment' has gained much appeal as a result of the perceived need to liberate environmental education from the narrow traditional focus of learning about/in the environment so that it can embrace critique of the political dimensions of environmental issues and engage students in the active resolution of environmental questions, issues and problems (Robottom, 1987; Stevenson, 1987; Huckle, 1983; Fien, 1993). For example, Fien (1993) promotes the concept of education for the environment as it addresses weaknesses of other approaches such as 'neglect of controversial environmental issues, and the avoidance of values and problem solving objectives . . . and a widespread avoidance of environmental politics and the political economy of resource use' (p. 9). For Fien and other writers, some of the defining criteria for 'education for the environment' are:

- to develop critical thinking and enable problem-solving
- to examine ideologies that underlie human–environment relationships
- to criticise conventional wisdom
- to explore material and ideological bases of conventional wisdom
- to analyse power relationships within a particular society
- to engage students in cultural criticism and reconstruction
- to foster political literacy
- to focus on real-world problems and participate in real issues
- to open students' minds to alternative world views
- to work and live co-operatively
- to realise that humans can act collectively to shape society

(Jickling and Spork, 1996, based on Huckle, 1983; Pepper, 1987;
Greenall Gough, 1987; Fien, 1993)

As Jickling and Spork point out, what is striking about this list is that it closely parallels broad conceptions about the very nature of education itself. Thus the slogan 'education for the environment' can retain advantages – as a symbol to highlight overlooked priorities – while advocating fundamentally educational qualities. Furthermore, as thinking about this term has developed, and the socially critical dimension of environmental education has been articulated and illuminated, the slogan has served (and indeed continues to serve) as a useful 'tool' or framework for teachers to analyse their work and discover overlooked dimensions of it.

Despite its acknowledged usefulness, these writers outline a series of interesting arguments against the continued use of the term, which can only be summarised here. They believe, for example, that when interpreted literally, 'education for the environment' reflects, through the language used, the values and predilections of activists more so than those of educators. 'Consequently, continued popular use of the term runs the risk of encouraging non-educative activities and alienating those whose vested interests are most obviously threatened' (Jickling and Spork, 1996, p. 21). More serious concerns are presented as 'programmatic definitions'. In this sense it is argued that 'education for the environment' is inherently deterministic and that it invites co-option by advocates of particular ideologies. They cite *Our Common Future* (WCED, 1987) as a clear indication of the programmatic nature of 'education for sustainable development'.

Sustainable development has been described here in general terms. How are individuals in the real world to be persuaded or made to act in the common interest? The answer lies partly in education, institutional development, and law enforcement.

(Jickling and Spork, 1996, p. 46)

'This statement suggests that sustainable development is in the common interest, and the public must be persuaded, or made to pursue this end. Further, education can contribute to the process of persuasion required' (p. 14). They present examples of approaches to education that appear to advance particular agendas, including 'sustainable development', yet also show inconsistencies between the advancing of their agendas and a number of the stipulated criteria of socially critical education. It is also argued that when 'education for the environment' is defined programmatically, 'there is a tendency towards narrowing of perspective, limiting of possibilities, anthropocentrism, and militating against the evolutionary tendencies of ethics' (p. 21). Having illustrated these points, it is concluded that the crux of the problem is actually structural.

> When we talk about 'education for the environment' we imply that education must strive to be 'for' something external to education itself. ... If we want students to examine ideologies, criticise conventional wisdom, and participate in cultural criticism and reconstruction, then we must accept that they may well reject the externally imposed aim that has been pre-selected for them. ... If we really want to open students' minds to alternate worldviews, it makes little sense to steer them, however gently, towards a particular vision. ... This prepositional use of 'for' ultimately leads, therefore, to either a literal or programmatic interpretation which is, in our view, deterministic.

(Jickling and Spork, 1996, pp. 21–22)

Thus it is concluded that perhaps it is time to retire the phrase, and develop new thoughts and directions to work with as researchers and educators seek to fill the void created. Finally, the writers offer tentative suggestions for a way forward. The first of these is a call for more conceptual and practical energy to be focused on the concept of education itself. It is suggested that if we lack confidence in education we may on the surface encourage students to be socially critical, yet feel the need to steer them towards a 'best' direction. 'Gaining confidence in "education" will require more clarity. We will need to be more clear about the nature of education and the problems of blurring distinctions between education and activism' (p. 22). Secondly, the deterministic tendencies inherent in constructions like 'education for the environment' need to be reversed. Indeed, perhaps we need to consciously ensure that indeterminacy is built into programmes and instruction.

> We can do this by acknowledging that our objectives are not external to education. ... Students will be encouraged to think critically about even the most environmentally enlightened practices available at present. To do

237

this they will need to hear a variety of theories, and participate in a range of activities. From these they can learn to critique new possibilities.

(Jickling and Spork, 1996, p. 22)

Thirdly, we should work towards the creation and adoption of a promising new environmental vision and an education process that is liberated from externally contrived agendas.

> To enable the success of our students, we need to acknowledge that shaping the future does not consist of being led to adopt some alternative vision. Rather, it involves the more indeterminate process of constantly examining and re-casting society. If we acknowledge that education should be free of specified ends, then we are ultimately led to challenge the way in which 'education for the environment' operates to predetermine educational aims.

(Jickling and Spork, 1996, p. 23)

In response to these well-articulated views that challenge the traditional categorisation of environmental education and call for a radical rethinking of internationally accepted terminology, I would ask a rhetorical question: how far actually are we from defining and accepting an alternative vision of education and the translation of that into the reality of education programmes that are liberated from assumptions and externally determined agendas? If the answer is 'near', then environmental education is well on its way to encompassing a new environmental vision, and so by all means let us abandon its time-honoured terminology. If the answer is along the lines that we have a fair way to go, then let us continue to debate the important and good points that authors such as Gough, Jickling and Spork raise. By such debate we may encourage the challenge rather than the casual acceptance of the categorisation and terminology of the field, and, most importantly, help educators to appreciate that the development of environmental awareness, concern and action in an individual is a function of the interaction of complex variables rather than merely the adoption of a deterministic position. As the debate goes on, however, surely it is important to retain goals and terms that have actually served and continue to serve the critical function of assisting teachers and other practitioners to discover overlooked and important dimensions of environmentalism. I would actually go further than this, and say that an understanding of the phrase 'education for the environment' and its inter-relationship with the other 'accepted' positions of 'education about the environment' and 'education in the environment' has been the bedrock stimulus for the practical development of environmental education programmes in classrooms around the world. A rereading of the fascinating overviews of international developments presented in Part V will confirm this view. The argument that the phrase 'education for the environment' necessarily means something that is patronising and anthropocentric, with the implication that there is a valuer who is 'external' (whatever that means) to the environment

238

and who is capable of determining what is good for it, seems hard to accept. Would the same be said for the phrases 'education for the later years of life', 'education for a global tomorrow'? Countless students and teachers have found the use of the word 'for' in relation to the environment most helpful when getting to grips with criticism of conventional wisdom, consideration of alternative world views and formulation of attitudes and values that will enable us to shape and recast society for the better. Furthermore, it is perhaps unfortunate to consider the phrase 'education for the environment' in isolation. As the conclusion of this text will make clear (pp. 266–273), it is surely the interlinking of all that is meant by education 'for' the environment with the acquisition of environmental knowledge and personal experiences in the environment that constitutes a holistic and balanced approach to environmental understanding. To lose sight at this stage of the accepted terminology is to lose sight of important research findings (see pp. 240–244) that reveal the critical role of 'in the environment' and 'about the environment' experiences in terms of illuminating an understanding of actions 'for the environment'.

A final argument for retaining, at least for the foreseeable future, the accepted categorisation of environmental education is that as the challenges and debate go on, perhaps the way ahead for the terminology of the field will become clearer. How difficult it is to find over-arching theories for human–environment relations. Capra (1982) talks of the present time as being a turning point, or at least one of transition. For this author, the time since Descartes and Isaac Newton was dominated by the metaphor of the machine, but a new metaphor, of a more organic kind, is emerging. As Simmons (1996) points out, this is in part a global consciousness facilitated by the implosion of electronic data transmission, which may supersede the binary division of environmental attitudes into ecocentric and technocentric (see, for example, O'Riordan, 1981 as discussed earlier in this text).

> There seems to be something of a parallel between the culture described by post-modernism (where nothing is permanent nor very substantial) and that of chaos theory where energy and matter synergise unpredictably.
>
> But we cannot yet know where globalisation, together with its likely countervailing forces, will lead. But the further entrenchment of only two basic attitudes towards the environment (one privileging humanity for all times and places, the other doing the same for 'nature') seems unlikely to last. In the whole domain of environmental thought, the old ways are dying but the new cannot be born. Further, the language to represent the new is as yet unformulated.
>
> (Simmons, 1996, p. 169)

Surely the related language of the field of environmental education similarly awaits the appropriate time for reformulation.

SMALL STEPS TO SUCCESS

The alternative to radical rethinking of the paradigms, approaches to and related language of environmental education is of course the taking of less radical steps in the desired direction to change or modify existing educational policy and practice. So we now turn to three areas of concern that illuminate appropriate steps that might be taken. These are: concern for significant life experiences, concern for content and concern for professional development. An outline of the salient points of each area will be given, followed by a case study for each that illustrates an example of educational policy or practice that has taken on board appropriate steps to success.

Concern for significant life experiences

The analysis of data relating to three separate research projects, as discussed on pp. 131–135, reveals that programmes of environmental education in the formal education service do indeed play a significant role, both in the development of people's knowledge and understanding of the environment and in their formulation of attitudes and feelings of responsibility towards it. Yet the data also reveal that the influence of environmental education is clearly not as dominant or successful as it ought to be. As we have seen, the research results show that even where successful programmes of environmental education do exist, their impact on long-term thinking and action is not as great as other significant experiences and formative influences in an individual's life. Presumably, then, it is very helpful to know more about the nature of the influences that do apparently have more substantial and long-term impact, as it may well be possible for formal educational programmes to 'tap into' or assist the promotion of these. It was mentioned on p. 133 that the 'Emergent Environmentalism' research study (i.e. the sub-study concerned with development of concern for the environment and influences and experiences affecting pro-environmental behaviours) (Palmer, 1993; Palmer and Suggate, 1996) reveals that experiences outdoors (particularly in early childhood) may well be the single most important influence affecting people's thinking in relation to the environment. Certainly this was the case for the initial 232 subjects in the 'Emergent Environmentalism' sample, and this finding confirms the outcomes of a previous study (Tanner, 1980). An elaboration of these findings will now illustrate key points relating to significant life experiences or formative influences of which educational programmes need take account. Of particular relevance is the obvious impact of what might be described as aesthetic or spiritual experiences. These would include such things as feeling a sense of awe, wonder and mystery; being inspired by the natural world or human achievement; experiencing feelings of transcendence, feelings that may give rise to a belief in a divine being, or the belief that one's inner resources provide the ability to rise above everyday experiences; reflecting on the origins and purpose of life, responding to challenging experiences of life such as suffering and death; developing a sense of community, involving the recognition and value of the worth of every human being and of relationships; exercising the imagination, inspiration and intuition; developing feelings and insights, being moved by beauty, hurt by injustice or aggression, and so on (based on NCC, 1993).

Both the initial and fine-grained analysis of the data show that whilst, as one would expect, such things as education courses, parents and other close relatives, friends, books, television/media, the impact of environmental disasters, travel, etc., all play a significant part in promoting environmental awareness and concern, the single most important influence overall centres around experiences in the natural world (see Table 4.1). Many of the subjects' fascinating life stories are rich with references to aspects of spiritual thinking and experience, particularly derived from being in the environment. There are accounts of the development of 'awe and wonder', of feeling 'mystery' and transcendence when describing time spent in the outdoor world – either living in a rural environment or engaging in activities such as walking, camping, bird-watching, practical conservation tasks, gardening and farming. Twenty-four subjects referred specifically to the spiritual influence of remote places, open space, and the experience of solitude or freedom to reflect on oneself, one's life, human relationships and the natural world. We estimate that over 90 per cent of the respondents referred at some point in their autobiographical accounts to spiritual ideas and experiences as key influences on their thinking. Aside from the mention of these in connection with being in the natural world, references in various other categories of response, notably the influence of parents, close relatives and friends, and the impact of environment disasters, portrayed clearly spiritual dimensions.

Following on from this analysis of autobiographical data obtained in the UK, the study has now been extended to incorporate parallel data from a range of international locations including Australia, Canada, the USA, Greece, Slovenia, Sri Lanka, Uganda, South Africa, Spain and Hong Kong. Ongoing analysis suggests a clear reinforcement of findings of the UK study – including the vital importance of early childhood experiences, and indeed experiences generally, in the natural world. Preliminary analysis also suggests the effect of spiritual, aesthetic and religious ideas, beliefs and experiences on people's thinking in relation to the environment – with, of course, fascinating cultural differences. Illustrative examples of comments include :

From the UK: 'I must have been born in a hedgerow for I realised that I got a better sermon from a beech tree than a bishop. . . . ' 'I'll never forget the sight of a barn owl flying across in front of me. . . . I can remember the exact incident when my imagination was fired. . . . '
From Sri Lanka: 'During a severe drought about 23 years ago when all the wells ran dry . . . my family contracted hepatitis . . . the sight of the hillsides being cut down . . . the paddy fields filled up for buildings . . . they were tremendous influences. . . . I thought of stories of Buddhist attitudes from my childhood.

... I came to realise that trees and the protection of animals and plants are so important.'

'My teacher accompanied me to her residence ... in the garden I came to a little chamber where I began to feel that I was in a smooth, cool, green heaven. ... I felt that I was moving with my close beloved ones. . . . '

From Greece: 'The most crucial feeling I feel in the forest is that there I feel at peace with myself, with the whole world. The wilderness seems to me like an "absolute" truth. In the wilderness I feel someone can find the real meaning of life.'

'My religious pursuits, my wanderings amongst the eastern religions and my arriving at the mysterious ceremony of Orthodoxism were the basic condition for my entering harmoniously into the natural and man-made environment and to respect every form of life.'

From Australia: 'There was one moment of pure stunning joy whilst watching a sunset over the ocean from the top of the highest peak around. I have striven to find such places and feelings ever since.'

'The most significant influence was probably tied up in the unbelievable survival skills of the aborigines – their mystical culture.'

From Canada: 'As a youngster, I played in the forest open to its life and amidst that life, I fell in love. Like any other lover, I wanted to be with my love, in the arms of my love, learning love's secrets, more than I wanted to be anywhere else. But I also learned, first with my heart and later with my head, that the purpose and goals of my civilisation were different from my love. They would show me that the price of this kind of bond, this felt sense of kinship with all life – the trees, the birds, the lichens and mosses, the 'coons and squirrels – would be spiritual violation, hurt, rage and finally fear.'

The two other on-going research projects referred to on pp. 133–135 provide further evidence of the importance of spiritual ideas, attitudes and values in the development of people's awareness of and concern for the environment. In the 'Global Environment and the Expanding Moral Circle' study, in response to the question 'what would you identify as the single most important influence or experience that has affected your attitude to our responsibility towards a) animals and b) the environment?', 62 subjects (35 per cent) provided a response for animals and 37 subjects (20 per cent) a response for environment that could be classed as being in the spiritual/aesthetic domain.

The question that asked subjects to provide an assessment on a scale of 0 (not at all important) to 5 (very important) of the influence of certain things (e.g. media images, television documentaries, books, intellectual argument, education courses, parents, friends, travel, etc.) on their attitude towards animals and the environment, resulted in figures relating to spiritual/aesthetic domain experiences (personal experience in or with nature) as shown in Table 6.1. Such experiences (average score 3.55) rank third out of 14 categories of influence, after television documentaries and media images.

Table 6.1 Subjects' assessment of the influence of personal (spiritual/aesthetic) experiences in or with nature on environmental responsibility

	Assessment						
	0	1	2	3	4	5	
Spiritual/aesthetic	1	16	23	35	39	56	↑ No. of respondents ↓

The student interviews for the research project on 'Subject and Community Knowledge in Environment Education' reveal a rich variety of responses, again including many references to the aesthetic/spiritual domain. For example, the lead question 'If you were designing an environmental education programme in a primary school, what would you consider to be the essential core content of it?' led to some very predictable and straightforward responses such as 'pollution . . . taking care of litter . . . protecting wildlife' and so on, but also to some far more reflective answers: 'An appreciation of who we are in connection with the natural environment . . . to understand that we are part of a world . . . to realise that although we are just one link in that chain, the effect we have on the environment is disproportionate.'

Responses to questions probing sources of students' knowledge are also extremely relevant to this text. As previously mentioned, responses were divided into two main groups: 'formal' sources, including school, higher education courses, books, television, media, etc.; and 'community or informal sources' leading to knowledge acquired by living and interacting with people in a community or locality and so absorbing knowledge, ideas and attitudes from their experiences 'in society'. Nineteen respondents, 38 per cent of the whole sample, said that community or informal sources had been the most important for their own learning and inspiration. A further 12 respondents (24 per cent) said that they gave equal weighting to formal and informal sources. Responses revealed the powerful influence of spiritual and aesthetic experiences; the students talked of such things as being moved by beauty and example; being hurt by injustice; being emotionally challenged by suffering and death; being aware of and reflecting on the meaning of experience, the development of insight and intuition.

Brief mention here should also be made of the key role of television and media images in developing environmental awareness and concern. Whilst apparently not as significant overall as personal experiences in the natural world and the influences of family and close friends in people's lives, such images are nevertheless very influential. In the 'Emergent Environmentalism' (Significant Life Experiences) study, television/media ranks fifth out of 13 categories of response (Table 4.1), and those who singled out disasters and negative issues as a major influence inevitably referred to media coverage of these. Indeed, if these two categories were combined, the ranking of media impact would be raised to third in the table.

Table 6.2 Subjects' assessment of the influence of television on environmental responsibility

	Assessment					
	0	*1*	*2*	*3*	*4*	*5*
Television documentaries	0	3	11	37	47	72

In the 'Global Environment and the Expanding Moral Circle' study, analysis of the assessment of influence question shows television documentaries to be the most significant influence overall: 72 out of 182 subjects gave this a rating of 5, as Table 6.2 shows (average score 4.02). Furthermore, television documentaries are followed in these rankings by media images in second position. When subjects were asked to identify the single most important influence affecting their attitudes to animals and the environment, 42 (23 per cent) of subjects provided a response for animals and 37 (21 per cent) a response for environment that was either television documentaries or media images.

By way of summary, a substantial research base encompassing data from several studies illuminates:

- The over-riding importance of the influence of personal experiences *in* the environment, particularly at a young age, in terms of developing environmental understanding and concern and inspiring action.
- The critical role of spiritual or other 'aesthetic domain' experiences in the development of environmental understanding, awareness and concern.
- The importance of 'community' knowledge: the absorbing of knowledge, ideas and attitudes from living and interacting in a particular society or locality.
- The key role of television and the media in influencing environmental thinking.

The importance of spiritual ideas and experiences in developing environmental concern, and the place of environmental education in this process, are discussed at greater length in Palmer (1998).

The following two-part case study illustrates one example of educational practice in which, unusually, the aesthetic and spiritual domains of environmental education are given prominent attention. The location is Norway, and the case study first outlines aspects of the National Core Curriculum, then describes how one school project successfully implemented the curriculum document's call for developing 'an environmentally aware human being'.

THE CORE CURRICULUM IN NORWAY – IN PRINCIPLE

In Norway, environmental understanding and awareness is placed at the heart of the published National Core Curriculum. The *Core Curriculum* for primary, secondary and adult education (Hagness, 1994) constitutes a legally binding foundation for the development of separate curricula and subject syllabuses at the different levels of education – the common core for the Norwegian education system. According to this policy, education of

the integrated human being . . . shall inspire an integrated development of the skills and qualities that allow one to behave morally, to create and to act, and to work together and in harmony with nature. Education shall contribute to building character which will give the individual the strength to take responsibility for his or her own life, to make a commitment to society, and to care for the environment.

(Hagness, 1994, p. 39)

Sections within the document, thus constituting the curriculum foundation, are 'the spiritual human being', 'the creative human being', 'the working human being', 'the liberally-educated human being', 'the social human being' and 'the environmentally-aware human being'.

It is recognised that:

Our living environment has become decreasingly dependent on nature and increasingly influenced by the man-made world. Our well-being depends on our ability to develop new ideas, to use advanced technology, to create new products and to solve traditional problems with more imagination and reason. . . . Human beings are a part of nature, and are constantly making decisions with repercussions not only for their own welfare, but also for other humans and for the natural environment as well. Our choices have consequences across geographic borders and across generations: lifestyle influences health; our nation's consumption produces pollution in other countries; and our society's waste becomes the plight of future generations.

(Hagness, 1994, p. 35)

Within the section on the environmentally-aware human being, statements within its sub-headings of Natural Science, Ecology and Ethics; Human Beings, the Environment and Conflicts of Interest; and the Joy of Nature, make it quite clear that this curriculum anticipates and encourages the crucial role of aesthetic and spiritual ideas and experiences in developing environmental awareness:

Education must counteract fragmentary and compartmentalised learning. Concrete facts are necessary, but by themselves are not enough – a holistic knowledge of the sciences and ecology is also needed.

Education must also kindle a sense of joy in physical activity and nature's grandeur, of living in a beautiful country, in the lines of a landscape, in the changing seasons. It should awaken a sense of awe towards the unexplainable, induce pleasures in outdoor life and nourish the urge to wander off the beaten track and into uncharted terrain; to use body and

245

senses to discover new places and to explore the world. Outdoor life touches us in body, mind and soul. Education must corroborate the connection between understanding nature and experiencing nature.

(Hagness, 1994, p. 38)

A curriculum based on statements such as these, with the structured inclusion of environmentally focused work across its whole spectrum of activity, would surely serve as an ideal basis for the nurturing of personal experiences in the environment; for a balanced approach to the incorporation of 'in', 'about' and 'for' environmental experiences; and for the consequent development of individuals' awareness, concern and actions.

Reference

Hagness, R. (ed.) (1994) *Core Curriculum for Primary, Secondary and Adult Education in Norway*, Oslo: The Royal Ministry of Church, Education and Research.

AESTHETIC EXPERIENCES IN PRACTICE

BY LILLIAN LARSEN

So how in Norway might such worthy guidelines be translated into practice? The following brief outline is of a project conducted with 8th Grade students at Tranby School, situated in a small, mostly rural township, 35 km west of Oslo. It illustrates one way in which Norwegian teachers incorporate artistic and creative dimensions into their environmental teaching. The chosen project title or issue to be considered was 'What Does the Forest Mean to Us?'. Seventy-six 8th Grade pupils and their teachers were totally immersed in inter-disciplinary studies relating to this for one week. Goals for the pupils were:

- the gaining of insight into processes involving human activity and the natural world
- the heightening of interest in what the forest means to us as individuals
- the learning of environmental skills relating to the conduct of practical project work

The week's programme

Monday: The intention of the day was to motivate, prepare for and begin the learning process. This involved orientation in classes, and a common programme incorporating administration; slides from the forest reservation on aspects of protection and responsibility in forest environments; a video on 'A Tree is a Tree, A Forest is a World'; an introduction to ecology; guidelines on how to behave in nature using the programme 'Guest in Nature'; and organisation of the pupils into project groups. One group was to have a particular focus on 'art in the forest'.

246

Tuesday: The intention for the day was for the students to experience nature, and diversity of living species, to develop a lasting interest in and sense of caring for the forest, and to acquire knowledge about outdoor activities. Teachers aimed to help students appreciate that they have outdoor rights, e.g. to walk, swim, camp, etc., outdoors, but that they also have responsibilities towards both nature itself and land custodians (farmers, foresters, community, etc.). The day's programme included reading of the work of Norwegian poets who wrote about nature (Boerli and Skjaeraasen); engaging in music (Michael Jackson's 'Heal the World'); watching a video about 'Forest and Animals in Buskerud' (the county in which the project took place); visiting the forest reservation for sensory experiences and engagement in a variety of outdoor activities; cooking an outdoor meal and working on practical nature protection/conservation tasks. Homework for the day involved the writing of personal logs on the day's experiences.

Wednesday: This was a day for group activities in the natural world. The art group adopted the phrase 'The Forest as a Source of Inspiration in Art' as a starting point for its endeavours. The day began with the pupils reading from their logbooks, describing what they had felt or experienced in relation to the forest. Then they studied the works of Norwegian painters who had used forests or trees as a theme or inspiration. They discussed why so many Norwegian painters were inspired by forests and trees (e.g. Kittelsen, Munch, Th. Eriksen, Astrup, J.C. Dahl, E. Enge, etc.). On realising that many artists are inspired by trees, they began to realise that forests are important not just for practical (scientific) reasons, but also in terms of personal feelings and experiences. They discussed ways in which forests are threatened, and the urgent need to conserve and protect forest areas. Students then followed individual interests in forest-related art, leading to the assembling of an exhibition of the pupils' creative work. Their art work depicted a range of themes, including damage to trees, and the beauty and richness of the forest. Each student then chose to study the way in which the forest has inspired one particular artist (involved in painting, music or literature), and linked this to the creation of their own works of art. For example, one student was familiar with Grieg's music 'The Hall of the Dovregubben' ('Dovregubben' is the 'head' of the trolls in Dovre, which is the Norwegian national mountain) and thus chose to work on the composition of forest music. Another student gained inspiration from the forest and wrote the words for songs for which he later composed music.

Thursday: Students continued with individual forest experiences and creative outcomes.

Friday: Projects were completed, presented for the whole group to share, and the week's work was evaluated. Questions for pupil evaluations included: What did you learn? What do you think the forest means to you? Why are forests important to the world? What is your opinion about practical project work of this kind? (What could have been done differently?)

The evaluations were overwhelmingly positive, and the students' works of art inspirational. They had worked seriously and enthusiastically with impressive creative outcomes relating to their personal forest experiences. The teachers are sure that their experiences and memories will be carried forward by the pupils into adult life.

Lillian Larsen MA is responsible for environmental education in vocational and technical studies (also art, craft and design) teacher training at Akershus College, Oslo.

With thanks to Randi Sylling Hersleth and Marit Skarstad Green who were two of the teachers of the project whilst following the part-time in-service course 'Environmental Education in Vocational and Technical Studies' at Akershus College.

Concern for content

Just as an analysis of significant life experiences affecting environment thinking has critical messages for the development of education programmes, so too does an analysis of what might be described as the 'content' of environmental education – that wealth of knowledge and facts about environmental problems, impacts, inter-relationships, issues and resolutions that is summarised in Part II. Indeed, that significant part of this text is devoted to outlining 'the global agenda' because of the significance of comprehensive coverage of it in educational pro- grammes. Adequate content of environmental education, i.e. an appropriate range of knowledge, concepts and understandings, is critical. Various published guidelines provide what might be described as a basic overview of areas to be covered. For example, the National Curriculum Documentation in England and Wales (NCC, 1990) suggests that seven areas of knowledge and understand- ing are identified that may form the basis for the development of worthwhile topics or subject-based interpretation (climate; soils, rocks and minerals; water; materials and resources, including energy; plants and animals; people and their communities; buildings, industrialisation and waste). This list is augmented with a set of objectives for the gaining of knowledge, e.g. 'pupils should develop knowledge and understanding of – the natural processes that take place in the environment; the impact of human activities on the environment; environ- mental issues such as the greenhouse effect, acid rain, air pollution; how human lives and livelihoods are dependent on the environment; how conflicts can arise about environmental issues', etc. Such lists are helpful. They at least indicate the range of topics to be covered, and questions and aspects to be focused upon. Yet surely they are also extremely limited, perhaps to the point of being misleading about an appropriate curriculum content and coverage. This serious challenge will be elaborated upon with reference to a number of serious limitations of suggested content for environmental education as found in 'typical' curriculum documents. Such documents are generally based on internationally agreed goals and objectives for instruction deriving from Belgrade, Tbilisi and other 'land-mark' events. The limitations cited will constitute a useful series of points to consider when planning educational programmes.

Firstly, the majority of curriculum guidelines and overviews of content of environmental issues (no doubt for good reasons of lack of space) fail to address the true complexities and inter-relationships that exist among people, their culture and bio-physical surroundings. More often than not, it is suggested that pupils should gain knowledge and understanding of environmental issues (such as the greenhouse effect, acid rain, air pollution, tropical forests). Indeed they should; but shouldn't they also gain an understanding of the fact that such issues cannot be understood and addressed in isolation from other issues? For example, air pollution from the increased use of fossil fuels is harming human health, causing acid rain, which in turn damages whole ecosystems and increases the build-up of atmospheric carbon dioxide and the likelihood of global warming and climate instability. Another example is unsustainable agriculture, i.e. the reliance on methods of food production that emphasise maximum short-term yields while causing environmental damage and long-term loss of natural productivity, which is an important or significant cause of a whole range of global problem impacts including unmet basic human needs, species depletion, habitat degradation, land degradation, desertification, loss of soil fertility, depletion of fresh water, water pollution, air pollution and human conflict. Environmental issues are an incredibly complicated web or network of inter-related causes and problem impacts. Relationships between issues may well be addressed within a single topic – for example, when studying rainforests, no doubt matters relating to biodiversity, endangered species, habitat degradation and so on will be incorporated – yet rarely is the complex web or network of inter-related causes and problem impacts addressed in a systematic way. By missing out on such systematic addressing of environmental complexities, it would seem that pupils and students rarely acquire any adequate comprehension of the true impact of causal factors and priority solutions. Indeed, small-scale research confirms this. Over a period of several years, intelligent undergraduate students enrolling on a course entitled 'Study of the Environment: Basic Principles and Global Issues' at the author's own university were asked in the course's first session what they considered to be the single most serious problem or issue affecting the planet today. Out of several hundred responses over the years, by far the most common were 'pollution', 'global warming' and 'destruction of the rainforests' – obviously topics that had been studied in school or had made impact through the media. The number of students that cited 'increase in human population' could be counted on two or three fingers. Yet research shows (see p. 59) that slowing population growth is the most effective single measure for alleviating the whole range of global problem impacts. Furthermore, experience shows that alongside a lack of systematic addressing of environmental complexities and inter-relationships is a situation in which the same, and rather limited, range of topics are taught over and over again in educational

249

institutions (notably global warming, acid rain, pollution, tropical rainforests, water resources) to the exclusion of a range of other equally significant ones, notably those focusing on 'human issues', poverty, inequality, etc. The reason that a fair amount of priority detail of specific global issues, of development and environment, and of the inter-dependence and complexity of problem impacts and causes is provided in Part II, is to provide indicative content or a framework for comprehensive coverage of the global agenda in education programmes – particularly at the level of teacher education.

A second limitation of many curriculum guidelines, which is in many ways linked to the first, is that they fail to emphasise, or even address at all, the distinctive role of human life in the ecological framework. Recommendations such as 'pupils should develop knowledge and understanding of the impact of human activities on the environment' (NCC, 1990) conceal the true complexity of such activities. Pupils may well learn about impact and interactions of living things in the biosphere, without fully appreciating the inequality of *Homo sapiens* as producer and consumer, and the injustice that typifies many of the relationships and activities in which humans are involved. Few texts that contain sound overviews of the science of ecology provide adequate or even scant coverage of humans' unique role in the biosphere. All of the basic principles and processes relating to ecological balance and stability can potentially be altered and disrupted by human activities. Such activities are peculiar in that they encompass biological, technological, industrial, economic and social interactions. Whilst, like all other species, people are dependent on natural ecosystems and the geophysical environment, we alone modify natural ecosystems, deplete non-renewable resources, generate pollution and produce non-recyclable hazardous waste substances. The impact of human life is edging natural systems close to the limit of the planet's carrying capacity, with international, inter-species and inter-generational implications (Palmer, 1995a). So many issues in educational programmes, the media and elsewhere are viewed and debated from a human-centred perspective. A good example is the threat to species and the need to conserve biodiversity. More often than not, a key argument given for this is the loss of a generic pool that is required for medical and other scientific advances. A sense of justice that extends to all species, in all locations, and which is not tied to the short-term needs of present generations, must surely encompass a planetary, ecological dimension, and, most importantly, must be incorporated into educational programmes in the field of ecology.

Thirdly, most 'lists' of objectives for the gaining of knowledge and understanding about the environment fail to be persuasive about the true inter-disciplinary nature of environmental understanding. Emphasis is almost invariably on the scientific knowledge to be gained, and at best encompasses some aspects of the social sciences. Debate and understanding of spiritual and aesthetic dimensions are very rarely documented as a priority. This fact reinforces the point already made several times in the text: that environmental education is grounded in and often perceived as 'the child of' science education.

It also aligns with the point made above, that school-based teaching programmes tend to address a limited range of common (and usually science-based) issues, to the exclusion of other significant ones, thus failing to address the true complexity of planetary inter-relationships.

Fourthly, the production of international, national or even local area guidelines and goals for the teaching of environmental knowledge leads to the inevitable assumption that these have some reified status. This point has already been considered on p. 101, but has renewed relevance here. Even without a *radical* shift in thinking about the status of guidelines and goals, surely it is important to move at least in some small way towards the view that guidelines and goals should be the subject of regular appraisal and reappraisal by educators themselves who function *within a particular community and context*. Thus the status-related limitations attributable to 'generally agreed' guideline statements are that they have a tendency to acquire lasting status (e.g. the statement of Aims produced by the NAEE still has considerable influence – albeit in revised form – on the delivery of environmental education in the UK today) and that they discourage educators from determining their own perhaps more locally appropriate goals.

A fifth limitation of generalised statements is that they mask the complexity, not just of the issues themselves, but of the teaching and learning process. They fail to address the importance of progression in learning, the relevance of prior knowledge, and learners' tendencies to acquire misconceptions and biased, stereotypical areas about people and places. Aspects of the 'Emergent Environmentalism' research project described on pp. 111–113 illustrate a range of erroneous ideas possessed by young people in the early years of schooling. Preconceptions or misconceptions can be held at any age or stage of learning, and research shows that they may actually be *reinforced* by school-based programmes. One of the environmental issues addressed in 'Emergent Environmentalism' is management of waste materials. Children aged 4 and 6 were interviewed with the aims of ascertaining what knowledge and understanding they had relating to this issue, and how knowledge develops during children's first two years in school. A concept map was constructed for each subject, recording the network of related scientific concepts referred to, explained and seemingly understood. Data confirm the view that many young children who are about to enter the stages of formal schooling know a good deal about their environment (Palmer, 1995b). Forty-nine per cent of the 4 year olds understood that waste products are 'managed' in the sense that they are collected in an organised manner; 23 per cent of the 4 year olds had heard of the concept of recycling and had some idea of what this means: the idea of using waste again or 'not throwing it away forever'. Still higher levels of understanding were demonstrated by 6 per cent of 4 year olds, who could explain that some waste can be recycled whilst other materials cannot, and 2 per cent of the sample understood the concept of conservation or reduction of waste, i.e. that recycling enables us to save materials because it uses waste again. Every 6 year old interviewed could explain that waste should not be left lying around; it should be placed 'in a bin'; 97 per cent of the sample could then articulate ideas relating to the organised collection of waste. Interestingly, very few 6 year olds could offer an explanation of why materials are recycled, i.e. the concept of reducing waste or conservation of materials. Beyond the 'new from old' explanation, the children almost invariably replied 'don't know' when asked at greater length about reasons for making new from old. No one in the sample could explain this in any greater depth than the 4 year olds. Some of the 6 year olds certainly demonstrated higher levels of understanding, for example they could explain that materials are selectively recycled; 21 per cent were so well informed that they could explain that only some of our waste is recycled (accurately naming materials that could be), and also suggest a realistic destination for that which is not. Yet a number of 'standard' or common confusions dominated the data from the 6 year olds (whereas as far as the 4 year olds are concerned, their incomplete answers tended to represent uncertainty or lack of knowledge rather than confusion and established misconceptions). A substantial number of the 6 year olds explained that *all* waste can and should be recycled. Other 'standard' confusions related to the recycling process itself. Probing beyond the 'using things again, new from old' concepts, discussions revealed that many children held the false idea that it is the very same can (crisp packet, bottle, etc.) that is used again for the same purpose for which it was originally intended. Only a very small number of children articulated accounts of the actual recycling process that touched on reality. Other substantial misconceptions surrounded 'genuine' recycling in the sense of a managed, factory-based process, and the use of waste for creative purposes. The point being emphasised here is that such misconceptions are held despite (or even reinforced as a result of ?) school-based teaching. An analysis of the sources of knowledge and misconceptions, insofar as these could be ascertained, suggests that school was the single most important influence on the thinking of 6 year olds. The misconceptions and blurred knowledge referred to above derived from children who had recently studied waste as a classroom-based topic. It would seem that such topics had focused exclusively on encouraging children not to throw waste around but to put it in the correct place, and on generally encouraging them to recycle materials. It would appear that scant attention had been paid to reasons *why* recycling is important, to details of the process, and to various methods of dealing with waste materials (Palmer, 1995b). In conclusion, then, it would seem that directives laid down within agreed guidelines – to teach pupils *x* (for example, issues such as the management of waste materials) – can actually do more harm than good unless teachers taking on board such programmes of instruction are themselves familiar with the range of accurate concepts to be acquired, how these may link together in the development of progressive understanding, and of common misconceptions and confusions that may arise in thinking, and that need to be addressed. This comment applies to all stages of education of course, not just teaching in the early years of schooling.

This tendency for guideline statements to mask the complexity of the learning process effectively leads into the next section of this text. This articulates a concern for professional development, and the urgent need for teachers to be aware, not just of environmental issues themselves, but of the teaching and learning process pertaining to them. First, however, we turn to a case study that illustrates good practice relating to the content of environmental education programmes. In particular, this example challenges the limitations of the scientific approach to environmental education, and potentially inappropriate goals. In other words, it addresses the third and fourth limitation of generalised guideline statements as discussed on pp. 250–251. The account that follows is persuasive about the true inter-disciplinary nature of environmental understanding. It is concerned in part with particular skills and scientific knowledge to be gained by pupils, but it also explores pupils' affective relationships with, and commitment to, action in the natural environment. It takes account of locally appropriate goals, and it is also an excellent example of 'teacher as researcher' in action.

OUTDOOR ACTIVITIES AS A SOURCE OF ENVIRONMENTAL RESPONSIBILITY

BY IRMELI PALMBERG AND JARI KURU

Background

This case study describes an investigation into the role and possibilities of outdoor education in environmental education. It was conducted at two locations in Finland, Vaasa and Rovaniemi, involving collaboration between staff at the Åbo Akademi University in Vaasa and the University of Lapland in Rovaniemi. The study was based on the premiss that outdoor environmental education programmes (including field experiences, hiking and adventure activities) are, through the first-hand and personal experiences involved, able to make a significant contribution to the development of pupils' affective relationship to the natural environment, their environmental sensitivity and outdoor behaviour, and their social relationships. Qualitative research methods were used to pursue this investigation, including the use of individual interviews, participant observation, photographs of landscapes, drawings and questionnaires.

Teaching hiking skills is one basis of the environmental education programme in the teacher training school of the University of Lapland (grades 1–6) including: trips to nearby forests (taking responsibility for themselves, their personal belongings and the environment by not littering and by tidying up); hiking in forests (learning about the terrain, animals and plants as well as the legal right of access to open country in practice); farming (learning about farm life); canoe trips to a national park (experiencing the national park by adventure); overnight skiing trips and a three-day hiking trip (learning about winter nature, taking responsibility for setting up camp, for equipment and for food).

Corresponding outdoor activities are also included in the programme of outdoor/environmental education in the teacher training school of Åbo Akademi University, with the additional inclusion of one-week camp schools in collaboration with the Department of Teacher Education. Outdoor education and environmental education are current projects at the Department of Teacher Education in Vaasa, including teaching programmes and research work that involve both student teachers and teachers.

The purpose of the investigation being reported here was to seek answers and tendencies in relation to the following questions:

1 Do nature experiences develop pupils' *self-confidence and action skills*?

- Are there any differences between pupils who have experience of outdoor activities and pupils who have not?

2 What kind of *relationships to the natural environment* do pupils have?

- What kind of conceptions of nature do they have?
- What do they appreciate in nature?
- How do they value nature?
- How important is nature to them (egocentric and/or ecological approaches)?
- What kind of personal meanings do they have?
- What kind of places do they prefer?
- Are there any differences between pupils who have experience of outdoor activities and pupils who have not?

3 What does *protection of nature* mean to pupils?

- Do they recognise/know about environmental problems?
- What kind of attitudes to environmental problems do they have?
- Do they have moral judgements from the point of view of ecological values?
- Do they worry about nature?
- Are there any differences between pupils who have experiences of outdoor activities and pupils who have not?

4 What kind of *responsible action/action skills* do pupils have?

- Do they want to take action for nature?
- Do they know how to take action?
- Do they themselves act according to their own attitudes?
- Are there any differences between pupils who have experience of outdoor activities and pupils who have not?

Methods

The participants in this study were 11-year-old pupils from the teacher training school of the University of Lapland (n = 22, 16 boys, 6 girls) and 11–12-year-old pupils from the teacher training school of Åbo Akademi University (Group

A: n = 8, 6 boys, 2 girls) and from a municipal comprehensive school (Group B: n = 6, 2 boys, 4 girls). The Vaasa pupils were selected on the basis of a survey of their experiences of outdoor education and outdoor life conducted in both schools. Group A comprised pupils who had the most experience of outdoor education. They attended the school that provided regular opportunities for such things as camping, fieldwork, sailing, hiking and canoeing. Group B comprised pupils who had the least experience of outdoor education. Their school had only one outdoor or sports day per year.

All participants were interviewed individually about their conceptions of, feelings for, and emotions towards nature – what it means to them and how they might protect it. They were invited to discuss local and global environmental problems and to describe pleasant and unpleasant experiences in nature. Further data were gleaned by asking Rovaniemi pupils to express their feelings and emotions by drawing a natural environment in Finland that they found especially attractive; by asking them to identify 'most' and 'least' attractive environments from photographs; and by observing and video-filming their actions during outdoor experiences. Pupils from Vaasa were observed and video-filmed during a one-day camp, to investigate such things as their practical skills, ability to take responsibility, to co-operate and to interact with others and the environment.

Findings*

The results of this study may be grouped under four headings.

Pupils' self confidence and action skills

It was found that personal experiences in the natural world develop pupils' self-confidence and feelings of safety, thus encouraging the desire for further participation. Pupils with more experience of outdoor activities had positive attitudes, knew their own limits and were spontaneously open-minded and co-operative. Less experienced subjects were considerably more uncertain and anxious about trying new things.

Pupils' relationships to the natural environment

Subjects' conceptions of nature varied considerably. The majority fell into what might be described as the ecocentric category (environmental problems are immediate and local, and the environment is something to be used – see Ballantyne and Packer, 1996). In general, the more experienced pupils had more comprehensive definitions/conceptions of the natural world than the inexperienced ones. Thus there were differences in how and what subjects appreciate in nature – some seek beauty from the natural environment, others privacy and peace, others freedom to explore and express themselves. Nature was important

255

to almost all subjects. To some it was an important place to go, to others it was important from an ecological point of view. Many expressed concern directed towards the welfare of animals. The pupils' drawings indicated that a pleasant natural environment was to them also a beautiful environment, e.g. a typical Finnish landscape. Among the displayed photographs they preferred places with smoothness, light, complexity, mystery and water. These preferences were connected to personal meanings, based on prior experiences and emotions (see Kuru, 1996). It was found that pupils who were more experienced in outdoor activities had a stronger and more clearly defined empathetic relationship to nature.

Pupils' knowledge of and values in the protection of nature

In addition to expressing concern about the welfare of animals, many subjects emphasised the importance of the protection of nature in general. Most of the values and concerns were based on personal feelings, e.g. 'it makes me sad when they fell trees and animals lose their homes'. Around 50 per cent of the sample expressed anxiety concerning environmental problems and the protection of the natural world, yet had difficulty in distinguishing environmental problems at different levels, i.e. local and global. For example, pollution of nature was described by the majority of subjects as a major problem, yet explanations of this ranged from descriptions of local litter, to air pollution and ocean pollution. Several pupils, mostly in the 'inexperienced' group, could give no examples of global problems. The most experienced subjects were more familiar with issues and showed a strong reactive empathy to nature (in association with pictures showed to them). The level of moral judgement from an ecological point of view was also found to be higher among the experienced pupils.

Pupils' environmentally responsible actions/action skills

The study was based on the premiss that responsible environmental behaviour is a learned response/action; that increased awareness and knowledge of environmental action strategies contribute to increased motivation to take action; and that self-esteem and pupils' beliefs and values are other factors related to action taking. (See, for example, Sia *et al.*, 1985; Dresner and Gill, 1994). Yet the findings reveal deficiencies in understandings of action competence, even in pupils with extensive experience of the natural world. For example, the most commonly suggested action for nature was to pick up litter. Whilst being able to suggest this, the subjects did not understand that the action was part of the sorting and management of waste in general. Hence minimising the amount of waste products we generate was not seen as an important action. Although most of the subjects mentioned non-littering as a key way to act 'for' nature, many of them confessed that they still occasionally threw litter in the streets (including some from the most experienced in nature group). Reasons for conflicts between environmental attitudes and behaviour may be explained in terms of conscious versus unconscious behaviour, and by the fact that fragmented knowledge does not reach the level of applied knowledge.

The study concludes that both knowledge and values play a major part in decision-making. Knowledge that enables the pupil to understand the dependence and interaction in relations between people and nature will, together with personal values, form a basis for willingness to act. Various activities in outdoor education can stimulate environmental education wherein the pupils learn about and experience nature while at the same time they learn the skills of and develop better understanding of action strategies. Experiences in outdoor activities have great possibilities for the development of a strong empathetic relationship to nature in the participants.

*Present space allows for only a brief overview of the study's findings. For a fuller account see Palmberg, I. and Kuru, J. (in press) 'Outdoor Activities as a Source of Environmental Responsibility', *Environmental Education Research.*

References

Ballantyne, R.R. and Packer, J.M. (1996) 'Teaching and Learning in Environmental Education: Developing Environmental Conceptions', *Journal of Environmental Education*, 27 (2) 25–32.

Dresner, M. and Gill, M. (1994) 'Environmental Education at Summer Nature Camp', *Journal of Environmental Education*, 25 (3) 35–41.

Kuru, J. (1996) 'Nature Experiences and Personal Meanings', paper presented at Northern Call for the Environment. International Conference On Environmental Education, Savonlinna, Finland, 26–30 June.

Sia, A.P., Hungerford, H.R. and Tomera, A.N. (1985) 'Selected Predictors of Responsible Environmental Behaviour: An Analysis', *Journal of Environmental Education*, 17 (2) 31–40.

Irmeli Palmberg PhD is Senior Lecturer in Biology Education, Department of Teacher Education, Åbo Akademi University, 65100 Vaasa, Finland.

Jari Kuru MEd is a teacher at the Teacher Training School, University of Lapland, 96100 Rovaniemi, Finland.

Concern for professional development

Many of the core ideas developed in this book obviously carry critical messages for initial teacher training and the continuing professional development of teachers. For example:

- the need to motivate teachers to want to spend time and resources on this area of the curriculum;
- the need for teachers to receive practical and accessible advice on how best to approach and implement environmental education, given already over-crowded timetables and other pressures;

- the need to help teachers acquire an adequate and appropriate range of subject matter knowledge themselves in order to be able to teach it effectively;
- the need to help teachers acquire pedagogic knowledge – i.e. knowledge of learning processes relating to environmental education; the importance of prior knowledge, progression in learning and so on;
- the need for teachers to understand different ideologies or perspectives on the root causes of environmental problems so that students can be exposed to a plurality of ideologies, thus developing their own set of environmental beliefs and values;
- the need to help teachers to understand and appreciate the various structural components and emphases of teaching and learning in the environmental education field (as depicted in Figures 4.2, 6.1, 6.2, 6.3).

Despite these needs, made obvious by the rapid growth of interest in environmental issues, and the many calls for promoting world-wide programmes of environmental education or education for sustainable living, it would seem that teacher education in these fields is far from widespread. Much has been written about the need for professional development, by national governments and international governmental commissions, by major groups such as UNESCO–UNEP (1990, 1992), and by individual researchers and writers. Research indicates that good practice in environmental and development education is not widespread, that few teachers appreciate the full range of objectives, resources and strategies in these fields, and that few have received either pre-service studies or undertaken in-service professional development in them (Fien, 1995 who also cites Stapp and Stapp, 1983; Fien, 1986; Spork, 1992). Where pre-service education courses have existed, doubts have been cast about whether a number of them have successfully met their goals (Stapp *et al.*, 1980; Wilke *et al.*, 1987). Tilbury (1992) discusses a number of 'models' for teacher education which emerged during the 1980s and finds criticism with them all. Some are claimed to be too content-focused (UNESCO–UNEP, 1990), some too specialised (Marcinkowski *et al.*, 1990), some insufficiently contextualised in the realities of the curriculum (Hungerford *et al.*, 1988), and some much too limited in their appreciation of the need for a strategic approach to change within teacher education institutions (Stapp *et al.*, 1980). Tilbury calls for a 'realistic model' that can match up the complexities of environmental education with the intricacies of teacher education programmes and institutions and which is accompanied by '... sound strategies which ensure its development ...' within pre-service teacher education (Tilbury, 1992 in Oulton and Scott, 1995).

For Robottom (1987), in line with his call for environmental education to move from its foothold in the positivist paradigm to the adoption of socially critical philosophy and practices, professional development should be inquiry-based. He provides a useful account of action research as an inquiry base for professional development, and summarises five 'guiding principles for professional development in environmental education' (both pre-service and continuing professional development), viz:

- Professional development in environmental education should be inquiry-based (encouraging participation at all levels)
- Professional development in environmental education should be participatory and practice-based
- Professional development in environmental education should be critical
- Professional development in environmental education should be community-based
- Professional development in environmental education should be collaborative

(Robottom, 1987, pp. 114–115)

An account follows that addresses the issue of providing realistic models for professional development with sound implementation and development strategies.

A REALISTIC MODEL FOR EDUCATING THE 'ENVIRONMENTALLY EDUCATING TEACHER'

BY CHRISTOPHER R. OULTON AND WILLIAM A.H. SCOTT

Introduction

Alongside the assertion that environmental education should be a component of the formal educational system (IUCN, 1970; UNCED, 1992) often comes a recognition of the need for pre-service and in-service teacher education programmes that prepare individual teachers to contribute to environmental education in school (IUCN, 1971; UNESCO–UNEP, 1976; UNESCO, 1978; Wilkie, et al., 1987; UNESCO–UNEP, 1990). This account critiques UNESCO–UNEP's ideas on what constitutes an environmentally educated teacher, and goes on to examine priorities for pre-service courses, drawing on a recent European Union initiative. The paper concludes with a series of organisational principles, explicated in the form of course aims, programme elements and didactics characteristics, which might inform the work of pre-service programmes.

Environmentally educated teachers: the priority of priorities

As a starting point for our critique we turn to UNESCO–UNEP's (1990) ideas on what constitutes an environmentally educated teacher. The paper defines the desired result of 'EE training programmes for teachers' as, firstly, 'foundation competencies in professional education' and, secondly, 'competencies in EE content', at four levels: ecological foundations; conceptual awareness; investigation and evaluation; environmental action skills.

Whilst we believe this analysis to be helpful, we do not see it as useful. Our three main concerns are set out below.

Firstly, the paper assumes that developing environmental education (EE) in teacher education programmes is unproblematic. This is unrealistic and we recognise a range of factors (Scott, 1994) that may militate against the inclusion of EE in such programmes. The lack of an overarching rationale for the particular competencies that the UNESCO–UNEP paper lists is a major omission that militates against the usefulness of the paper as a whole. Such a rationale might begin to persuade colleagues in pre-service programmes that this is worth doing, and that they should be involved.

Secondly, the paper is inappropriately conceptualised. In particular, it is too heavily focused on ecology, without acknowledging the role of other disciplines. There is also an implicit assumption that teachers act alone, and have a large degree of influence or control over curricula. Team-building and team-working competencies are lacking from the list. The paper, at times, presents a technicist view of teaching and learning that is problematic, as we support Robottom's (1989) critique of such technicist approaches. Inevitably, the paper is locked into a pre-UNCED (UNESCO–UNEP, 1992) view of the way forward, and for this reason alone revision is required.

Thirdly, the paper is orientated to ends rather than means in that it presents a daunting and unrealistic list of competencies to be achieved. This is exacerbated by a lack of differentiation between the needs of in-service and pre-service programmes; primary and secondary courses; fundamental and subsidiary priorities. The text also assumes that conditions are right in schools for EE to develop, and that all that is needed is for teachers to have the requisite competencies. There is no suggestion that there might be considerable constraints and that management of innovation issues and processes are involved, which means that there is a need to introduce teachers and novice teachers to the theory and practice of the management of innovation in order to prepare them to take an active role within schools. We prefer the phrase 'environmentally *educating* teacher' as this signifies the dynamic nature of the process we are considering.

Beyond UNESCO–UNEP: other perspectives

The largest question that remains unaddressed, and which underpins the issue of how we achieve desired ends, is that of who is going to do this? The UNESCO–UNEP paper does rather assume that the skills, resources and motivations required to effect such goals are in place. In terms of pre-service courses, this is simply not the case. Universities and schools are not, with a few notable exceptions, repositories of such expertise (see Williams, 1992 and the studies discussed by Fien, 1994) . Tutors' competence needs to be developed, and their awareness raised. In other words, programmes are needed whereby experts work with teacher educators on this area. Where is the staff development for this to occur?

Whilst all these questions need attention, we wish to focus on what we feel is the important question as far as pre-service programmes are concerned, that is, what limits do you realistically place on the focus and goals of such programmes? What should the priorities be for pre-service programmes in terms of organisation, content and approach, given the limited state of EE within such programmes currently?

Tilbury (1992), as already mentioned above, having largely dismissed a range of 'models' proposed over the last 15 years for the inclusion of EE into pre-service teacher education, calls for a 'realistic model' that can match up the complexities of EE with the intricacies of teacher education programmes and institutions, and which is accompanied by ' . . . sound strategies which will ensure its development . . . ' within pre-service teacher education.

What, then, might a 'realistic model' be?

Developing a realistic model

Experience of two research and development programmes – *Thinking Futures* (Bullock *et al.*, 1996) and EEITE (Brinkman and Scott, 1994) – suggests that a multicomponent strategy will be needed if EE goals are to be realised in pre-service programmes. There are two sets of issues here: managing the introduction of the innovation, and managing the aims and outcomes of the EE innovation itself.

Managing the innovation

In terms of *innovation*, the following need to be considered:

- Positional and/or professional authority
- Course committees and academic boards
- The course team and course management
- Individual tutors
- Partnership schools
- Novice teachers

Positional and/or professional authority

Kanter (1983) has suggested that:

> Any new strategy, no matter how brilliant or responsive, no matter how much agreement the formulators have about it, will stand a good chance of not being implemented fully – or sometimes at all – without someone with power pushing it.

This reality calls for a dual approach. It argues for a continuation of the external pushes aimed at making the intellectual case for EE, within pre-service courses; it also argues for tutors within institutions and schools to continue, formally and informally, to press the case internally, and to support this by carrying out persuasive research studies.

Course committees and academic boards

Academic boards and committees that adopt policies and generally validate, monitor and evaluate courses and programmes are also open to persuasion and are susceptible to the push of external persuasion. Their approval of an initiative can confer considerable respectability and status.

The course team and course management

These are significant 'gatekeepers' to any innovation, and any internal *push* will need to persuade such groups. It is here that battles are likely to be fought over the prioritisation of curriculum time, and where arguments must be won if EE is to be seen as an entitlement. For success, there needs to be clarity in the defining of purposes and practice, precision in timetabling and organisational requirements and a shared understanding.

Individual tutors

It is here that most flexibility exists. Wherever individual tutors are both willing and able to deliver EE goals through their particular programmes, there are few logistical or other reasons to prevent them. However, it is clear that most tutors are not currently involved, so how might a transition most appropriately be effected? The research report in *Thinking Futures: Making Space for Environmental Education in ITE – A Handbook for Educators*, by Bullock *et al.* (1996), highlights one route.

Bullock *et al.* comment on an initiative where a number of tutors from varying disciplines worked together with experts and resource support from the

Resources and conditions necessary for staff-development programmes

Phase 1	• tutors willing to come together and explore ideas	• time for working together as a group on EE itself and its pedagogical facets
	• a source of expertise to guide the development, acting as a consultant to all tutors involved in the initiative	• appropriate resources; some of these will be EE-specialist materials; others will be subject- or phase-specific
Phase 2	• time for individual experimentation; ideally this involves working with novice teachers trying out a small number of ideas; guidance from the consultant	• the opportunity to share outcomes and plan for future activity, ideally on a co-operative mutually supportive basis guided by the consultant
Phase 3	• time to build on developments, ideally by building an aspect of EE into the subject didactics programme and reviewing progress	• collective review of developments and joint action-planning for future individual and collective work; guidance by the consultant

World Wide Fund for Nature in a conscious attempt to make the shift discussed above. The outcomes of this development suggest that resources and conditions needed for such a shift are eight-fold and need to be organised in three phases. This is shown in the three-phase model on p. 262.

Phase 1 itself might usefully occur in more than one stage, and be integrated with the beginnings of Phase 2, rather than requiring a strict sequence. This model is very flexible and adaptable.

Partnership schools

Given that the prime purpose of having environmentally educating teachers is to further EE in schools, it seems appropriate to involve schools and teachers in practice within pre-service courses. Where particular expertise resides in a school, that should be drawn upon, and where EE courses are run in schools, novice teachers need to get involved.

Even where none of this is found, every school affords the interested novice the opportunity of experimenting with approaches in their own work, subject only to the agreement of the school or subject department in this process. Ideally, to support this, EE developments within pre- and in-service work need to be focused around IT-INSET work in partnership schools.

Novice teachers

Novice teachers are crucial participants in the innovation. There are two issues here. Firstly, part of their awareness-raising might usefully involve sharing the importance of such developments both in terms of EE, and in respect of the need to encourage novices' own competence, and that of schools. Secondly, many novice teachers themselves have both experience and expertise to contribute to this process.

Aims and outcomes

In terms of aims and outcomes, we need to consider what the outcomes of our ambitions for EE within pre-service programmes ought to be, and to ask what might environmentally educating teachers have experienced, and what skills or awareness might they have acquired by the end of a course? We should also consider the extent to which it is appropriate for novice teachers to define their own developmental objectives. The answers to such questions will determine what limits the pre-service course should set itself.

Finding responses to these questions has been at the heart of the EEITE project (Brinkman and Scott, 1994) which drew up a series of organisational principles to underpin the work of pre-service courses in this regard. These are set out in the following case study.

Case study of pre-service course development – the EEITE project

This case study sets out a number of organisational principles in the form of course aims, programme elements and didactics characteristics that might inform the work of pre-service teacher education.

The course aims are that as a result of pre-service teacher education programmes, novice teachers should be both willing and able to make a contribution to environmental education through their own work with learners;

- *willing* in a sense that they understand the importance of environmental education and have a personal commitment to it that is both practical and intellectual;
- *able* in a sense that they have a repertoire of management of change and curriculum innovation strategies upon which they can draw in co-operation with others.

These are ambitious aims, and in order to achieve them, pre-service programmes will need to contain two *elements*. These elements are listed here separately, but this should not be taken to mean that these will necessarily be separate in practice; rather, tutors will have the responsibility of deciding the inter-relationships between these (and other) elements for themselves – and for determining the patterns of organisation and support that their development work will have. It will also be necessary to encourage diversity and to monitor practice in order to gain insights into the transferability of particular approaches and programme designs between institutions.

The two programme *elements* are:

I aims and practice

- a consideration of the aims and practice of environmental education, particularly as it relates to compulsory schooling;
- an examination of curriculum practice and extra-curricular opportunities and the desired learning outcomes associated with these;
- the identification of these characteristics which mark out curriculum activity as contributing to environmental education;
- an exploration of particular strategies and approaches that can be employed in environmental education.

II personal experience in environmental education

- working with teachers and children in schools on suitably small-scale activities;
- evaluating this practice and building on the foundations laid through reflection and systematic planning;
- in particular, evaluating the effects of this practice on both their own and children's awareness of the possibilities and priorities of environmental education.

It is necessary to emphasise the incremental and iterative nature of such developments, and the consequent necessity of taking a small-step approach, coupled with a focus on the management of innovation.

The EEITE project evolved a number of didactics characteristics that each institution's developmental project would try to follow. These might themselves describe desired characteristics of pre-service programmes.

The didactics characteristics are:

- in part at least, a local focus, drawing from, and contributing to, expertise and awareness in the local community;
- integration in initial teacher education programmes, rather than being an addition;
- a clear set of aims and desired learning outcomes, which are related to the goals of the pre-service programme;
- action-orientated, in that novice teachers will be involved in the planning, implementation and evaluation of the work, and will be encouraged to have an individual commitment to reflection so as to build the experience into their own professional development;
- values and attitude development are key features;
- processes and outcomes of the work can be shared with other subject didactics groups;
- an inter-disciplinary approach, involving more than one subject area or curriculum focus;
- a dual focus, in which tutors and teachers work with novice teachers, who for their part work with students in school;
- reflection on European and non-European and global aspects of environmental issues;
- a contribution to better citizenship through novice teachers being more informed and more active participants in a democratic society;
- a contribution to professional growth and development of novices as teachers and as reflective practitioners.

It is our contention that this model provides a realistic basis for the development of a wide range of environmental education activities in a variety of teacher education contexts. Support for this claim may be found in the case studies of EEITE projects that are reported in *Environmental Education Research* 2 (1) (1996).

References

Brinkman, F.G. and Scott, W.A.H. (eds) (1994) *Environmental Education into Initial Teacher Education in Europe (EEITE) 'the State of the Art'*, ATEE Cahiers No. 8, Brussels: Association of Teacher Education in Europe.

Bullock, K.M., English, T., Oulton, C.R. and Scott, W.A.H. (1996) 'Reflections on an Environmental Education Staff Development Initiative for Teacher Educators', in Champain, P. and Inman, S. (eds) *Thinking Futures: Making*

Space for Environmental Education in ITE – A Handbook for Educators, Godalming: WWF.

Champain, P. and Inman, S. (eds) (1996) *Thinking Futures: Making Space for Environmental Education in ITE – A Handbook for Educators*, Godalming: WWF.

Fien, J. (1994) 'Learning to Teach for a Sustainable World: Two Asia-Pacific Projects in Environmental Education for Teacher Education', paper presented to the ATEE Annual Conference, Prague.

IUCN (1970) *International Working Meeting on Environmental Education in the School Curriculum*, Paris: UNESCO.

IUCN (1971) *International Working Meeting on Environmental Education in the School Curriculum*, USA: IUCN.

Kanter, R.M. (1983) *The Change Masters*, London: Allen & Unwin.

Robottom, I. (1989) 'Social Critique or Social Control: Some Problems for Evaluation in Environmental Education', *Journal of Research in Science Teaching*, 26 (5) 435–443.

Scott, W.A.H. (1994) 'Diversity and Opportunity – Reflections on Environmental Education Within Initial Teacher Education Programmes Across the European Union', in Brinkman, F.G. and Scott, W.A.H. (eds) *Environmental Education into Initial Teacher Education in Europe (EEITE) 'the State of the Art'*, ATEE Cahiers No. 8, Brussels: Association of Teacher Education in Europe.

Tilbury, D. (1992) 'Environmental Education within Pre-service Teacher Education: The Priority of Priorities', *International Journal of Environmental Education and Information*, 11(4) 267–280.

UNCED (1992) *Agenda 21. The United Nations Programme of Action from Rio*, New York: UN.

UNESCO (1978) *Final Report: Intergovernmental Conference on Environmental Education*, Paris: UNESCO.

UNESCO–UNEP (1976) 'The Belgrade Charter', *Connect*, 1(1) 1–8.

UNESCO–UNEP (1990) 'Environmentally Educated Teachers: The Priority of Priorities?', *Connect*, 15 (1) 1–3.

UNESCO–UNEP (1992) 'UNCED: The Earth Summit', *Connect*, 17 (2).

Wilkie, R.J., Peyton, R.B. and Hungerford, H.R. (1987) 'Strategies for the Training of Teachers in Environmental Education', *International Environmental Education Programme; Environmental Education Series No. 25*, Paris: UNESCO–UNEP.

Williams, R. (1992) 'Report of a Survey of the Provision for Environmental Education in Initial Teacher Training', *Environmental Education and Teacher Education – Preparing for Change and Participation*, Sussex University, UK: Education Network for Environment and Development.

Bill Scott is a Senior Lecturer in the School of Education at the University of Bath, and is Director of the Centre for Research in Environmental Education Theory and Practice (CREE). Chris Oulton is Deputy Director of CREE and is Director of Studies for the School of Education's school-based PGCE in Partnership programme. He is also editor of the journal *Environmental Education Research*.

MODEL FOR ENVIRONMENTAL EDUCATION: TOWARDS PROGRESS AND PROMISE IN THE TWENTY-FIRST CENTURY

As the text draws to a close in this final part, an attempt will be made to summarise and draw together some of the central theoretical and practical aspects of environmental education that have so far been addressed, and to identify imperatives for action if progress is to be made in the new century.

It has been established that environmental education has the task of addressing an extremely wide-ranging and bewildering array of content. This is a dynamic, ever-changing content, characterised by highly complex inter-relationships, priority problem causes, impacts and solutions. The knowledge base of environmental education is made all the more difficult to comprehend because the human race often simply cannot understand environmental issues or their potential resolutions in any definitive or permanent sense. It is a highly value-laden content, and one person's solution may be another's catastrophe. It is a content that incorporates aesthetic, spiritual, social, political and economic dimensions alongside (not separate from) the purely scientific. Furthermore, it is a content that does not and should not focus solely on environmental disasters and negative issues. Environmental education is not simply about 'saving the whale' or indeed 'saving the world'. It is equally about the development of an appreciation of the wonders and beauty of the world, and of a sense of *wanting* to save it – in short, the development of ecological thinking or of an environmental ethic.

It has also been established that there are a number of different ideologies or perspectives on the root causes of environmental problems, which give rise to various implications for education. In particular, students should be exposed to a plurality of ideologies in order that they might develop their own set of environmental beliefs and values, and can then go on to pursue actions that are considered necessary and justifiable (according to their own reasoned thinking) to achieving environmental reform in accordance with the personal ideological position that has been adopted.

This position (i.e. relating to both content and ideologies) is in conflict with current educational practice. A series of inconsistencies and limitations has been established that suggest that the gap between the rhetoric and the reality of environmental education is wide. Various statements of internationally agreed guidelines and goals have been well publicised, yet, at best, attempts are made to implement them as unchallengeable 'givens', and more often than not, educators possess neither the time nor the motivation and training to implement (or appraise) them. A number of exciting and forward-thinking case studies have illuminated this text, yet regrettably they remain the shining examples of good practice rather than the global norm. Research shows that the influence of formal 'quality' environmental education is not as successful as it could or ought to be for two reasons: firstly, the logistical problems of its widespread implementation ensure that there is not a sufficient amount of it, and secondly, even when well-designed and seemingly appropriate programmes of environmental education do exist, it would appear that other influences on people's lives are far more significant than education programmes in the development of their environmental understanding, awareness, concern and action – and formal programmes take little or no account of these. Indeed it is extremely difficult to match up the complexities of environmental education with the intricacies and demands of formal education curricula and with the principles and processes of learning – at any stage of education, be it the early years of schooling or within teacher education programmes.

So what are the priorities for attempting to solve these problems? For some, as we have seen, the answers lie in major paradigm shifts: substantial changes in thinking and practice that may apply not solely to environmental education, but perhaps to education itself. Alternatively, solutions may be approached by the adoption of less radical charges in practice, for example, by taking account of and building upon prior knowledge and formative experiences; by setting locally appropriate goals; and, most importantly, by planning coverage of all of the core components of environmental teaching and learning.

For this latter task to be accomplished, a framework for guidance is surely necessary. So we return to an overall model for planning teaching and learning, which provides an elaboration of the model presented in Part IV, and takes account of other critical factors that have since been introduced.

In the first instance, the curriculum's essential 'elements' (empirical, ethical, aesthetic) deserve emphasis; hence stage 1 of the revised model (Figure 6.1) includes them. As explained in Part IV, these components of the model are useful in that they help make the critical links between the three-fold framework of environmental education and the dimensions of learning. It should be noted that a fourth element (previously introduced as the 'synoptic' element) is omitted since surely this is an all-embracing concept. Indeed the whole of the model is concerned with helping learners to realise the complex nature of the environment and making sure that they are introduced to the inseparable nature of the various components of an environment and to the inter-relations of these. This overarching complexity should be central to all planning. Any curriculum review needs to consider whether the essential elements are adequately covered by asking such questions as:

- do the pupils/students have as many opportunities as possible for empirical investigations *in* the environment; for observation, measuring, recording, interpreting and discussing what has been observed? Research has shown conclusively how important '*in* the environment' experiences are;
- are pupils made aware of the complex nature of the environment? Do studies help pupils realise the inter-relationships and complexities within and among issues; the inseparable nature of the various components of the environment, and the unique position of human life in relation to other things?
- is there a focus on aesthetic dimensions and qualitative study? '*In* the environment' experiences do not necessarily have to focus on quantitative investigations. Research shows the critical importance of aesthetic and

spiritual experiences, of realising that there is no right or wrong answer in absolute terms to aesthetic questions;

• are the pupils/students introduced to the ideas of personal responsibility for the environment and the concept of stewardship? In other words, does the programme contain ethical dimensions; encouraging learners to ask if the criteria of proposed actions are based on morally justifiable values?

Whilst this static model (Figure 6.1) shows the three elements as primarily located within one of the three approaches to teaching and learning (about, in and for the environment), it should be emphasised that inevitably they merge and overlap. Such are the limitations of two-dimensional representation. How useful it would be if the diagram's three circles were revolving spheres, whose surface elements similarly rotated and blended with each other.

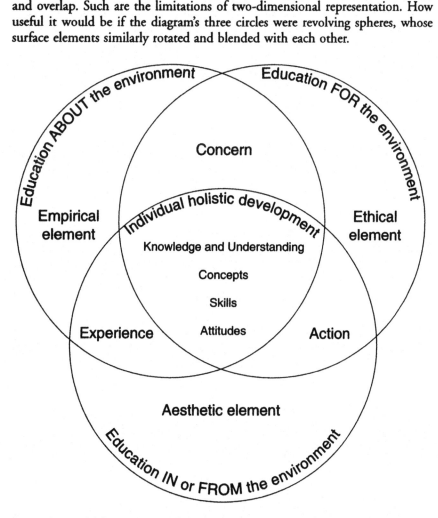

Figure 6.1 Model for teaching and learning in environmental education: components of the planning task (2)

A second and extremely critical elaboration of the original model is also required. Figure 4.2 and Figure 6.1 represent components of the planning task, yet there is a major omission on these diagrams, namely the wealth of formative influences or significant life experiences that individuals bring *to* their further learning. Research has demonstrated that these may indeed be more significant than planned formal educational programmes in the development of environmental understanding and concern, and, wherever possible, educators need to be aware of prior knowledge and build upon it in a meaningful way. Thus the centre, or the 'core', of the diagram ought to contain this powerful base of formative influences upon which all further learning depends, and which most educational programmes and practice seem to ignore (Figure 6.2). From such formative influences, through a combination of 'life' (i.e. further significant experiences) and

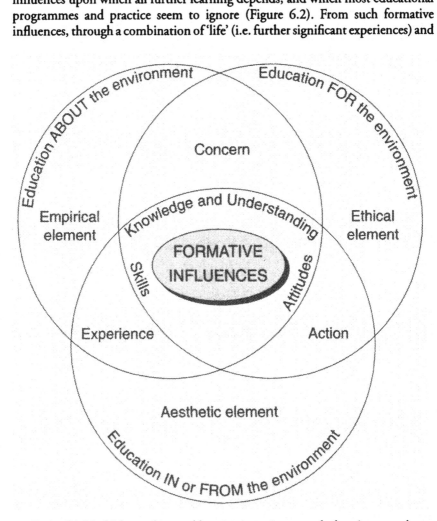

Figure 6.2 Model for teaching and learning in environmental education: complete planning framework (1)

formal education programmes, hopefully, individuals may acquire the necessary range of knowledge and understanding, skills, attitudes and values that foster personal concern and enable the ability to act in pro-environmental ways.

Perhaps one further, and indeed 'final', revision of the model should be made, which returns us to the issue of the limitations of two-dimensional representation. So far the model's components have been presented solely in two dimensions, suggesting that relationships between them are comparable. In reality this is not the case, since the 'core' of formative influences is *pre-supposed* and cannot be planned for in the same sense as other components. The core is independent of, yet inter-relates with, the experiences of planned programmes, and so is better regarded as a 'foundation' that continues to feed into and nurture other experiences (Figure 6.3).

By way of summary, priorities or imperatives for enabling environmental education to meet its promise and potential in the twenty-first century include the widespread design and implementation of planning models and related instructional programmes at all levels of education (pre-school through to higher education, initial teacher training and the professional development of teachers) which:

- recognise and build upon the importance of prior knowledge and of formative influences and significant life experiences influencing people's thinking and behaviour;
- recognise the importance of knowledge gained through living and interacting in communities, socially acquired knowledge, as distinct from 'formal knowledge' gained in classrooms and from other formal sources including television and the media;
- recognise the importance of education *in* the environment, and of aesthetic and spiritual experiences;
- are to a dominant extent issue-based, action-orientated and critical (i.e. they involve the development of critical reflective knowledge, critical thinking skills and democratic skills and values);
- take account of the complexities of inter-relationships and priorities in the field of environmental knowledge, and provide a systematic coverage of such knowledge, a coverage that recognises the inequality of and injustices caused by the actions of human beings, and is truly inter-disciplinary;
- take account of but allow for appraisal and reappraisal of internationally agreed guidelines and goals, and incorporate locally appropriate goals when it is desirable to do so;
- build in planned progression in learning and attend in a systematic way to learners' gaps in knowledge, misconceptions and biased and stereotypical ideas;
- provide exposure (for students at appropriate levels) to different ideologies or perspectives on the causes of and solutions to environmental problems;
- take account of research findings that illuminate the teaching and learning process in environmental education.

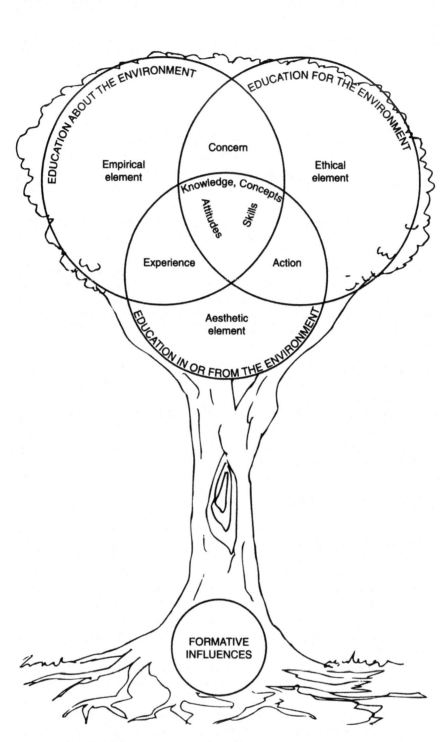

Figure 6.3 Model for teaching and learning in environmental education: complete planning framework (2)

272

If the suggested model and priorities for action are to be successful, they will take account of balance (of the model's components) and will place emphasis on one or more of them as and when necessary. *All* components should be addressed in a systematic way. None should be left to chance or an opportune moment. Whilst being in agreement with those educators who advocate a shift in emphasis away from environmental education as being *about* the environment (grounded in the scientific domain) towards an all-encompassing education *for* the environment, it is argued here that whilst a shift of emphasis is to be welcomed and indeed promoted, a total rejection of other approaches is not. What is needed is an appropriate balance. Perhaps the pendulum has swung too far in favour of calls to educate *for* the environment – an education that focuses exclusively upon a particular issue as an organising principle and that draws upon knowledge opportunistically rather than systematically. I agree that education *about* the environment should go *within* socially critical education, but surely if any degree of true and comprehensive understanding of the world is to be achieved (even in a small measure) then education *about* the environment should go *alongside*, inter-linked with, issue-based, action-orientated, socially critical education. So too can education *in* the environment – that essential foundation for formative influences of the personal, aesthetic kind. Research findings and case studies of good practice cited within this text show that all of these aspects of the environmental education framework have a significant role to play alongside and inter-linking with each other.

The immediate practical consequences of these recommendations are:

- the need for every educational institution to have a well-designed policy document for environmental education that includes details of aims, objectives, components of the planning task, methods, style and timing of teaching, content (details of issues, knowledge, skills, concepts to be addressed), resources and organisation of resources, assessment, record-keeping and evaluation (see also Palmer and Neal, 1994);
- the need for every institution to have a co-ordinator for environmental education;
- the need for institutions to establish adequate mechanisms for review and revisions of policy and practice;
- the need for on-going programmes of in-service professional development for teachers;
- the need for widespread attention to be paid to environmental education in the initial training of teachers;
- the need for on-going research in the field and for the outcomes of research studies to be accessible to all concerned with environmental education – policy makers, curriculum developers and educators alike.

(For further details of developing a school policy and the role of the co-ordinator, see Palmer and Neal, 1994.)

Finally, and in some ways by way of postscript, an imperative for the twenty-

273

first century is the internalisation of the realistic view that formal programmes of environmental education alone cannot educate people to 'save the planet'. Strange as it may sound, this view is rarely, if at all, articulated in the relevant educational literature which focuses almost entirely on how to plan, implement and evaluate environmental education programmes so that they succeed in their task of educating people 'for sustainable living'.

There is no intention whatsoever here of delivering the totally unexpected message that formal programmes of environmental education are, in colloquial terms, a 'waste of time'. It is, however, being suggested that until such times as a major paradigm shift in education (in the direction of ecological thinking) takes place – and even the most optimistic amongst us would surely say this was not imminent – then formal environmental education programmes can and will form only a small part of an individual's education relating to the environment. The sooner this is recognised – by governments, NGOs, educators and community groups alike – the better.

Environmental education, in its broadest sense, is about 'empowerment' and developing a sense of 'ownership', improving the capacity for people to address environment and development issues in their own communities. It is about touching people's beliefs and attitudes so that they *want* to live sustainably, providing sufficient information to support these beliefs, and to translate attitudes and values into action. Of course this process includes formal teaching, but it also encompasses another whole dimension – that which has been placed at the 'core' of the teaching and learning model – the dimension of 'informal' education sources. As we have seen, these include communication and information that results from living and interacting in a particular locality and community, newspapers, television, radio, other media forms, 'events' in one's life and in the wider world, and interacting with relatives and close friends. Environmental education depends upon the totality of an individual's experiences relating to the world – of which formal education is but a small part. *Caring for the Earth* (IUCN/UNEP/WWF, 1991) emphasises the need for all sections of the community to engage in education and communication relating to sustainable living:

> The effective implementation of the world ethic will only be possible if it is taken up by all sections of the community. The range of actions that could be taken is very large, but should include:
>
> - parents teaching their children to act with respect for other people and other species;
> - educators incorporating the world ethic into their teaching;
> - children helping their parents to become aware and change their behaviour by explaining at home the new ideas they learned at school;
> - artists in all media using their creative skills to inspire people with a new understanding and respect for nature, and a wish to conserve it;
> - scientists improving understanding of ecosystems, their sensitivity to

human impact and their capacity to meet human needs, and at the same time ensuring that findings are communicated accurately and applied reasonably;
- lawyers evaluating the legal implication of the world ethic, and drafting the laws required to support it;
- technologists, economists and industrialists entering into dialogue with the coalitions and groups (concerned with respecting and caring for the community of life, and with the consequent personal and social obligations) and establishing new technologies and business approaches to implement the world ethic;
- politicians, other policy makers and public administrators working similarly to evaluate the changes needed in public policy, and then to put them into effect.

(IUCN/UNEP/WWF, 1991, action 2.3, p. 16)

Clearly, 'education' and 'communication' are inseparable processes that impact upon people's thinking and actions. As I have argued elsewhere, since education and communication both deal with the transfer or exchange of ideas, information and skills in a two-way process, they inevitably shade into one another. Environmental education (formal as well as informal) builds the motivation, skills and understanding on which environmental citizenship may be based. Environmental communication is aimed at changing practices and behaviour, and inviting participation or action in relation to environmental issues. It has a short-term, action-specific goal (Palmer *et al.*, 1995). A published, edited collection of papers (Palmer *et al.*, 1995), delivered at a workshop on 'Changing Personal Attitudes and Practices' at the IUCN General Assembly of 1994, provides a series of case study examples of good practice that go some way towards answering the three critical questions:

- how can education and communication be used to change the attitudes and behaviour of people?
- how can education and communication be focused effectively on sustainability?
- how can we promote, plan and carry out education more effectively?

A number of key messages portrayed by the case studies (from both developed and developing nations) go some way towards answering these questions. Firstly, both education and communication have a very different starting point from science and other disciplines, and from research. They begin with the perceptions of their target audiences, and try to improve these perceptions by providing better and more reliable information. In seeking to change knowledge, attributes or behaviour, scientific facts and data are in themselves insufficient. They may even be counter-productive. They have to be translated into concepts and messages that make sense to a target audience, and to be relevant to them. In many cases, communications experts have proved that knowledge of facts

275

alone is of no consequence when it comes to changing behaviour. Linking information to personal benefit is more important (Palmer, 1994).

Secondly, action for environmental education and communication has to be integrated into wider policies and into plans for environmental care and for sustainable resource use.

> It has to be combined with legal, economic and technical instruments for change . . . different kinds of communication and support for education are needed at different stages in the action . . . to start with, people need to be enthused to join in discussion of the problems and how they may be solved. Then they need to be motivated to join in the action.
>
> (Holdgate, 1996, commenting on Palmer et al., 1995)

Thirdly, communication strategies must be flexible and adaptive. New insights must be used to improve policy. Education and communication programmes need a four-phase, cyclical approach leading from research through planning to implementation and on-going evaluation (Palmer, 1994; Holdgate, 1996).

Fourthly, people need to feel 'ownership' of problems and solutions and to derive benefits from the new policies they adopt as a result of the programme of education and communication (Palmer, 1994; Palmer et al., 1995).

> For information alone does not necessarily lead to changed behaviour: the latter is far more likely if the change will bring personal benefit. This can take many forms, including social acceptance, enjoyment, greater environmental or financial security, and a healthier life for children.
>
> (Holdgate, 1996)

To be effective, education and communication have to be seen as relevant, and they have to offer the prospect of an improvement in people's lives.

As we have seen through the accounts and case studies within this text (see also Palmer et al., 1995 and Holdgate, 1996), progress in establishing environmental education around the world is uneven in many respects. In developed nations, it tends to be far more institutionalised, with much stronger support from governments. Education and communication tend to be separated, with 'formal' environmental education being seen as the task of schools, colleges and universities and 'informal' environmental education being left to chance in the hands of the media and NGOs. In the developing world, on the other hand, the existence of structured, comprehensive programmes of formal environmental teaching and learning is still quite rare; where such programmes exist, they are relatively new. Here, more attention has been given to informal education, via the media and through local community projects, often supported by a government. As Holdgate points out, where formal programmes do exist in developing countries, they tend to be weakly structured, weakly developed and poorly supported socially. As a result, a 'negative feedback loop' is established:

environmental education does not pervade the whole educational system, because it lacks high level institutional support; it is not informed by efficient educational research because the system is not attuned to using the results of such studies; and it becomes discredited further because what is done does not produce useful results.

(Holdgate, 1996, p. 155)

Where examples of success are found (in both developed and developing countries) they tend to fall into two categories, admirably illustrated by the case studies in Palmer *et al.* (1995). These are: successful action to establish organisational structures for environmental education; and successful actions for conservation, based on education and communication at community levels, which provide public information for action.

The world's *most* successful programmes in the twenty-first century will surely be those in which the formal and informal elements of education are supported alongside each other. Many countries have made and continue to make excellent progress in the establishment of organisational structures for environmental education – obviously a fact to be welcomed. Yet formal programmes cannot 'do it all' and neither should they. Formative influences and informal educative experiences do not simply precede and 'feed into' formal programmes that can then 'take over the task' in a linear progression. Formative influences occur before, within and after formal programmes, and interact with them. It is a combination of these 'life' experiences, general maturation and exposure to 'environmental education' at a variety of levels and degrees of formality that will lead to individuals gaining a sense of personal concern for the environment, a desire to live in sustainable ways, and the ability to act appropriately.

Our task as environmental educators in the twenty-first century is to recognise this complexity of experience, and to assist the overall process – by striving to implement programmes of education that *inform* our students about the complexities of the environment in which they are growing up; *empower* them to address environment and development issues in their own lives; and provide them with opportunities to be *inspired* by the joys, wonder and mysteries of the natural world and human achievement.

REFERENCES

Capra, F. (1982) *The Turning Point*, London: Flamingo Books.

Devall, W. and Sessions, G. (1985) *Deep Ecology : Living as if Nature Really Mattered*, Salt Lake City, Utah: Gibbs M. Smith.

Elliot, J. (1991) *Developing Community-focused Environmental Education Through Action-research*. Monograph. Norwich: Centre for Applied Research in Education, School of Education, University of East Anglia.

Fien, J. (1986) 'Development Education in Teacher Education', paper to Joint National Development Studies Centre – Australian Council for Overseas Aid Conference on Development Education: Practical Policies for Australia, Canberra. October.

Fien, J. (1992) *Education for the Environment: A Critical Ethnography*, Brisbane: University of Queensland.

Fien, J. (1993) *Education for the Environment: Critical Curriculum Theorising and Environmental Education*, Geelong, Victoria: Deakin University Press.

Fien, J. (1995) 'Teaching for a Sustainable World: The Environmental and Development Education Project for Teacher Education', *Environmental Education Research*, 1 21–33.

Fox, W. (1987) *Approaching Deep Ecology: A Response to Richard Sylvan's Critique of Deep Ecology*, Environmental Studies Occasional Paper No. 20, University of Tasmania, Hobart: Board of Environmental Studies.

Gough, N. (1987) 'Learning with Environments: Towards an Ecological Paradigm for Education', in Robottom, I. (ed.) *Environmental Education: Practice and Possibility*, Geelong, Victoria: Deakin University Press.

Greenall Gough, A. (1987) 'A Political History of Environmental Education in Australia; Snakes and Ladders', in Robottom, I. (ed.) *Environmental Education: Practice and Possibility*, Geelong, Victoria: Deakin University Press.

Holdgate, M. (1996) *From Care to Action*, London: IUCN/Earthscan.

Huckle, J. (1983) 'Environmental Education', in Huckle, J. (ed.) *Geographical Education: Reflection and Action*, Oxford: Oxford University Press.

Hungerford, H., Peyton, R. and Wilkie, R. (1983) 'Editorial – Yes EE Does Have a Definition and Structure', *Journal of Environmental Education*, 14 (3) 1–2.

Hungerford, H.R., Volk, T.L., Dixon, B.G., Marcinkowski, T.J. and Archibald, P.C. (1988) 'An Environmental Education Approach to the Training of Elementary Teachers: A Teacher Education Programme', *International Environmental Education Programme; Environmental Education Series No. 27*, Paris: UNESCO.

IUCN/UNEP/WWF (1991) *Caring for the Earth: A Strategy for Sustainable Living*, Gland, Switzerland: IUCN.

Jickling, B. and Spork, H. (1996) 'Environmental Education for the Environment: Retained? or Retired?' Paper presented to the Special Interest Group on Ecological and Environmental Education at the Annual Meeting of the American Educational Research Association, New York, April 1996.

Marcinkowski, T.J., Volk, T.L. and Hungerford, H.R. (1990) 'An Environmental Education Approach to the Training of Middle Level Teachers: A Prototype Programme', *International Environmental Education Programme; Environmental Education Series No. 30*, Paris: UNESCO–UNEP.

NCC (1990) *Curriculum Guidance 7: Environmental Education*, York: National Curriculum Council.

NCC (1993) *Spiritual and Moral Development. A Discussion Paper*, York: National Curriculum Council.

O'Riordan, T. (1981) *Environmentalism*, London: Pion.

Oulton, C.R. and Scott, W.A.H. (1995) 'The "Environmentally Educated Teacher": An Exploration of the Implications of UNESCO–UNEP's Ideas for Pre-Service Teacher Education Programmes', *Environmental Education Research*, 1 (2) 213–231.

Palmer, J.A. (1993) 'Development of Concern for the Environment and Formative Experiences of Educators', *Journal of Environmental Education*, 24 (3) 26–31.

Palmer, J.A. (1994) 'Changing Personal Attitudes and Practices.' Rapporteur's Summary of Workshop 7, at the 19th Session of the IUCN General Assembly, Buenos Aires, Argentina, January 1994.

Palmer, J.A. (1995a) 'Just Ecological Principles?', in Cooper, D.E. and Palmer, J.A. (eds) *Just Environments*, London: Routledge.

Palmer, J.A. (1995b) 'Environmental Thinking in the Early Years. Understanding and Misunderstanding of Concepts Relating to Waste Management', *Environmental Education Research*, 1 35–45.

Palmer, J.A., Goldstein, W. and Curnow, A. (eds) (1995) *Towards Better Planning of Education to Care for the Earth*. Volume based on papers delivered at Workshop on Changing Personal Attitudes and Practices, held during the 19th Session of the IUCN General Assembly, Buenos Aires, Argentina, January 1994. Gland, Switzerland: IUCN.

Palmer, J.A. (1998) 'Spiritual Ideas, Environmental Concerns and Educational Practice', in Cooper, D.E. and Palmer, J.A. (eds) *Spirit of the Environment*, London: Routledge.

Palmer, J.A. and Neal, P.D. (1994) *The Handbook of Environmental Education*, London: Routledge.

Palmer, J.A. and Suggate, J. (1996) 'Influences and Experiences Affecting the Pro-Environmental Behaviour of Educators', *Environmental Education Research*, 2 (1) 109–122.

Pepper, D. (1987) 'The Basis of a Radical Curriculum in Environmental Education', in Lacey, C. and Williams, R. (eds) *Education, Ecology and Development: The Case for an Education Network*, London: WWF & Kogan Page.

Robottom, I. (1987) 'Towards Enquiry-Based Professional Development in Environmental Education', in Robottom, I. (ed.) *Environmental Education: Practice and Possibility*, Geelong, Victoria: Deakin University Press.

Robottom, I. and Hart, P. (1993) *Research in Environmental Education: Engaging the Debate*, Geelong, Victoria: Deakin University Press.

Simmons, I.G. (1996) 'Environmental Thought: The Last 25 Years', *International Journal of Environmental Studies*, 29 163–170.

Spork, H. (1992) 'Environmental Education: A Mismatch Between Theory and Practice', *Australian Journal of Environmental Education*, 8 147–166.

Stapp, W.B. and Stapp, G.L. (1983) 'A Summary of Environmental Education in Australia', *Australian Association for Environmental Education Newsletter*, 12 4–6.

Stapp, W., Caduto, M., Mann, L. and Nowak, P. (1980) 'Analysis of Pre-Service Environmental Education of Teachers in Europe and an Instructional Model for Furthering this Education', *Journal of Environmental Education*, 12 3–10.

Stevenson, R.B. (1987) 'Schooling and Environmental Education: Contradictions in Purpose and Practice', in Robottom, I. (ed.) *Environmental Education: Practice and Possibility*, Geelong, Victoria: Deakin University Press.

Tanner, T. (1980) 'Significant Life Experiences', *Journal of Environmental Education*, 11 (4) 20–24.

Tilbury, D. (1992) 'Environmental Education within Pre-Service Teacher Education: The Priority of Priorities', *International Journal of Environmental Education and Information*, 11 267–280.

UNESCO–UNEP (1990) 'Environmentally Educated Teachers the Priority of Priorities?', *Connect*, 15 (1) 1–3.

UNESCO–UNEP (1992) 'UNCED: The Earth Summit', *Connect*, 17 (2) 1–7.

WCED (1987) *Our Common Future*, Oxford: Oxford University Press.

Wilkie, R.J., Peyton, R.B. and Hungerford, H.R. (1987) 'Strategies for the Training of Teachers in Environmental Education', *International Environmental Education Programme; Environmental Education Series No. 25*, Paris: UNESCO–UNEP.

INDEX

Lightning Source UK Ltd.
Milton Keynes UK
UKOW05f1804010317
295675UK00016B/359/P